Heroic Efforts

Heroic Efforts

The Emotional Culture of
Search and Rescue Volunteers

Jennifer Lois

NEW YORK UNIVERSITY PRESS

New York and London

NEW YORK UNIVERSITY PRESS
New York and London

Library of Congress Cataloging-in-Publication Data
Lois, Jennifer.
Heroic efforts : the emotional culture of search and
rescue volunteers / Jennifer Lois.
p. cm.
Includes bibliographical references and index.
ISBN 0-8147-5183-0 — ISBN 0-8147-5184-9 (pbk.)
1. Mountaineering—Search and rescue operations—
United States—Case sudies.   2. Volunteer workers
in search and rescue operations—United States—
Psychology—Case sudies.   I. Title.
GV200.183 .L64 2002
796.52'2'0289—dc21   2002015945

New York University Press books are printed on acid-free paper,
and their binding materials are chosen for strength and durability.

Manufactured in the United States of America
10 9 8 7 6 5 4 3 2 1

This book is dedicated to Tim

Contents

Acknowledgments

When I graduated from college in 1989, I had no idea what I wanted to do with my life, so I moved out West and taught skiing for a few years. I had always wanted to write a book about a little-known subculture or group, but I didn't know how to approach it, so I abandoned the idea and decided that I wanted to be a sociology professor. Strange, especially since I had no idea what sociologists really did, but I was pretty sure that they were interested in the same kinds of things I was. Through a coincidental series of events, in the fall of 1993 I enrolled in a Ph.D. program and got my first real taste of sociology: we started reading Durkheim and learning quantitative data analysis. I began to seriously question my new career path. The next year, I hit the jackpot when Patti Adler introduced me to ethnography. I couldn't believe my good fortune—here I was wanting to study people's experiences from their perspective, and here she was telling me I could do just that! She took me under her wing and helped me initiate an ethnographic research project, which turned into my Ph.D. dissertation, and later evolved into this book. She worked closely with me for six years, listening to every concern I had, poring over every word I wrote, and devotedly chairing my dissertation committee. I could never have completed this project without her expert guidance, support, friendship, and (thank god) her sense of humor. Peter Adler, too, contributed in many of the same ways. I owe them both the deepest debt of gratitude for the extensive effort they put into helping launch my academic career.

There are also several other people who, over the years, have contributed significantly to this book. My dissertation committee members were instrumental in helping me make this work cohesive and coherent. I am grateful to Nan Boyd, Dan Cress (who sensitized me to the question, "What's your theoretical hook?"), Jim Downton, Leslie Irvine, and Joyce

Nielsen. I could have never kept up my momentum with this project if it weren't for the immense support of my peers, who started with me in graduate school and are still with me today: Alice Fothergill, Joanna Higginson, Katy Irwin, and Adina Nack. They tirelessly read and commented on many early drafts, improving this work substantially. Other sociologists have also read portions of this book and provided me with vital feedback. I would like to thank numerous anonymous reviewers, and David Franks and Steven Lyng especially, for giving my work such detailed attention over the years. I am also grateful to my colleagues at Western Washington University, particularly Karen Bradley, Adam Resnick, and Jay Teachman, for providing me with encouragement and support for completing this book. Jennifer Hammer at NYU Press has also worked very closely with me on this project, and her editorial support and advice have been invaluable.

The personal and emotional support I have received from my friends and family has been the most important thing in keeping me grounded and motivated. The friends I made in Peak Volunteer Search and Rescue have contributed perhaps most uniquely to this book. They trusted me, sharing their stories and lives with me; obviously, this book would never have been possible without their willingness to do so. I hope I present their experiences in the true spirit that they lived them. I also owe a great deal of gratitude to Rollie Reinholtz, Lois Reinholtz, Rhonda Reinholtz, Joseph Colletti, Claude Goldberg, and Lance Badger, who have always been supportive of my goals. I also thank my grandparents, Mary Lois, the late Joseph Lois, the late Villette Thompson, and the late Evelyn Thompson, whose spirit and determination have always inspired me. I am eternally grateful to my parents, Jackie and Joe Lois, and my sister and her husband, Sara and Gary Brown, who never had any doubt that I would complete this book, and, despite dealing with serious illness, they still had enough love and emotional support to provide me with unlimited supplies. Sophie, Jacob, Noah, and Calvin were charged with the duty of revitalizing our family, and they've done a fantastic job. Last but not least, I am forever grateful to my husband, "Gary," who sacrificed a great deal in the years it took me to complete this project. As my hero, he is the strongest person I know and the inspiration for this book.

Portions of earlier versions of chapters 3 and 8 have appeared as: Jennifer Lois, "Socialization to Heroism: Individualism and Collectivism in a Voluntary Search and Rescue Group," *Social Psychology Quarterly*, vol. 62, no. 2 (June 1999). Portions of earlier versions of chapters 4 and 8 have appeared as: Jennifer Lois, "Peaks and Valleys: The Gendered Emotional Culture of Edgework," *Gender and Society*, vol. 15, no. 3 (June 2001), by permission of Sage Publications. Portions of earlier versions of chapters 5 and 8 have appeared as: Jennifer Lois, "Managing Emotions, Intimacy, and Relationships in a Volunteer Search and Rescue Group," *Journal of Contemporary Ethnography*, vol. 30, no. 2 (April 2001), by permission of Sage Publications. I am grateful to Sage Publications for granting New York University Press permission to use this material.

Introduction

On a dark November morning in 1999, I awoke to the squelching emergency tones emanating from the pager next to my bed. Rolling over, I glanced at the clock: 6 A.M. The dispatcher's voice came across the pager next: "Attention all Peak Search and Rescue members. Report to the base for a search in the Mount Alpine area. Time now o-six-hundred."[1] *Mount Alpine?* I thought. Who in their right mind would be hiking a 14,000-foot mountain at this time of year? True, it had been a dry season so far. There was no snow yet in our Rocky Mountain resort town (a mere 7500 feet above sea level), and we'd had a warm, dry fall. But up in the high-alpine wilderness, there had been some snow, and the temperature was dropping well into the single digits at night. I hoped this lost person had brought the proper equipment.

I debated whether to get out of bed. I was finished collecting data for my research, I reasoned, so perhaps I should go back to sleep; after five and a half years, I had plenty of information on the rescuer experience. What's more, they'd probably call off the search once we all got rolling anyway. I'd most likely spend all day hiking up one of the two trails to Mount Alpine (again) only to find that the missing person miscommunicated his travel plans to his friends (again), who were now reporting him missing (again). Or, maybe someone really *was* lost. Cursing my conscience, I stumbled out of bed, got my gear together, and headed down to the base building to meet the team.

I walked into the rescue base just as Joel, the mission coordinator, was beginning to brief the eight other volunteer rescuers who were also able to get out of their commitments today. We'd be looking for Bill Brown, a white male in his late thirties from Springfield, a town in the foothills about 100 miles away. A sheriff's office dispatcher had called Joel at about five o'clock Friday afternoon, saying that she had received a 911 cell phone call from a man who was lost on Mount Alpine. She still had him on the

1

line, and patched him through to Joel, who was the "on duty" volunteer search and rescue coordinator. Joel talked to Bill for less than five minutes before the line went dead. In that time he tried to help Bill get his bearings by having him describe what he saw. Joel guessed at his likely location, described some prominent landmarks Bill should look for, and gave him directions back to the trail based on those landmarks. Joel was also able to learn that although Bill was unfamiliar with the area, he was in good health and was fairly well prepared to spend a night (albeit an uncomfortable one) in the wilderness. By Saturday afternoon, however, deputies confirmed that Bill's car was still parked at the trailhead. Joel sent two rescuers up the first part of the Mount Alpine trail, hoping they would run into Bill, who might have been on his way back to his car. He wasn't. Night fell, the two rescuers returned to the base, and Joel launched a full-scale search this morning. It had been 37 hours since Bill reported himself lost.

Joel divided the rescuers into four two-person teams. I went on a team with Matt, a new member who had never been on a search or rescue before. We were, as I had predicted, to ascend west along the first three miles of the main "Mount Alpine Trail" that Bill had taken. A second team would ascend southwest, up the seven-mile "Lower-Access Trail," that began 10 miles away but led to the same general area. Two more teams would be lifted by helicopter and dropped off above tree line, in the giant boulder field that constituted the top 3000 feet of Mount Alpine. The helicopter would then search this wilderness area—over 50 square miles—by air.

As the two teams departed from the helicopter—one at 11,000 feet, the other at 12,500—they quickly realized that their searching would be slow. Two inches of snow were covering the giant boulders—not nearly enough to fill in the three-foot-deep gaps between them, but plenty to make travel across the rocks treacherously slippery. One wrong step could snap a rescuer's leg or dislocate a shoulder.

After driving for about an hour, Matt and I set out on the main access trail by 8 A.M. It was slow going since we began at an elevation of 10,500 feet and, although there was not a cloud in the sky and it was a balmy 50 degrees in the sun, we were loaded down with winter survival gear. Furthermore, the trail was covered with patchy snow and became more consistently blanketed as we gained elevation. As we hiked along, we periodically called out Bill Brown's name, a standard practice on searches, but one that still made me self-conscious anyway. "Bill!" we would shout every minute or so, then stay silent, hoping to hear a response. In my five and a half years in Peak, I had never had anyone call back.

We climbed for an hour, surpassing the tree line, and finally reached an 11,500-foot saddle on top of a ridge. From here, with Mount Alpine to our left, we could see five miles straight ahead to the mountain ridge that rose up on the other side. The valley in between stretched for eight miles to our right and was flanked on one side by the trail we had just come up and, on the other, at the base of that ridge we were looking at, by the Lower Access Trail the second team was ascending (though it was too far away for us to see). The two trails almost converged in a "V" at the base of Mount Alpine, but the mountain was so massive that they arrived at different sides, still a couple of miles apart.

Matt turned to his left and tried to spot the two boulder field teams that had been dropped off on the mountain. I laughed. "The size is deceiving; they're too small to see. If we're still out here tonight, we'll be able to see their headlamps, but you'll never spot them in the daylight from here." Matt was astounded at the sheer size of the search area and wondered aloud how these four small teams had any chance of ever finding Bill Brown. I reminded him that this was only the *likely* search area; Bill Brown could easily be on the other side of the mountain, an area we were not covering on foot today. I empathized with him, though. "It's totally overwhelming, isn't it? You don't even know where to *start* looking for these people. But it's amazing—we always find the people we're looking for." I radioed in to the base to let them know we were at the saddle and to ask which way Joel wanted us to proceed. From our location there was a spur trail that went off in another direction, and we had found lost people on it before; so Joel might want us to check that out instead of continuing on the main trail toward the mountain. Elena, another volunteer who was running the radio, told us to stand by while she relayed our position. Within moments, she came back on the radio and told us to continue down the main trail. At the bottom, we were to go off it and follow a creek for a while. "Sometimes lost people follow streams downhill. I think kids' scouting groups teach that or something," I explained to Matt as we began the descent down the other side of the ridge toward Mount Alpine.

By 10 A.M. both boulder field teams, although miles from each other, had reported seeing a single set of footprints in the snow; in each case, whoever had made them was alone. We listened as the teams compared them over the radio by describing the size of the foot (about a man's 11) and the design of the sole pattern. The descriptions matched; they were from the same shoes. Both teams then followed their set of tracks, which were curiously undirected; they went up, down, and wound around in circles. By noon, one team had followed their tracks down into the valley where they saw them descend the banks of an icy-cold, thigh-deep river and emerge on the other side—all within 20 feet of a bridge! What's more, the tracks continued on the other side of the river, crossed *over* the well-marked Lower Access Trail, and carried on up a steep clifflike hill, over rocks and fallen trees, toward the far ridge Matt and I had seen from our rest stop. Everyone who heard these reports over the radio was stymied. Even someone who was hypothermic and disoriented would surely use a bridge to cross a river and choose to take a trail instead of bushwhacking!

Around the same time, team 2—Nick, Patrick, and Nick's search-dog-in-training, Skip—were six miles up the seven-mile Lower Access Trail. Periodically they yelled Bill Brown's name, just as Matt and I had been doing. While we could not hear their voices from where we were, we did hear a faint horn echoing through the valley, which seemed oddly out of place in the pristine wilderness. Apparently the boulder field teams heard it too and got on the radio to ask what it was. Nick answered that his father, who owned a boat in another state, had given him an air horn recently, which Nick thought might be useful on a search, as he routinely went hoarse from yelling all day. Matt and I had a good laugh over that, feeling envious of his ingenuity.

Forty-five minutes later, around 1 P.M., Nick and his team reported hearing someone yell in response to his air horn. Apparently Skip, the search dog, heard the voice first, and became quite agitated. As Nick and Patrick followed the dog, they got close enough to hear the voice themselves. Matt and I became visibly excited upon hearing this news. We started hiking faster, talking about how this *had* to be Bill Brown, and speculating about where he was. We expressed our amazement at how unlikely it seemed that we could find someone in this vast expanse of wilderness. In the next 20 minutes, team 2 was able to get close enough to the sound of the voice to verify that it was indeed Bill Brown, but they could not find him. Through their shouting back and forth, they repeatedly asked him where he was, but he kept saying he didn't know. The terrain was playing tricks on the team, creating echoes and dead spots that prevented them from pinning down his location. One minute they thought he was right around the bend, and the next they seemed to lose him altogether. Even Skip was confused, running in circles and barking in different directions.

Joel redirected the helicopter to fly the area, and told Nick's team to stay put and maintain voice contact with Bill. Then Joel radioed Matt and me and had us return to the saddle to find a suitable "LZ." When I explained to Matt that an LZ was a landing zone for the helicopter, he almost burst with excitement. "We might be the most convenient team to pick up," I told him. "You ready to fly in a helicopter today?"

By 2:30 P.M. we were back on top of the saddle. The helicopter had been searching for Bill for almost an hour, and was still unable to locate him. I walked around looking for the best LZ possible, then radioed in. We were told to sit tight. From our location, we could periodically hear the *wump-wump-wump* of the helicopter passing up and down the ridge on the other side of the valley. Matt looked for it, but I reminded him that he was probably expecting to see something bigger than it was. I told him to look for a glint in the sky where the sun reflected off the metal. When he did spot it, he was amazed at how small it was.

We sat atop the ridge for the next 45 minutes, becoming just as frustrated as Nick's team, who could still hear Bill's voice but couldn't find him. Apparently, Bill could not see the helicopter, but he could hear it, and he said he was frantically waving his arms. As we discussed it, Matt and I agreed that something wasn't right. Why couldn't Bill see the helicopter? Was he in the trees? Why didn't he get out into the open? Nick and his team were not able to ask Bill these questions either, since the sound from the helicopter, for the most part, overpowered their voices. By 3:15 the helicopter pilot radioed in to Joel, saying that he had 10 more minutes of search time, and then he would have to return to his base to refuel. By that time, it would be too late to resume the search since it would be getting dark. The upshot: if they could not find Bill in the next 10 minutes, we would not have helicopter assistance until the next morning.

Five minutes later the pilots spotted him. He had climbed almost to the top of the 800-foot ridge but had encountered a 40-foot sheer cliff wall, blocking his ability to ascend farther. If he could have made it up that wall, he would have been able to hike the last 200 feet to where the helicopter could land because the ground was then more level. But he was stuck on a ledge at the base of this wall. The pilots radioed to Joel: because they were "bingo fuel" (quickly running out of gas), they needed to pick up a rescue team immediately to help them reach Bill. Matt and I jumped up and began throwing our gear into our packs. Our adrenaline was rushing as Joel radioed to ask us if we were ready for pick up. We were. Then Joel began radioing other teams to see if they were in suitable LZs. Although

Nick and his team were closest to Bill, they were in the trees on the Lower Access Trail, which made them inaccessible to the helicopter. Gary and Cody, however, were in a good LZ and, furthermore, were in the boulder field, which was much closer to the helicopter than our location. They got to go.

Matt and I, slightly disappointed, unpacked and made ourselves comfortable again. We listened intently to the blow-by-blow radio transmissions of the rescue. Within 15 minutes, team 3 had Bill in the helicopter (which was now seriously pushing its fuel supply), and they were headed for the waiting ambulance in town. Matt and I packed up our gear and headed out. When we reached the car I radioed in: "Team 1 is out of the field."

"Copy that, team 1," said Elena, who was still working the radio. "We'll do the debrief at the Mineshaft, so meet us there instead of coming back to base. Time now, 16:47."

Matt and I arrived at the restaurant just as the rest of the team was coming across the street from the base building. Everyone was ecstatic, grinning ear-to-ear, laughing, and high-fiving one another. The eleven of us pushed some tables together, sat down, and ordered several pitchers of beer. The whole team was abuzz with excitement. We were talking about Nick's air horn, and the footprints, and the stream Bill Brown had crossed. Why couldn't he see the helicopter? Why couldn't he describe where he was? What kind of shape was he in when Gary and Cody reached him? Finally, after many disorganized side conversations, everyone settled down enough to let Gary and Cody tell the following story.

On Friday night when Bill Brown called to report himself lost, his cell phone battery died, which cut his conversation with Joel short. As he tried to follow Joel's directions, he slipped on a snowy boulder, fell, and hit his head. The fall caused him to lose his glasses, without which he was legally blind. To make matters worse, he was disoriented from hitting his head. By the time he regained his senses, he found himself without his pack, which contained his food, water, survival gear (like matches and a compass), cell phone, and extra clothes. All he had left was what he was wearing: a long underwear shirt covered by a long-sleeved, cotton tee-shirt, socks, hiking boots, and running tights. Night had fallen, and he was cold.

He began descending the mountain in the dark, sliding from boulder to boulder on his backside. In the middle of the night he tried to curl up under the branches of a pine tree, but he got too cold, so he kept moving.

He warmed up on Saturday, but still had no idea where he was or where he was going since he could not see anything without his glasses. He was petrified of blindly stepping off a cliff, so found it more comfortable to go up than down. This explained why his footprints were so undirected. Sometime Saturday night, he made it down to the valley. After another almost unbearably cold night, he came upon the river and knew he had crossed one on his way in (he thought it was the creek that Matt and I had followed for a time). Bill hoped he'd found the right creek—he hadn't—and that he was going the right direction—he wasn't. His blindness explained why he crossed the creek within 20 feet of a bridge and why he crossed the obvious trail and began bushwhacking up the steep hillside: he didn't see any of it! He headed uphill because, if he had crossed the right creek, he knew he had to ascend up to the saddle where Matt and I had been. Unfortunately, he was getting farther and farther away from where he had started.

By Sunday morning, crawling around in the rocks near the top of the ridge, he heard the helicopter. A couple of times he thought it was close, but couldn't see without his glasses, so he waved his arms and yelled, but wasn't able to attract any attention. Finally, he heard Nick's air horn blasts, and he shouted in response to them. When Nick established voice contact with him and asked him where he was, he could not answer because he had no idea; he couldn't see.

When Gary and Cody jumped from the helicopter and made their way down the ridge to the edge of the cliff just above Bill, they noticed a gully to their right, which skirted around the sheer face, down to Bill's ledge. It was steep and rocky, but they thought they could scramble down it safely. When they reached Bill, he clung to them and began to sob. "Are you the guys with the air horn?" he choked. "I didn't think you were going to find me!" He began to collapse in relief. Gary and Cody looked at each other, knowing this was a problematic response. They worried about how they would get this 200-pound guy, who, in Gary's words, "had turned into a big pile of goo," up the gully and to the helicopter.

"So what'd you do?" someone around the table asked.

"We yelled at him," Cody quipped.

Everyone laughed. "Oh, that's nice!" commented Elena sarcastically.

"We weren't trying to be nice, we were trying to save his life," Gary sternly explained. "He couldn't even stand. We had to get him fired up enough to climb up that gully."

"So what'd you say?" I asked.

"We said, 'We *cannot* carry you out of here. You've gotta climb. Bill! Get off your ass, *now!*'" Gary led the way up the gully so that Bill, with his severely restricted sight, could follow him, placing his hands in Gary's footholds. Cody climbed up behind Bill, steadying him and making sure he didn't fall backward. If he did, he'd kill them both.

At the top of the gully, Bill collapsed again. The adrenaline push had been all he could handle. Cody picked him up, fire-fighter style, and carried him, as fast as he could, halfway to the awaiting helicopter. He traded off with Gary, who brought him the rest of the way. As I sat there, riveted to the story, I thanked my lucky stars that the helicopter had picked up Gary and Cody instead of Matt and me. There was no way Matt and I could have accomplished that task with even a fraction of the efficiency. The helicopter, short on fuel, would not have been able to wait for us.

When they got him into the ship, Gary, who was an Emergency Medical Technician (EMT), began his medical assessment of Bill but had a hard time getting him to answer any questions since he couldn't stop "blubbering." He was intermittently sobbing, thanking them profusely, and telling them what happened.

"So what kind of shape was he in?" someone asked.

"Bad," said Gary. "He wasn't shivering, which means he was so hypothermic that his body had lost the ability to warm itself. We cranked the chopper's heat, stuck heat packs in his armpits and crotch, and wrapped him in blankets. We got him shivering again by the time we dropped him at the ambi, so that was good. But he was bumped and bruised and scraped and disoriented. He was really dehydrated and had frostbite on his fingers and toes. His clothes were pretty much falling apart. His tights had big holes in the butt from sliding on the rocks. He took off his socks after he crossed the river 'cause they were wet, but his boots were still drenched, so his feet were like ice. He did *not* have another night in him, I'll tell you that. If we hadn't found him, he would've died tonight for sure. I can't believe he survived the two nights he did. They're gonna keep him in the hospital for a couple of days—check his kidney function and treat the frostbite."

Someone ribbed Nick: "He sure is lucky you brought that air horn!"

No one could believe this set of circumstances. What a terrible run of bad luck Bill had, and what good luck the team had! Everyone felt absolutely euphoric. We toasted a job well done, finished the pitchers, ordered another round, and continued to toast throughout the night: "To the air horn!" "To the fumes the helicopter was flying on!" "To Bill Brown!" "To the spare set of glasses I'm going to put in my pack!"

I looked over at Matt, who was beaming. "Are all the searches like this?" he asked.

"Nope!" I replied. "Enjoy this while you can!"

This is a study of heroism. The members of Peak Search and Rescue voluntarily interrupt their lives when they are spontaneously called upon to help strangers. They awake in the middle of the night to cover miles of terrain in search of overdue hunters or lost hikers, like Bill Brown. They regularly relinquish their leisure time to recover the bodies of victims killed in planes that crash in the wilderness. They frequently sacrifice income, leaving work to search potential avalanche zones for missing skiers, snowboarders, and snowmobilers in blizzard conditions. And they are repeatedly pulled away from family obligations, putting their own lives in danger to rescue stranded, hypothermic kayakers and rafters from rivers. They help others by donating their time, forfeiting their income, risking their lives, and receiving no material rewards for doing so. They are heroes.

The Sociology of Heroism

Several fields of sociology have theoretically examined how and why people help others. Altruism, those acts that benefit others while providing no benefits to the self, has been the most widely investigated phenomenon.[2] Although acts of altruism do not benefit the actor, they may not have any substantial costs to the actor, either. For example, stopping to help someone who has dropped a large stack of books may not substantially impinge on helpers' time or effort, especially if they are not involved in something important at the moment. Many altruistic acts, though, more clearly carry costs to the actor. People must sacrifice their time and comfort to donate blood or to help a stranger change a flat tire. Helping may even cause helpers to become embarrassed in the event that they misinterpret a situation and try to help someone who does not need it. People may also help others even when the costs seem to be exceedingly high—perhaps a threat to the helper's own life and limb, which makes this phenomenon seem almost illogical. Some researchers have labeled this subset of altruism—action that carries with it potentially huge (and seemingly irrational) costs to the helper—as heroic.[3]

Risky intervention on the behalf of others is a significant feature in the theoretical literature on heroism, yet this body of work remains fairly distinct from the theory and research on altruism.[4] In theorizing about heroism, these works share three assumptions. First, heroism differs from altruism because it must be socially recognized. Altruism can exist in the absence of others' recognition of the act; heroism, theoretically, cannot. Heroes only exist when they are labeled as such by others, as Edelstein has explained: "Generally, to be regarded as a hero . . . one must have done something daring and gallant and, critically, one must be recognized . . . as having done something daring and gallant. . . . That is, having performed a heroic act does not automatically confer the status of 'hero' on the actor. . . . [T]here must also be recognition of the actor as a hero" (1996: 35–36). Other heroism scholars concur with this basic assumption and have used it to build theory. Goode (1978), for example, suggested that heroism operates as a potent form of social control precisely because the great public recognition granted to heroes is highly prestigious and desired.

The second similarity in most definitions of heroism is that heroes are a celebrated class of citizens in any society because they embody a culture's most highly prized values. Klapp (1962) has analyzed the hero as a distinct "social type," or cultural model, whose meaning epitomizes a culture's values. Klapp claims that cultural definitions of heroism serve as models for individuals to draw on in interpreting their own and others' actions. By representing a culture's most valued traits, heroes promote social stability as community members band together to celebrate heroes and aspire to live up to the culture's revered values.[5]

Third, although cultures may have different values that represent heroism, one value seems to be common to most cultural definitions of heroism: heroes serve the group at the expense of the individual; they sacrifice themselves for others, in part or in full, symbolically or literally. Most societies label such self-sacrifice as heroic, granting the utmost prestige and status to its heroes; in this way, they entice all community members to conform to this important societal value—to behave in ways that benefit the group.

Although this set of theories on heroism exists, there has been virtually no empirical research that incorporates and extends this body of knowledge.[6] In this study, I use the empirical evidence from my six years in a participant-observation role with Peak Volunteer Search and Rescue to examine the meaning of heroism as it relates to the heroes themselves, as well as to those who label them heroes.

The Self, Emotions, and Gender

As I studied the lives of Peak's rescuers, several sociological phenomena emerged as integral to the heroic experience. First, rescuers' understandings of heroism and the acts that they performed through their work in Peak influenced their selves and their identities. Sociologists generally think of a "self" as an idea that we develop about who we are because of others' reactions to us. We can only see ourselves as we think others see us—by interpreting their words and actions toward us. Thus, the idea of a self is distinctly social. We understand who we are only through our interactions with others in social life. Conversely, who we believe we are influences our behavior. We structure our interactions with others based on these ideas, which, of course, affects the interactions we have, and circularly, how we see ourselves.[7] Peak's rescuers developed ideas about themselves and others through their participation in the search and rescue subculture. These ideas then affected how they approached subsequent rescue work. For example, within the context of the group, rescuers were socialized to downplay any kind of self-aggrandizing or selfish behavior. So when Matt and I were passed over for the helicopter pick-up in favor of Gary and Cody, we had to display acceptably humble selves rather than be disappointed or angry that we were not given the chance to rescue Bill Brown. Throughout this book, I deal with such situations and show how rescuers' selves were both driven by and a result of their idea of heroism.

Rescuers' emotional experiences is a second theme that runs throughout this study. Sociologists view emotions much like they view the self: as interpretive and socially derived. Our feelings are not purely innate or instinctual but depend largely on how we interpret other situational information as well as on cultural and historical beliefs about particular emotions.[8] Interaction among people in different cultures and historical periods has resulted in culture-specific meanings for many emotions. People of those cultures and time periods, in turn, have drawn on these emotional meanings to structure their interactions with others. Gordon has discussed the shared and symbolic nature of emotions, calling it an "emotional culture," which he defined as "the patterns of meanings embodied in symbols, by which people communicate, perpetuate, and develop their knowledge about and attitudes toward emotions" (1989: 115). These meanings are not always shared within one large culture or one vast historical time frame; meanings may vary from group to group. Thus, small groups, like Peak for example, may construct emotional cultures by developing norms and vocabularies to express and reinforce their beliefs about particular emotions. Just like members of a larger culture, these group members interact with one another and their environment based, in part, on their shared emotional belief system, such as their beliefs about what emotions they will feel in particular situations and how they should interpret, act on, and express these feelings. These beliefs, by definition, vary from one emotional culture to the next. In Peak, for example, rescuers quickly learned what emotions were appropriate for certain situations, such as becoming emotionally detached when dealing with death or controlling a victim's panic during a dangerous or difficult rescue (like Cody and Gary did by yelling at Bill Brown). These ways of understanding emotions influenced rescuers' ideas of who they were. In the pages that follow, I show how Peak's emotional culture was intricately tied to the heroic work rescuers performed as well as to their understanding of their selves.

Gender was an important part of Peak's emotional culture, as it is in many others as well. Pervasive gender stereotypes yield distinct beliefs about women's and men's capacities for experiencing various feelings. Gender stereotypes also produce cultural rules about what feelings are appropriate for whom and how those feelings should be handled. For example, the stereotype of the emotionless male suggests that men do not cry; the stereotype of the irrational, overreacting female suggests that women are emotionally weak.[9] These gendered ideas often reinforce stereotypical beliefs about the nature of women and men, which affect how people view themselves and how they think about their emotions. Rescuers' beliefs about gender shaped their experiences, especially when it came to dealing with emotions and performing acts of heroism. This book uncovers many aspects of heroism by illuminating how ideas about the self, emotions, and gender affect heroes' lives.

Research on Risky Occupations and Leisure

There have been several fictionalized media portrayals of search and rescue teams, including the ones in Sylvester Stallone's blockbuster film *Cliffhanger*, in Robert Conrad's made-for-TV-movie *Search and Rescue*, and in the short-lived dramatic television series in the mid-1990s, *Extreme*. There have also been some nonfiction accounts of mountain-environment rescue groups, like one in Colorado profiled by a journalist, and those that are part of the television show *Rescue 911* and other shows of that genre.[10] But there has yet to be any in-depth scholarly examination of search and rescue groups or their volunteers.

There have been several studies, however, on environments in which workers incur considerable risk, experience intense excitement, and help others as part of their occupational duties. For example, some studies have examined how EMTs, paramedics, military personnel, and police officers seek thrilling experiences and, as such, are drawn to the sometimes dangerous and always unpredictable nature of their work.[11] Other research has examined nonoccupational settings in which individuals undertake risk as part of their leisure activity, such as mountaineering, whitewater rafting, and high-ropes courses.[12] These thrill seekers carefully calculate the dangers and rewards of pursuing high-risk activity, as Lyng (1990) comprehensively discussed in his theory of "edgework."[13] Using his own ethnographic data on skydiving as well as other data on fire fighting, race-car driving, and other high-risk pursuits (both occupational and leisure oriented), Lyng detailed how risk takers negotiate the boundary, or "edge," between safety and danger. He defined "the archetypical edgework experience [as] one in which the individual's failure to meet the challenge at hand will result in death or, at the very least, debilitating injury" (1990:857).

Lyng contended that edgework is alluring because it gives individuals a feeling of control over their lives and environment while they push themselves to their physical and mental limits. On a psychological level, surviving the edge leads them to experience intense highs.[14] This sensory experience on the edge compels the edgeworkers to pursue it repeatedly, each time pushing their physical and mental limits farther to control the seemingly uncontrollable.[15]

Some studies of high-risk activity have noted that risk is a highly masculinized domain, largely because of the physicality involved in many risky activities as well as the powerful socialization toward risk and aggression for men. Some research has focused on the difficulty women commonly have in breaking into high-risk professions, such as police work, fire fighting, and the military, which are overwhelmingly male dominated.[16] These women are often marginalized, which may make it difficult for them to build solidarity with other high-risk workers, most of whom are male. One ramification of this weak solidarity is that women may be trusted less often than their male colleagues. Furthermore, in these risky environments that require a great deal of physical strength, women may have a hard time gaining the respect they feel they deserve because some of their coworkers may view them as inferior.

Research on Heroic Activities

This study is about heroes: rescuers who volunteer to risk their lives to help others.[17] Volunteer search and rescue shares some features with risky occupations and risky leisure, yet is distinct from each as well. Like professional ambulance workers, police officers, military personnel, and fire fighters, Peak's rescuers risked their lives to serve others; like recreational mountain climbers, skydivers, and whitewater rafters, Peak's rescuers were not paid for undertaking risk. By most definitions, "true" heroes perform acts that are independent of material rewards; thus, people who undertake risk as part of their everyday occupational duties would not theoretically be considered heroes.[18] Indeed, candidates for the Carnegie Hero Fund are eligible for the award only if they do not work in a "heroic" vocation or if their heroic acts clearly surpass their occupational duties; likewise, the Congressional Medal of Honor also requires that its recipients have risked their lives "beyond the call of duty."[19]

Of course, professional fire fighters, military personnel, police officers, and ambulance workers often perform above and beyond the call of duty, which would indeed qualify them as heroes in those instances. But sociologists have yet to study this type of incident, and thus this type of heroism. Moreover, since heroism is defined, in part, by voluntarily putting one's own life at risk to help others, recreational risk takers would not theoretically be considered heroes, either, since their activity is primarily self-gratifying. Thus, aside from a few studies of volunteer fire fighters, one survey on volunteer search and rescue workers in Australia, a content analysis of the dedications awarded with the Congressional Medal of Honor, and an in-depth examination of rescuers of Jews in Nazi-occupied Europe, very few studies have examined true heroes.[20]

The Setting

In 1994, I joined Peak Search and Rescue and began a six-year ethnographic study of the group. I was completely unskilled and inexperienced in all backcountry knowledge, but in those six years I learned a great deal about the group and forged lasting relationships with several of its members. The next chapter explains my role in the group and in the research, as well as my methodological trials and tribulations in negotiating a foothold in this world. For now, however, I set the stage by describing the setting.

Peak Search and Rescue (also frequently called "mountain rescue" by its members) was located in a small mountain resort town in the western United States. The group was under the direction of the Peak County Sheriff's Department and served as a volunteer-based extension of that division. Peak County consisted of 1700 square miles, 1300 of which were undeveloped national forest or wilderness-area lands. Local residents and tourists alike used this "backcountry" land year-round for various recreational purposes such as hiking, camping, hunting, rock and ice climbing, mountain biking, whitewater rafting and kayaking, snowmobiling, snowshoeing, and skiing outside of the ski area boundaries. Occasionally these recreational enthusiasts became lost or injured in this remote area. Because the sheriff's deputies and ambulance workers lacked the means to reach injured parties as well as the specialized skills to aid them in these wilderness areas, the county sheriff commissioned Peak to oversee all backcountry emergencies.

Peak's members had many specialized rescue skills to reach and help victims who were incapacitated while engaged in this wide variety of recreational activities. For example, some members were adept at riding snowmobiles and were frequently sent to search for lost snowmobilers and snowshoers. Others possessed honed whitewater skills, and as such, their expertise was utilized for rafting and kayaking accidents. Many members, however, had only basic skill levels in several areas, for example, operating the rope and pulley systems used to maneuver victims and rescuers over cliffs, surviving for several days in the wilderness while searching for a missing person, and using radio signal receiving devices to locate skiers buried in avalanches. Some members held emergency medical certification as well. There were approximately five emergency medical technicians, one paramedic, and one doctor in the group.[21] All members, however, were required to have at least basic first aid and CPR certification.

Since Peak was the community organization charged with handling all backcountry emergencies, the group was involved in a wider variety of searches and rescues (collectively termed "missions") than just tending to wayward recreationalists. For example, members occasionally searched for suicidal individuals. The family would phone 911 and report that their loved one was missing, suicidal, and likely to have gone up a favorite hiking trail. Peak would be dispatched to the trail while sheriff's deputies would search likely spots in town. Another of Peak's duties was searching for planes (and their passengers) that crashed in the wilderness. It was clearly stated in the county's disaster contingency plans that Peak was in total control of such search, rescue, and recovery efforts. Members also occasionally took their backcountry technical expertise to accidents that happened in more urban environments, for example, extracting victims from the cars that they had driven over cliffs or into rivers, or searching public establishments and town streets for missing children. Finally, in my six years, Peak was called twice to search for evidence at crime scenes: one time to search a riverbed after a drug bust, and another time to scour an arson scene.

At any one time, the group consisted of approximately 30 active members who had from zero to 25 years of experience in search and rescue. Of the 75 or so members who were active at any time during the course of this study, all were white, most were middle- to upper-middle-class, and most were permanent, year-round residents of the resort area that constituted much of Peak County. Furthermore, of these 75 members, only one had been born and raised in Peak County; all other members had migrated to Peak County in their adult lives, drawn largely by the resort industry, which dominated the local economy. The group's ratio of men to women was about two to one, although this low ratio was a relatively recent development as many of the newer members were women. Members ranged in age from the early twenties to mid-fifties; their educational levels ranged from high school through the M.D. degree.

Peak had an official hierarchy that delineated members' abilities. The most highly skilled and experienced were "lead" members, whose job it was to lead teams and direct the rescue effort on missions. They were in charge of choosing the most suitable mission procedures; for instance, which members to send into an avalanche zone to dig for a buried skier, or the safest way to reach a rafter stranded in the middle of a river. This category contained approximately 11 members: nine men and two women.

The "mission coordinator" position was an offshoot of the lead category and was equal in the status hierarchy. For the most part, mission coordinators were longtime lead-status members who rotated through the duty of receiving the group's emergency calls. When a call came in, the mission coordinator collected information about the victim's condition and likely whereabouts and then called out members for assistance. During the missions, the coordinators organized many different resources: they communicated with field teams via two-way radios and charted their progress on maps laid out in the group's base building; they mobilized outside support such as rescue helicopters, search dogs, or volunteers from other counties; they continued to probe the reporting parties or family members for new clues; and on long missions, they prepared statements for the press.

Those at the next level were "support" members. Their main function was to aid the lead members in any way they could. For instance, they made up the team that a lead-status member led into the field, or they set up a system of ropes and pulleys to lower a rescuer down the side of a cliff. Often they carried heavy rescue gear and did what they were told. Support members had to possess a basic level of skill, and were advanced to this category only after they had proved themselves. Most of Peak's active members, myself included, occupied this status.

At the bottom of the hierarchy were the "new members," who were the most inexperienced or yet unproven members. They occasionally served the same function as the support members. Their skills were unknown or undeveloped, however, so they were given roles in the missions less frequently and more cautiously.

As an official nonprofit organization, Peak had to have a board of directors, which comprised five rescuers elected by the membership. Board members were in charge of the organizational functioning of the group, and each held a standard board-of-directors-type position such as treasurer or president. The board did not hold scheduled meetings but only met when it had to vote on an issue facing the group, such as what equipment to buy or how to discipline a problematic member.

In addition to participating in missions, Peak's members had several other responsibilities. First, the group held biweekly business meetings, run by the board of directors. Some meetings were more highly attended than others, but at least half (about 15) of the members were usually there. The group also held training sessions for the members, especially for the newer, inexperienced members, which were run by one of the board members, the "training officer." "Trainings," as members called them, consisted of practicing a variety of skills and rescue scenarios. Rescuers might work out some map and compass puzzles, set up a series of rope and pulley systems to lower a team down a steep hill, learn how to operate the snowmobiles, or get acquainted with where all the different supplies were located in the base and in the rescue truck. These trainings were held sporadically, depending greatly on members' interest, time, and availability to attend.

Some rescuers also saw each other socially, although this varied a great deal throughout my time in the setting. When I first joined the group, many members attended trainings and went out for drinks immediately afterward. Later on in my career, this happened less often. Some members were friends outside of the group setting, making dates to ski, rock climb, or just go out to dinner. I became close friends with several members, and acquaintances with all.

Member Portraits

This section features portraits of some rescuers I knew well.

Jim

Jim, a founding member of the group, was a robust, balding man in his late forties, with a scraggly beard, a booming voice, and a commanding demeanor. A former marine, he was a veteran of the Vietnam War, where he had been a medic and a crew chief on a medical evacuation helicopter. His duties had included operating the helicopter's machine gun to lay down cover-fire when the ship entered enemy territory to rescue wounded soldiers, as well as medically tending to them during the evacuation. At one point, his helicopter was shot down by enemy fire, and of all the people on the ship, he was the lone survivor (it was rumored that he had lost some of his hearing in the accident, which was the reason he talked so loudly).

After the war, Jim moved to Peak County, arriving in the mid-1970s. He got a job working the front desk at one of the few hotels in the newly established mountain resort town. One day, the local radio station put out a call for anyone to help with a river accident. Five people had been thrown from a raft and were missing. Jim felt he could help, given his military search and rescue experience, so he drove down to the scene and spent the next three days riding the search raft down portions of the river, getting tossed around by the whitewater, and even capsizing on several occasions. He thought his wild rides in the raft were "great fun," although his fellow searchers disagreed, getting others to replace them after only one swim through the rapids.

After that search, Jim was invited to the fledgling, unorganized monthly meetings of the group that would later become Peak. Jim and one other member, Richie, took charge of the group and between them, responded to every backcountry emergency call for the next 10 years. Meanwhile they actively recruited members, but in those days, Peak County had only a fraction of the population it did when I lived there, so it was hard to find willing volunteers. But Jim never gave up trying to recruit people. Approximately a third of the members in this study (20–25 years later) said they joined the group because Jim recruited them.

By the mid-1980s, Jim was balancing the demands of work, his wife and two young daughters, and Peak. He had been able to recruit some highly skilled mountaineers and pushed for the group to become accredited in one of two national-level search and rescue organizations, which it did. The group became bigger and more organized, and Jim stepped up his commitment by serving on several regional and national search and rescue boards. In 1987, Jim's past caught up with him and collided with his intense commitment to rescue work. He realized that he was experiencing some "deep psychological ramifications" from his role in the war, which took the form of overwhelming survivor's guilt: "[What] stuck in my mind the most was all those guys that didn't make it in Vietnam. I carried that around for 20 years. That it was *my* fault that the squad got wiped out. That it was *my* fault that our helicopter got shot down. Why was I the only one that lived? I have no idea."

Jim dropped out of the group and sought therapy, where he was diagnosed with Post-Traumatic Stress Disorder. After attending counseling sessions twice a week for 18 months, he returned to Peak, healthier and ready to begin rebuilding his search and rescue career. This time he maintained his high levels of commitment to his wife and (now three) daughters, to Peak, and to his job (seemingly in that order), continuing to leave work whenever he could to run missions.

Jim's reputation as an extraordinary mission coordinator grew and reached the national level. He successfully resolved some high-profile missions, which garnered him the respect of many search and rescue teams, and in the mid-1990s, he was elected president of one of the national search and rescue organizations. Once he took over the helm of the national office, his involvement in Peak dwindled somewhat, but he was still able to make himself available for big missions. After three years as national president, he stepped down and sharply curtailed his search and rescue participation. By the end of this research, he was still a dominant force in Peak, serving on the board as well as attending meetings and other scheduled events, but he had rearranged his priorities. He had taken a management job that gave him more work responsibility, which precluded him from leaving work to run missions.

Meg and Kevin

Meg and Kevin were a married couple in their early forties when I joined the group in 1994. He was tall and slender, with thinning hair and a weathered complexion, the result of working outside year-round. He was also congenial and diplomatic—everyone loved Kevin, and he was often asked to serve on the board of directors (including Peak's) for community-based organizations. Meg was softer. Physically, her 5'7" frame was fuller than Kevin's, and socially, she was more outgoing and talkative. Her vivacious but down-to-earth manner made it easy for people to talk to her, and she held close friendships with many people in Peak County.

Meg and Kevin moved to Peak County in 1989, leaving behind their white-collar corporate jobs in the Midwest to be seasonal workers at the resort. They had always planned to move to the mountains once they had saved enough money; but when Meg survived a sudden, life-threatening complication from routine surgery, they immediately packed their bags, sold most of their belongings, and moved to Peak County. Their child-free lifestyle left them open for volunteering in the community, so within a month they attended their first search and rescue meeting.

Not knowing many people, nor knowing anything about the mountains, Kevin and Meg learned a great deal from participating in Peak. They attended trainings and missions regularly and forged some lasting relationships with members in the group. Many of the missions produced rewarding experiences for them, and they persisted in their involvement. Kevin, after a few years, advanced to lead status, and although Meg could have achieved it too, she never desired that position; she preferred to remain a support member. While both were often sent into the field on searches and rescues, Meg migrated toward fulfilling one particular (but only occasionally needed) role: staying behind with the family members during long searches. Here she found that she had a unique ability to connect with people, as she provided them with the emotional support they needed while others searched for their loved one.

Kevin and Meg also weathered several difficult group transitions, maintaining their dedication to the group by disengaging from "political issues," or intragroup conflicts and personality clashes. One example of this disengagement was their tacit refusal to go out for drinks after trainings or meetings. They felt that these informal, cliquish events were the breeding ground for the group's political struggles, and they disapproved. In this way, they were able to remain neutral parties and put their energy toward helping the group survive some tumultuous times.

Nick

Nick, who found Bill Brown with his air horn, was a 29-year-old support member when I joined the group in 1994. He stood six feet two inches, although his thick, spiked brown hair added an inch or two. Despite his long, skinny legs, his shoulders were broad, and he was quite strong. Temperamentally, he was moody and inexpressive, often appearing sullen and reserved, yet he was usually friendly once approached. He was also a risk taker. As a teenager growing up on the East Coast, Nick had raced motorcycles and driven fast cars. When he was 16, he lost control of the car he was driving and ended up in a two-week coma. Later he resumed his thrill-seeking activities, taking up with a wild crowd of boys in the neighborhood. When he was 17, his mother and stepfather sent him away to military school, where he became involved in some highly profitable but illicit activity. Upon graduation, he ended that career and got a job in a retail sports store. There he had an affair with the owner's wife, and together they left the East Coast and moved to Peak County in 1989. They lived together for three years before breaking up in 1992.

Nick was attracted to Peak in 1990, when Shorty, a member he worked with, convinced him that he could learn to ride snowmobiles if he joined the group. The idea of zooming around in the backcountry appealed to Nick, so he began attending meetings, trainings, and missions. Over the next seven years, he accumulated a great deal of experience on missions, as well as one of the thickest files in the local emergency room. He had more accidents than anyone else in the group, and according to the nurses in the ER, more accidents than most people in Peak County. For example, on several occasions he fell from construction scaffolding (he had become a drywall hanger); one time he broke his leg, cracked some ribs, and got a concussion in a dirtbike crash; and once he accidentally nailed his foot to the floor when he misfired a nailgun. Despite his propensity for injury, Nick was always willing to perform any job on missions, particularly if it was challenging or dangerous. In 1997 other members began to tell him that he was close to being advanced to lead status. The main obstacle to this was that Nick, ironically, hated the sight of blood and had been unable to sit through the graphic (although fake) films shown in the CPR certification classes. Eventually, though, he got his medical certification and was promoted to lead.

Within the group, Nick was one of what I called the "Ironmen." This was a group of young, experienced men who practically salivated at the thought of undertaking a dangerous or difficult task during missions, especially if it involved flying in a helicopter. They were extremely physically strong, most of them were of lead status, and they comprised the core of the subgroup who went drinking together after meetings, trainings, and missions. Although others were welcome to tag along, the members of this clique dominated the interaction at the bars.

Elena

Elena, who worked the radio during the Bill Brown mission, was a first-generation American of German descent. She was 28 years old when I joined the group in 1994. A transplant from the East Coast like myself, she moved to Peak County in 1990, two years after graduating from college. Elena was five feet two inches tall, had shoulder-length blond hair, a stocky build, and a muscular disorder in her calves that caused them to become easily overworked and to cramp severely under strain. After two years in Peak County, Elena was looking for volunteer opportunities when a friend told her about search and rescue, suggesting she call Jim to find out more about it. Jim was receptive and encouraged her to come to a meeting. There she felt out of place, noticing the large number of men in the room and feeling like there were "absolutely no girls," even though three women were present (including Meg). But Elena persevered. She tried attending some trainings but felt even more out of place there, so she quickly limited her participation to meetings only.

In addition to having very little backcountry experience, one reason Elena felt like she did not belong was because of the physically demanding nature of the missions and trainings. With her calf-disorder, she could not reliably hike miles through the woods, and with her short stature, she did not have much upper body strength for carrying injured victims or hauling rope systems. Thus, in her first year of membership, Elena's participation waxed and waned as she tried to find her niche. Because she attended meetings sporadically and did not attend trainings or missions at all, the other members only vaguely recognized her.

One event transformed Elena's experience: the group's annual fundraiser. She got involved in the project with several other members and put an enormous amount of time into it. The effort netted $12,000 that year—doubling the old record—and Elena felt proud and important to have played such an integral role. Others started to recognize her and eventually she felt more accepted. She began attending trainings and missions that spring, just as a new crop of inexperienced recruits (including myself) entered. The new recruitment cohort helped her keep up her momentum and solidify her commitment as we all studied and practiced rescue techniques together. Furthermore, now that there was a group of new recruits, we were able to tag along to the bar and socialize with some more established members, easing our adjustment and, we hoped, raising our status.

Throughout the next six years, Elena carved out several different roles for herself: she volunteered to do some administrative work, like typing and copying; she organized future fundraisers; and she served on the board of directors. One of her biggest accomplishments, however, was becoming a mission coordinator. Although the group had never had a mission coordinator who was not of lead status, Elena pushed for it so that she could contribute more to missions. This situation also allowed the group more leeway in utilizing its most skilled rescuers in the field instead of having them run the base operations.

In the chapters that follow, I tell the stories of Jim, Meg, Kevin, Nick, and Elena, as well as those of many other rescuers. I begin in chapter 1 by describing in more detail how I entered the setting, how I negotiated a role in Peak, the methods I used in gathering and analyzing my data, and several methodological problems and issues I encountered during the course of this study. In the next two chapters, I detail and analyze members' early experiences in Peak, including their motivations for joining as well as their confrontation with and eventual socialization to the group's strict heroic norms. Chapters 4 and 5 focus on members' emotional experiences during missions and how they managed both their own and others' intense feelings during crises. In the next section, chapters 6 and 7, I discuss how the outcomes of the missions and members' sustained participation in Peak influenced their heroic and emotional selves. Finally, in chapter 8, I examine the theoretical confluence of heroism, the self, emotions, and gender.

1

Studying Peak Search and Rescue

Ethnography (also known as "field research" or "participant-observation") does not conform to the tenets of the deductive scientific approach. The latter assumes that people can be studied the same way as objects, by formulating hypotheses from established theories, then gathering data that support or refute the hypotheses. This approach assumes that there is an objective reality that exists outside of human experience; that the "facts" are out there waiting to be discovered by using a controlled and standardized procedure. While this deductive model can be useful in answering certain questions, it would not have been able to answer my main questions: How do Peak's members understand their rescue experiences, and how do these understandings affect their lives? The answers to these questions depended largely on how rescuers interpreted and made sense of their experiences as well as on how they understood reality.

People come to define reality based on their experiences in social life. They assign meaning to social processes and objects (including themselves and others) based on their experiences with them. They then act based on the meanings these processes and objects hold for them. One way to understand behavior, then, is to investigate how people assign meaning to social phenomena. This is best accomplished through ethnographic research: observing and participating in people's lives in a natural setting, as well as talking to them in depth about their experiences.[1] The data gathered in ethnographic research take the form of field notes, in which researchers record what they see, hear, and feel, and of interviews, in which researchers ask their subjects to provide their own accounts of their experiences.

There are several advantages to ethnographic research. First, it provides a deep and intricate understanding of how and why social processes happen because it captures the nuanced meanings people give to social phenomena; it uncovers the reality they create.[2] The researcher can examine this reality not by imposing and defining it at the outset of the research, but by allowing it to emerge from the data. Second, although ethnographic research does not produce findings that are generalizable to other social settings, the data are not totally idiosyncratic. Ethnography allows the researcher to abstract general social principles and suggest where else they may be applicable, a quality that Glaser and Strauss (1967) termed "theoretical generalizability."[3] In this way, ethnographic research is inductive and theory generating. It produces tentative theories that may later be tested deductively to establish where, when, and how they may be counted on to explain other social phenomena.

I studied Peak Search and Rescue ethnographically because I wanted to explore specific aspects of rescuers' lived experience: why they volunteered to risk their lives to help others, how they handled risky situations, how their rescue experiences—both good and bad—affected their sense of self, and how they interpreted the rewards of rescue work. I could answer these questions only by achieving an intimate familiarity with rescuers' lives through participating in their world, by doing the things they did and feeling the things they felt.[4]

Getting In

I first decided to join search and rescue in the spring of 1994. I was looking for a unique social setting to enter in preparation for a sociology graduate seminar I was taking the next fall: ethnographic methods. A friend suggested that Peak Search and Rescue would be an exciting and fun setting in which to conduct participant-observation research. Naïvely, I thought the group would feel lucky to have someone like me, with my basic CPR training, volunteer to rescue people. (I later learned that there were several EMTs, paramedics, and even one doctor in the group. I also discovered that my level of medical certification did not even meet the group's minimum requirement.) When I called Peak in late June to find out how to join, I spoke to Gary, a well-respected rescuer. He told me that the group was always looking for people, so I should come to one of the business meetings, which were held on the first and third Sundays of every month.

I told a friend of mine, Barbara, that I was planning to join Peak to study it for a sociology project. She jumped at the chance to join with me, saying that she had always been interested. I thought that sounded like fun as well as academically productive because Barbara could provide me with a perspective of everyday life to enhance my own sociological observations.[5]

In July 1994, Barbara and I attended our first business meeting in the group's base building. Although we tried to enter unobtrusively, we felt highly conspicuous and quickly took seats in the back. Because it was a holiday weekend, there were only eight people in attendance (seven men and one woman), three of whom were on the board of directors and sat behind a table, facing the rest of the group. One member, Jim (whom I later learned was the founding, 20-year member), spent 15 minutes recounting a rock climbing rescue he had recently worked in another state. His point was that the standardization of search and rescue techniques made it easy for him to coordinate with other rescuers on the scene, and probably saved the victims' lives. I was much more fascinated, however, with his blow-by-blow description of the rescue, which sounded exciting. It did not occur to me, however, that rescuers would need highly specialized skills.

Barbara and I remained silent throughout the meeting, until the very end when the president asked if we were new. He told us to see Meg, a 10-year rescuer, who would show us around and give us some paperwork to complete. Meg was friendly as she gave us a tour of the base building, pointing out the radio room, the rescue truck, and the upstairs loft where much of the rescue gear was stored. At one point, though, she bluntly told us not to expect the other group members to welcome us with open arms. I was thrown off kilter by her frankness. She explained that many people joined and soon quit because they did not get what they expected from the group, which was to be assigned exciting roles on missions. The established members responded to this dynamic by remaining aloof until newcomers proved some kind of commitment to the group.[6] Meg recommended that we get involved in the weekly trainings so that we could begin what seemed to be a long, slow process of establishing trust. She gave us our paperwork and told us to hand it in at the next business meeting in two weeks. Now somewhat apprehensively, Barbara and I made plans to attend the two trainings in the interim.

When Barbara and I began to fill out the paperwork, it suddenly became very clear that we were totally unqualified, which made us even more apprehensive about going to the trainings.[7] We were asked to rate our skill in several areas using a scale from 1 (no experience) to 10 (expert). I scanned the list: whitewater rafting/kayaking; rock climbing;

summer wilderness survival; winter wilderness survival; snowmobiling; mountaineering; ice climbing; avalanche training; map and compass knowledge; medical certification; backcountry skiing; physical fitness. I rated myself a "1" in everything except physical condition, for which, after much debate, I circled "5" (fighting the urge to place myself higher, I suspected that my standards were not as high as the group's). Barbara did the same. We started to realize where we would stand in Peak.

With much less confidence, we began to attend trainings. As it turned out, there was a group of nine newcomers who had joined several months earlier, all of whom were enthusiastic and eager to become involved with Peak (this was the largest incoming "class" of recruits in my six years). Five of these members were also very inexperienced, so although Barbara and I were still the newest and least experienced, we were not as far behind as we had anticipated. We fit in reasonably well with this group of newcomers in other ways, too. We were similar in age (most were mid-twenties), race (white), and social class (middle–upper-middle). Furthermore, there were five other women in this group of nine, which made us feel more comfortable.

In the first month, I tried to get involved in the training exercises while simultaneously trying not to overstep my bounds, which can inhibit rapport and trust. I also tried to talk to people at the trainings, which was difficult because few people ever remembered my name, although sometimes they knew it was either Jen or Barbara. Barbara's interactional style was more effusive than my own, so I was often relieved when she developed an initial rapport with some members with whom I had more trouble.[8] Barbara had more luck than I did with one particular member, Elena, who seemed to be the leader of this group of newcomers. She was quite resistant to my friendly overtures. Every time I tried to talk to her, she gave me a one-word response and walked away.[9] I persisted, though, trying to engage her and other newcomers in conversation about the rescue techniques we were learning and making small talk with them during breaks. I rarely spoke to the few lead-status members who were running the trainings. For the most part they were the Ironmen: the highly experienced, risk-taking, thrill-seeking, intimidating young men. All in all, I felt awkward and out of place, common sentiments for fieldworkers entering new settings.[10]

After these first few encounters, I decided not to suggest that I study the group. I was taking field notes, however, in journal form so I could remember my early experiences, but I was under what Fine (1993) called "deep cover": I did not tell the members that I was conducting research. I reasoned that this might inhibit my ability to earn their trust, which looked like it would be hard enough to gain anyway. This decision proved to be a good one methodologically, as in early August the group spent an hour of its business meeting discussing an incident that had occurred two weeks before: Kevin, who had recently taken over the post of treasurer, discovered that a three-year, highly committed member had embezzled over $20,000 of group funds and equipment.

Members were shocked at the news. They felt betrayed and exploited, and thus became even more guarded than before, often openly stating their suspicions about why people joined the group. Several popular explanations revolved around how individuals used the group for their own benefit. One was that outsiders were seeking the prestige of membership. These people were derogatorily called "rescue rangers," a term that cast their enthusiasm as a desire for self-glorification.[11] It was widely believed that these glory seekers became interested through the burgeoning rescue-type television shows of the mid-1990s, such as *Rescue 911* and others, which, according to members, attracted droves of people looking for a glamorous, heroic experience. Another selfish reason people joined Peak, according to the subcultural lore, was to secure good prices on expensive outdoor gear. These people knew that group members could get discounts on equipment like snowshoes and sleeping bags, so rescuers believed that these outsiders joined the group, ordered their gear, and then quit when they received their merchandise. The third unacceptable reason people might join Peak was to acquire skills. Rescuers feared that people took advantage of the trainings run by experienced rescue personnel and then quit after they learned the techniques they sought. When the embezzler was caught, one month after I joined, members closed ranks and became highly suspicious of newcomers' motivations.

I continued my participation that summer, though I remained fairly marginalized throughout. Sometimes several members went for drinks after the trainings, but I did not feel comfortable doing so, even though one or two rescuers halfheartedly invited me a few times. I befriended a member who joined after I had, and one day she told me that Elena (who wouldn't talk to me) had explained to her that the only way to gain acceptance in this group was to go to the social events; trainings and meetings weren't enough (this new member, incidentally, quit several weeks later). I decided I had to step up my participation.

After one training at the end of August, I accepted the invitation to go to the bar for drinks (Barbara was out of town). By the time I got there, however, one large table was completely filled with well-established core members, as well as with some new members. A small satellite table had been started next to it, where Brooke, a young southern woman in her early twenties, sat alone. I knew that Brooke, although only a one-year member, dated Nick, a core member, but he wasn't there so she was feeling isolated and left out. She waved to me and loudly beckoned, "I'm at the loser-table! Come sit with me at the loser-table!" How could I refuse such a complimentary invitation? Within minutes, two other new members wandered in and sat with us. I began to make the posttraining trips to the bars a habit, which proved to be an excellent setting for developing rapport and gathering data, in part because of the lubricating effect of the alcohol on members' sociability.

During that summer, I employed various techniques to ingratiate myself with the established members as well as with the newcomers. I tried to be outgoing and entertaining, a feat I accomplished by using a great deal of lighthearted self-deprecation during social events. Self-deprecation also allowed me to project a nonthreatening persona, which I used to engage others in conversation, even if it was to make myself the butt of the joke.[12] During trainings I tried to be a bit more serious and less self-effacing, but I continued to remain subordinate, deferring to others who had more knowledge and experience than I, which was everyone. All in all, I worked hard to befriend the members by earnestly complimenting them, appearing interested by asking them about themselves, and when I thought it would be well received, gently teasing them about things they said or did.

Yet I was making slow progress. One day, however, I got a break. In late September, two and a half months after I joined, Barbara and I were at a bar with several new members and our trainer, Roy, a 15-year veteran of Peak. Barbara referred to me as a "professor" during the conversation, and this caught everyone's attention. Several times in the past I had explained to members that I was a graduate student and a teaching assistant in sociology, but no one had seemed to care, or perhaps no one understood exactly what I was talking about. But the word "professor," inaccurate as it was, piqued the members' interest, so they asked (again), "Wait—what do you do?" Thankful for the opening, I carefully explained it again and tried to focus on some of the more interesting aspects of my job, like leading class discussions on social issues and doing research on social interaction. They became more interested and began asking me to give them personality profiles. I tried to explain that I was not a psychologist, but rather a sociologist, who studied interactions between people and behavior in small groups. Then they wanted me to give Peak a "group-profile" analysis. When I declined, saying that Peak was "too complex," they persisted, saying things like, "Oh, come on, take a potshot at it." Luckily, Elena interjected: "Hey, if you ever need a project, you can study mountain rescue! You can study this group!" Others chimed in, "Yeah! Study us!"

This was indeed a lucky break. After several months in a covert researcher role, fearing the group members would be resistant to my studying them, I now had several members begging me to do so.[13] I decided to bounce the idea off Roy, our trainer, because of all the core, well-established members, I knew him best. It took me several weeks to approach the board of directors officially, because Roy agreed to pave the way for me by talking to some of the board members in advance. When I did approach the board, they consented after I allayed some of their concerns, and they put aside some time for me to explain the project to the entire membership at the next business meeting. The members received the idea well, making jokes during my presentation, such as if I undertook this "year-long" study, at least I would stick around for that long. Some members, like Brooke, who had invited me to sit at her loser-table, even thought it was a great idea and offered to help me any way they could.

My role in the group changed after that. Once I became an overt researcher, people began to trust me more—they talked to me more, anyway, although in the beginning the idea of "research" was foreign to them. As they realized I was not going to show up to all Peak functions wearing a white lab coat or carrying a note pad, they relaxed and eventually forgot about it, a common response to ethnographers.[14] My overt researcher role also allowed me to network further, as it gave me a reason to talk to the more established, higher status members. In the interest of research, I could more comfortably engage them in conversation, and they suspected me less, presumably because my motives were clear to them. I began going to Peak's social hours at the bars with more frequency, even when new members were not going to be there. I also received a pager and started to be called out to go on missions.

Getting Established: Acceptance Processes

In my first two years, I focused heavily on acceptance processes, a theoretical interest that arose out of my own difficulty breaking into the group, and a topic that shaped my first paper (see chapter 3). During that time, I gained a great deal of knowledge and experience through trainings and missions, and numerous times I was able to prove myself a valuable member. For example, I tried to perform at high levels and show enthusiasm for undertaking difficult tasks, like being on a team of three to carry the heavy stretcher miles up a steep hiking trail to reach an injured victim. I also, however, tried not to overestimate my abilities in these areas since I had quickly surmised that appearing unsafe was one way to lose status in the group.[15]

One particular mission serves as an example of the conflict I felt between wanting to prove myself in challenging situations and not wanting to fail. One winter evening in my second year, Peak was called out to search for some lost snowboarders who were last seen eight hours earlier snowshoeing up a valley carrying their boards on their backs. Jim, the mission coordinator, was putting together two teams to track the party that night, while reserving most members for a full-scale search the next day. I wanted to go on the all-night search team, so I told Jim I was available. He asked, "Are you prepared to spend the night out and bed down with the victims if you find them?"

Oh. I had not thought of that. I was prepared to walk all night, even if the temperatures dipped below zero, because hiking with a pack would keep me warm. I was not sure, however, if I had the right gear to stay in one place all night. I considered it for a moment: "I don't know," I said, but then quickly acquiesced. "So I guess that means I'm not prepared to do it."

Jim said, "Good. Smart decision. If you don't know, then we can't take a chance on ya." I was disappointed (and embarrassed) because I had wanted a chance to prove myself, but I realized that "proving" I was careless and inexperienced by getting frostbite or becoming hypothermic carried a greater risk, both to my own status in the group as well as to the victims' and other rescuers' safety.

Another way I tried to prove myself was by being in good physical condition, since that was one of the ways rescuers got to go on missions and gain status. Ideally, I wanted to be able to keep up with the pace of any field team because I was afraid of being left in the dust by the Ironmen. However, since that was a pipe dream, I settled for respectably pulling my weight (for a "girl"—see chapter 2) and physically pushing myself to my limits. At least others would know I was trying. After a year in Peak, I was promoted to "support" status.

During this time, I also began to familiarize myself with the various recreational activities and corresponding skills in which Peak's members were involved, such as backpacking, map and compass route finding, and telemark skiing (a cross-country/downhill skiing hybrid) in the backcountry. As I got more involved in these activities, it was easier for me to ask the more established members if they wanted to accompany me on recreational outings. We made ski dates and went mountain biking, where we got to know each other better. These members eventually became my closest friends. We socialized often, pet-sat for each other, and even took vacations together. In the first two years, Barbara and I became particularly close to Nick, Brooke, Elena, and Roy.[16] After year two, Barbara moved to another state, and in the following four years I expanded my circle of close friends in the group to include Maddie, Meg and Kevin, Cody, and Vincent. I also became romantically involved with Gary at this time, and married him at the conclusion of this research.[17]

By my third year in the group, I was a core member. I had responded to enough missions that the members considered me dependable, and I had been in enough challenging situations that others considered me competent to handle the less to moderately challenging tasks. I was also fortunate to have achieved a reputation for being one of the women in the group who was physically fit.

Dating Gary did not hurt, either. My role in Peak expanded to include that of Gary's girlfriend, and I gained status from this association. After a year of dating, we moved in together, and the next year he was elected president of the group. Since he was so involved in Peak's inner workings, I was able to get an extensive look behind the scenes. Board members would frequently call our house or come over to discuss group business. In these ways, I was privy to the most highly sensitive group information. Living with Gary helped me understand the group workings in other ways, too. I often shared my developing analyses with him, and he offered his own from the perspective of a highly skilled man—two perspectives I, personally, did not hold. His viewpoints proved to be enlightening on many occasions, as he provided me with the perspective of a native in the setting.[18] In this way, we were able to use some of the breadth-and depth-enhancing benefits of team research.[19]

During this period, Gary also became involved in search and rescue work at the regional and national levels. He was elected to an officer position in our geographical region, which included nine other teams. As part of his post, he was in charge of running several weekend-long meetings a year where rescuers from around the state gathered to practice rescue techniques and conduct "reaccreditation" tests for teams whose certification had expired. Any rescuer from one of the regional teams could attend these retreats, so I went regularly. I spent the 12-hour days observing other teams in mock-rescue scenarios and consulting with other evaluators about their own experiences, which were invaluable learning experiences for me.

Gaining Experience: Emotions in the Field

My theoretical interest in emotions arose later in the research as I gained enough experience on critical missions to notice some patterns. The first time I became aware of intense emotions on a mission was on New Year's Eve in 1995. I responded to a call to search for a tourist from Kentucky who had been buried in an avalanche. He, his wife, and stepson had come to Peak County to snowboard for several days. They budgeted their money, boarded for as many days as they could afford, and were preparing to drive home when a snowstorm hit. They stayed one more night because the husband wanted to snowboard in the fresh powder the next day. Since they had run out of money for ski lift tickets, he asked his wife to drive him to a steep hill he had seen from the road so he could hike up and board back down. She dropped him off, ran some errands, and when she came back to pick him up, she could not find him. Not knowing that what she was looking at was an avalanche, she drove back to the hotel, thinking he might have hitched a ride back to town. Meanwhile, several motorists reported seeing fresh avalanche debris from the side of the road, with a snowboard track going into it but not coming out.

By the time the sheriff dispatched Peak, it was late afternoon. I responded to the page and arrived on the scene with several other rescuers. While Jim, the mission coordinator, was putting together a team to check out the debris zone, the wife and her 15-year-old son drove up. This mission was unique because the accident scene, about 200 feet away, could be seen from the side of the busy road where we were stationed. Jim assigned me to stay with the family members, both to keep them from running into the dangerous avalanche zone as well as to make sure they did not wander into traffic.

We watched two rescuers enter the danger zone as others waited in a safe area, ready to dig them out should they become buried in another slide. The son was silent, staring at the ground and pacing back and forth on the side of the road. The wife was frantic, tightly gripping my arm and constantly asking me what was happening. I felt okay about describing what we were watching, but I was much less comfortable answering her other questions, like how many people survive avalanches (almost none if they were buried as long as her husband) and did I think he was alive (doubtful). Instead of telling her what I thought, I tried to give her hope without implying that he would survive by telling her that our rescuers, some of the most experienced in the country, would do everything they could. Within 10 minutes, rescuers found her husband, already dead. Jim came over and informed her: "I'm sorry, he didn't make it." She began wailing and collapsed in my arms. Her son began to swear, kick the ground, and hit the side of their car. I felt sad for them, and I tried to comfort her, but I really did not know what to say, which made me even more uncomfortable. I had no idea how to respond to her emotions, and I felt guilty for not having the courage to have answered her questions during the mission; perhaps I could have done a better job to prepare her emotionally for this outcome. Soon the sheriff arrived along with a victim's advocate volunteer, and they took her away. The next week at the business meeting, Jim reported on the mission and thanked me specifically for "volunteering" to stay with the family during the ordeal. Several other rescuers turned to me and most sincerely said, "Yeah, thanks for doing that, we really appreciate it." I got the feeling it was the least coveted position on a mission.

About a year later, I was on another mission that caused me to feel particularly strong emotions. A private plane carrying five passengers—a father, mother, and three young daughters—was missing and presumed to have crashed in Peak County during a November snowstorm. All downed planes emit an emergency locator transmitter (ELT) signal, so rescuers spent all night driving and skiing to the highest points in the county with radio signal receiving devices trying to zero in on the plane's location. The process often takes hours because mountainous terrain causes the signal to bounce off the uneven geography, producing many inaccurate readings. At three in the morning, upon returning to the base building from one of these assignments, I was told that several field teams were very close to finding the plane so I could go home. But I didn't want to. I was very emotionally involved, speculating that some of the victims could be alive. I was particularly disturbed by the possibility that the parents were dead but the young girls were alive and freezing to death in the snowstorm. This image kept entering my mind. I wanted to stay and help. The mission coordinator assured me that he would call me if he needed me, so I went home. Several hours later, a team reached the plane. All the passengers had been killed upon impact.

Later that day, I told Gary about the persistent image I experienced during the mission, and how it made me feel. He told me that rescuers cannot allow images like that to affect them emotionally because those "got in the way" of rescue work:

> If you let those concerns bother you—"Oh God, there's three kids out there freezing to death"—you're losing sight of your task. And you're jeopardizing your own safety and your team's safety by not being focused on what your task is. If you're out there searching for a plane crash, the odds are you have an ELT signal. You're not looking for those three little kids, you're looking for that signal. And if you start thinking about those three little kids, you're going to get off your task. Emotions just get in the way on missions.

I found these ideas intriguing and began to examine rescuers' strategies for emotion management during critical situations. Thinking back to the avalanche rescue, I also began to explore how rescuers managed the emotions of family members during missions.

Once I became sensitized to emotions in rescue work, I started to interpret all of my experiences through this lens and asked other rescuers to describe their emotional experiences on missions. I then thought about these strategies when I was confronted with emotionally demanding rescue situations. In the winter of 1999, I responded to a page for a car that had rolled off a steep embankment. When several other rescuers and I arrived on the scene, a sheriff's deputy informed us that the victim was dead; the deputy had hiked down the embankment from above and discovered that the driver, a seventeen-year-old man, had been killed. Our team got ready to snowmobile into the scene from a trail at the bottom of the ravine to recover the driver's body. There were five of us, and Nick was in charge. He told me I did not have to go in to recover the body since it could be upsetting. After hearing many stories from other rescuers about body recoveries—both in casual conversation and in interviews—but having never been on one, methodologically I thought it would be a good idea to participate in the recovery.[20] I was prepared to suppress my emotions, like many rescuers told me they did when they encountered graphic sights (see chapter 4), and I realized I might have flashbacks for some time afterward.

When we arrived on the scene, we saw that the victim had been thrown from his car and had rolled most of the way down the hill when the back of his pants caught on a tree branch, which stopped him, upside down, about 20 feet above the trail. The tree branch had pulled his pants down around his knees, exposing his white boxer shorts with red hearts—a humiliating way to be found dead, I thought. His eyes were open, and he had a small cut on his temple. The deputy hypothesized that he had died from this head injury.

We climbed up, extricated him from the tree, and tried to carry him down to the trail when someone slipped, sending his frozen body sliding the rest of the way on its own. Back on the trail, we pulled his pants up and packaged him in the body bag, which took some maneuvering since his knees were bent and frozen in position. Even though I was wearing winter gloves, I found touching him a bit creepy, so I manipulated him by his clothes, avoiding contact with his skin. We brought him back to the rescue truck where other deputies were stationed, and where six of his family members, along with their priest, were now waiting. A deputy opened up the body bag upon the family's request, and the priest performed a ceremonial blessing while we five rescuers stood by quietly. After the blessing, a deputy ushered the family away, while one young woman cried, "My brother! My brother!" Personally, I found her crying to be the most upsetting aspect of the mission.[21]

We loaded up the truck and took off. On the ride back I shared my thoughts with Patrick, a rescuer who had been working on an ambulance for the past two years. I thought seeing my first dead body would have been much more upsetting, but I was not that bothered by it. He told me that it was easier when victims were frozen and the trauma was not too apparent because they looked like "mannequins."

Three days later I drove by the accident site, which suddenly reminded me of the mission. I was surprised because I had not thought about it since, even though I had been expecting to have some emotionally disturbing flashbacks from seeing and touching the body. I shared these thoughts with Gary, who told me that missions and rescuers were all different: some body recoveries are easier than others, and some rescuers have a harder time than others.

By becoming a full-fledged rescuer, I took on a "complete membership role" (Adler and Adler 1987) in the setting. I was not a removed researcher, but rather participated in the same things the other rescuers did and felt the same things they felt. These emotionally demanding situations gave me a sound experiential basis for probing others about their own emotions on missions and greatly aided me in gaining this intimate familiarity with rescuers' emotions—much more so than a more distant, less involved role would have.[22]

Gathering and Analyzing Data

During my six years in the setting, I kept detailed field notes of my participation in group activities, including missions, training sessions, post-training and postmission social hours at bars, and the biweekly business meetings. In addition to observing the action in these settings, I also conducted hundreds of focused conversations with rescuers, which I also recorded in my field notes. At first, my notes were quite extensive since so much was new to me, but as I became more familiar with the workings of the group, the sheer number of pages I was writing each time began to decline.[23] In the first year, most of my notes centered around group acceptance processes, one of the major "sensitizing concepts" (Blumer 1969) for me since acceptance was one of the major hurdles I had to overcome. My notes during this time focused mostly on the interaction that occurred during the trainings, meetings, and social hours, but relatively little on the missions since I had not been highly involved in very many.

After a year in the setting, I constructed a "theoretical sample" (Glaser and Strauss 1967) of members to interview by choosing those whose experiences were most relevant to my theoretical interests. I interviewed a range of rescuers, from newcomers (Mitch and Patrick were one- and two-year members then) to old-timers (Jim and Roy were 20- and 15-year members at that time) to those in between. I also tried to interview members of both sexes, various ages and occupational fields, as well as of different skill and experience levels. These initial 13 semistructured, in-depth interviews ranged from 75 to 120 minutes each and provided me with "thick description" (Geertz 1973) of rescuers' motivations, rewards, and acceptance experiences. Only after two and a half years did I accumulate enough experience with Peak to understand that emotions were integral to missions. I then conducted ten more in-depth interviews (bringing the total to 23) during my third and fourth years, this time focusing the questions around rescuers' emotional experiences on particularly risky, fulfilling, or otherwise memorable missions. These data are especially valuable because they reveal members' innermost feelings, something these macho rescuers did not usually talk about. I feel fortunate to have spent as much time in the setting and to have developed such rapport with the members that they entrusted me with deeply personal information they would normally guard quite closely.

Throughout my six years, I also had considerable contact with rescuers from other teams. For example, some searches were so large and so protracted that they became statewide events. After 24 to 48 hours of unsuccessful searching, a call for volunteers would go out to the rescue teams around the state, and some of their members would arrive within hours to assist in the search. On many occasions, I was placed with rescuers from other teams and sent into the field for 12 to 15 hours at a time. I also attended one national-level search and rescue meeting, as well as seven regional-level meetings. I recorded these events in my field notes, which gave me ample opportunity to compare the dynamics I noticed in Peak to those in other teams. These findings served as a way for me to cross-check my data, ensuring that the social processes I was discovering were not idiosyncratic to Peak's rescuers.

I also talked to dozens of victims and their families during and immediately after missions, and I recorded these experiences in my field notes as well. Furthermore, over the course of this study I collected 46 thank-you letters that victims and their family members sent either directly to Peak or to the local newspaper's editor. I used these letters to enhance my understanding of rescuers' relationships with victims and their families during and after missions.

As I collected these field notes, interviews, and thank-you letters, I formulated tentative theories about rescuers' experiences. I revised subsequent interview questions to reflect my new suspicions and continued to collect new data, which would yield still more variation from my developing analysis. I then used this new information, once again, to refine my theoretical framework and revise the content of subsequent interviews, which made the data gathering and analysis an interactive, dialectical process in accordance with Glaser and Strauss's (1967) model of grounded theory. After six years, these data reached what Glaser and Strauss called "theoretical saturation": No new conceptual patterns were emerging, a situation that Taylor (1991) referred to as one's fieldwork yielding "diminishing returns."

Problems and Issues

I encountered several problems and issues during the course of this fieldwork, some of which held potentially disastrous consequences for my presence in the setting as well as for the relationships I had built with members. The first and most logistical impediment to my gaining entrée into this setting was that I lacked the required gear. When I joined Peak, I did not own several important (and expensive) items: a pair of good hiking boots ($200), a quality backpack ($150), a climbing harness ($75), or even a waterproof jacket ($300) and pants ($150). There were countless other little things I needed to buy as well, like a compass, fire-starting fuel sticks, and water purification tablets, but the big purchases set me back both in money as well as in time, because on a student's budget, it took me a long time to save up for each item. Until I was properly prepared, I would not be sent into the field on missions. Furthermore, on a more informal level, not having this specialized gear drew attention to my suspicious motives. How interested in backcountry search and rescue could I be if I did not even own hiking boots?[24]

A second problem occurred during my second year in Peak. Political infighting made this a particularly difficult time for many rescuers, as several longtime members vied for control of the group. I was very involved in the new member trainings at that time, and the other new members and I became highly concerned with this debate. After trainings we went to the bar and complained about Peak's problems. Although our involvement was not formal, these informal griping sessions clearly aligned us with one of the members, thus pitting us against the other side. Eventually this situation blew over, and the member with whom we were aligned quit the group when he was not elected president. Following that event, the political climate relaxed, and the membership was able to jell together. My access to any of the members was not permanently affected by the temporary split, but in retrospect, I realize that being involved in this political issue could have been methodologically disastrous.[25] At the time, though, I did not care because I had "gone native."

This brings me to the third problem. During my second year, I became too engrossed in becoming a respected member of Peak to maintain my objectivity, a common problem for researchers who enter a setting intending to take a less active role but who are "converted" to complete membership.[26] I was making new friends and doing fun things so I neglected my work. Although I continued to take field notes during this time (in fact, I did so more frequently than during any other time), I was not engaging in productive analysis. I had completed my first paper on acceptance and socialization (although it would go through many more substantial revisions later), but I was having trouble finding new topics to analyze, probably because I was so focused on the norms, violations, and sanctions of group membership.

Eventually, I regained my perspective. One thing that helped me do so was having new members join the group. Although I had joined the group two years before, no new members had committed since, so my cohort and I remained the newest, least experienced members until newer people came in. This event suddenly put me in the role of more experienced member, and this new role gave me a fresh perspective; I did not see everything from a newcomer's standpoint anymore. Another thing that aided me in recalibrating my perspective was going on more missions. With more mission experience, I was able to analyze interactions that did not have to do with group members' volatile relationships with each other. It was then that I began to notice the strong role that emotions played in search and rescue.

My status as a female rescuer presented some interesting dilemmas as well. In some ways it was an advantage. Since women are less threatening than men and often act as the "sociability specialists" (Douglas 1976), subjects may have felt comfortable opening up to me, especially when it came to talking about emotions, which are often considered women's domain.[27] In other ways, being a woman in Peak inhibited my aspirations to blend into the group. The missions were often highly physical and sometimes risky, and as a result, they were often considered a highly masculine domain.[28] Physically, I was less capable than a physically fit man, so I was sent on difficult tasks less often and missed out on some data-gathering opportunities. It was also difficult to penetrate the Ironmen clique, whose members spent a great deal of time at the bar trying to one-up one another with war stories from the field. While they welcomed me as an observer to this interaction, I was not qualified to participate in it. Yet, on the other hand, a man with my paltry qualifications would not have an "excuse" to be so inexperienced—by virtue of his gender, others might have expected him to have engaged in these risky and daring activities before. Thus, being an inexperienced woman at least allowed me to gain acceptance by conforming to the gender norms associated with my subordinate status. I elaborate on this gendered component of group life in chapter 2.

I also had some ethical concerns throughout the course of this study. First, I was not entirely comfortable entering this setting covertly, although, as I explained, it turned out to be necessary in order to establish trust with highly suspicious members. Although some may object to my use of the covert role, I believe it was an appropriate methodological tactic to aid me in gaining entrée. Second, I have blatantly deceived members on two fronts in order to gain permission to study the group and maximize my research goals. In one instance, I misrepresented my research interests by omitting potentially alienating topics such as conflict and power struggles in the group.[29] Although I wrote about these issues in my field notes, they never evolved into any major themes and thus were never published, so my ethical concerns with this issue have dissipated. Furthermore, after the group gave me permission to study it, two members thanked me separately for asking permission to study Peak because I "could have just gone ahead and done it anyway." I told them that I would never consider that approach since it would be unethical. While that was not exactly true, since I had been taking field notes in a covert researcher role for several months, it was true that I would not have continued in that capacity without the group's consent. A third ethical issue was that of harm: I would feel quite guilty if Peak lost one or more dedicated volunteers because they felt alienated by my research. Fortunately, to my knowledge, this did not happen. Finally, I have tried to protect the privacy of my subjects. Much of the information they have shared with me has been of a sensitive and personal nature, and I am grateful to them for allowing me to probe into their innermost thoughts and feelings. I have done my best to present their experiences as accurately as they presented them to me.

Disengaging

I left Peak slowly; over a period of eight months I began "drifting off" (Glaser and Strauss 1968). While Gary was still highly involved, I began attending meetings less often and participating in missions more selectively. One reason was that I needed to write up a substantial portion of my analysis in a relatively short period of time, which gave me less time to donate to Peak. A second reason was that I had accepted a job in another state, and Gary and I were going to move away. It was emotionally difficult to leave Peak and the friends I made there, and I experienced a variety of emotions: I felt sad because I would miss many of them, I felt nostalgic

because I would miss the emotional rush of finding lost victims and rescuing injured people, and I felt relieved because I would *not* miss getting up
in the middle of the night to respond to a mission (nor would I miss the
guilt from deciding to stay in bed).[30] Snow (1980) noted that disengaging
from setting members may be particularly difficult when the relationships
are intense and intimate. I felt especially close to those rescuers who
shared their private emotional experiences with me in interviews; thus the
nature of my data contributed greatly to the intensity and intimacy I
shared with many members.[31]

2

Joining Up

Joining Peak was not effortless. Potential members came to the group with many different motives and expectations, which could influence whether they continued to participate. Members' demographic characteristics also indirectly influenced how involved they could be in Peak.

Members' Motives

People joined Peak for a variety of reasons. New members often had their expectations disconfirmed upon joining, a common experience for newcomers to any organization.[1] Some of these people quit the group after discovering it was not what they expected, while others, despite their disconfirming experience, stayed and committed to the group.

All of the members I interviewed stayed with the group for at least one year, so my research only reflects the motives of those who displayed some kind of commitment to Peak. This sample limitation makes it impossible for me to assess how members' motives contributed to their decision to stay in or quit Peak. Rescuers, however, had very definite ideas about the relationship between motives and commitment. The prevailing belief was that people committed to the group because they had the right reasons for joining; those who joined for the "wrong reasons" subsequently quit (I discuss what effect this belief had on group socialization in chapter 3). Whether this was true can never be known, yet casting quitters' motives as unacceptable allowed committed rescuers to interpret their own motives through this ideological framework.

When I asked them what brought them to Peak Search and Rescue, members talked about their experiences in three stages. They explained what generally attracted them (and others) to search and rescue, what specific event actually impelled them to join, and, in some cases, how their initial motives were changed or expanded as they gained experience with the group.

Initial Attractions

Many rescuers said that meeting people was either their primary or an auxiliary reason for joining the group. In some cases, the would-be members were new to town and were looking for a way to get to know others in the community. They were attracted to Peak as opposed to other community organizations because they believed they would encounter a certain type of person in a search and rescue group. When I interviewed Brooke, she had been a member for two years (one year after she invited me to sit at her "loser-table"). She explained her motives:

> I wanted to join because I wanted to meet people. Because being straight out of college, working at ski stores where I was working at the time, I was coming in contact with a lot of ski bum-, transient-type people. I mean "ski bum" in the highest sense of the word, of course [laughs]. I mean, great people, but I guess I kind of wanted to become more a part of the community, and I was sort of looking for a way to meet people who were locals. And I figured if I was gonna be a local, those were the kind of people that I wanted to meet.

Brooke was not alone in her desire to meet year-round residents. Because Peak County was dominated by a skiing resort town, many residents were seasonal and temporary members of the community; they were around for the winters, but left for the summers. Several members joined Peak, like Brooke did, in an effort to become more firmly rooted in the community.

Mitch, a one-year member who, like Brooke, moved to the resort area right after college, also said he was attracted to Peak because of the type of people he would (and did) encounter there. At his first meeting he talked to Roy, the member of 15 years who was in charge of training the new members. Roy spoke about his extensive mountaineering experience, and Mitch respected him from the start:

> I was just impressed by someone with [Roy's] skill level [who] was applying it to sort of a greater good. Because climbing's a very self-serving sport, and it's awful nice if you take something that's really self-serving

and use it to try to benefit someone else or help someone else [through] search and rescue. And someone who's world-class like Roy is, who's still doing that on a basic, county level—that was, like, a tribute to his character. And so I guess I was impressed by the type of people that would be brought into the group.

Mitch was lured to the group by what he perceived to be members' high moral, or heroic, character, as evidenced by their willingness to be self-sacrificing. A climber himself, he was particularly awestruck by Roy's mountaineering accomplishments.

Meg, too, told me how when she and Kevin moved to Peak County from the Midwest 10 years earlier, they joined Peak because they wanted to meet people who had interests compatible with their own:

> We had made a commitment that this is where we wanted to live, and we wanted to get involved in the community in a big way and get to meet people. I mean, it's kind of scary being in a strange place, a new place, [and we] didn't know anyone. We did a lot of outdoorsy things back home. We did quite a bit of rock climbing, so we had some skills, and we liked the outdoors, so we thought that it would be a fun way to meet people with those same skills and to learn about the new environment we were in. 'Cause we found that [to be], actually, a little intimidating. You know, a couple of flatlanders all of sudden in the mountains, there were things that we obviously didn't know, and so we thought that would be a great way to get something out of it for ourselves, to participate, to meet people, and to get involved in the community. So that's how we started. And it was right that first summer that we moved here.

Members often thought that they might fit in well with the other group members because of the nature of Peak's work. For example, several members, like Meg, described themselves as "outdoorsy" people, and migrated to Peak, as opposed to other volunteer organizations, because of the work Peak did in the wilderness. In this way, members sought "focused sociability" (Fine 1998), hoping that organized contact with others who had similar interests might lead to friendships. Benny, a construction worker and seven-year member in his late thirties, told me that he originally joined the group because he felt an "affinity" with the other members who all had similar interests in outdoor recreational activities; he said it was a "powerful pull" for him to join.

The concept of individual-group "fit" applied to skills too. Jim originally showed up at the river rafting accident because he "had a fair background in search and rescue activity from being in the Marine Corps"; and Roy, our trainer and the accomplished mountaineer, gave similar reasons for initially being attracted to Peak in the early days, when the membership's skill base was shallow: "I had a lot of experience and a lot of depth, and a lot of mountaineering experience. And they were deficient in that. They were very good on medical [skills]. . . . And they had a basic mountaineering guy, . . . but they were kind of thin [on more advanced mountaineering skills]." Roy saw that he could offer something to the group by contributing needed skills to enhance Peak's functioning level.[2]

Meg had also named providing skills as one of the forces behind her and her husband's membership, but she also added that they had wanted to acquire new skills as well. In a trade-off, she and Kevin would contribute the skills they had in exchange for learning some new skills specific to their new environment. Other members, too, believed that Peak was a good fit for them since they wanted to learn certain skills, and Peak seemed like a good place to get them. While acquiring skills is a common motivation for joining voluntary groups, it was only an acceptable motive in Peak under certain circumstances (I deal with this issue in greater depth in chapter 3).[3]

Some members also felt the pull of public service and joined Peak as a way to contribute to the community. Kevin, Meg's husband, identified the same motives for joining as she did, but added that the most important of them was that "we had the opportunity to give back, be helpful to our community. Service, civic-minded stuff." Martin, a 53-year-old construction supervisor who had joined the group with my cohort five years earlier, was also motivated by the desire to contribute to the community. He chose Peak as the way to make his contribution because the nature of the work was suited to his recreational interests:

> I'd always been an outdoors person. I'd always been a climber, a hiker, [and I'd begun] kayaking also lately. And Shorty had mentioned it to me and then [another member] had mentioned it to me. They thought I'd be good for it. And I'd just found that I was sitting around bitching about everything in town, the government wasn't working, nothing seemed to be working right. Town was growing and I didn't like it. And I just said [to myself], "Why don't you get off your ass and do something instead of

bitching?" And I thought of what I could do where I could make some kind of a difference, and mountain rescue just fit in perfect.

Finally, the last major reason people joined Peak was to help others. Vince was a 24-year-old member of two years who had dropped out of college to become a paramedic. When I asked him what drew him to search and rescue, he told me it was the same thing that had drawn him to emergency medicine—his desire to help people:

> *Vince:* I joined mountain rescue because I like helping people. That's also why I made the decision to go to paramedic school and not fin-ish college. It was like, "I *could* finish college, I could do that, it'd be okay. But that's not really what I *want* to do. I want to help people, I want to do something like that." And I think I've also been really picky about the environments in which I want to help people.
> *Jen:* You could always help people as a social worker or a teacher, could-n't you?
> *Vince:* Oh, yeah, you could. Definitely, you could. I hate to even say it, but I like to help people who really *need* lifesaving help. And I'm not sure why that is, I've thought about it before. I don't know if it's be-cause they are in a life-threatening situation, and I am there to take care of that problem, or if it's just a genuine desire to help people. You know, as a paramedic, I am that person's chance for survival. You know, 'cause I can help people [at work] in my ski shop too, and I *hate* helping people in my ski shop [*laughs*]! Oh my gosh! Oh, they stress me out so bad.

Other members, too, expressed the desire to help people in critical situa-tions. They chose Peak because they could perform good deeds in an ex-citing and thrill-seeking environment.[4]

Yet established members made it clear that solely seeking excitement was not a valid reason for joining Peak. Prospective members had to have more respectable reasons for wanting to participate, and thrill-seeking was simply considered too self-serving a reason. In his 20 years of search and rescue, Jim had developed some staunch convictions about the people who were attracted for the "wrong" reasons. Because he felt so strongly about it (and because he tended to be long winded), he provided me with a very detailed and articulate description of the change in the types of re-cruits Peak had begun attracting when I interviewed him in 1995. He blamed the recent proliferation of emergency-rescue television shows for romanticizing search and rescue activities:

> I think that in the last three or four years there seems to be a tide of people wanting to get involved in search and rescue, [and] I question whether or not they have that same commitment to the individual victim's survival [as others have in the past]. . . . I see a lot of glory seekin', and I know it's driven by [some] television programs, and the glamorization of a not very glamorous activity at all. The 911 [shows] are all signs of people wanting to take something that's a very humanitarian effort, I think it's a very *selfless*-based effort, and make it into something more than what it is. To glamorize it—and it ain't. There ain't nothin' glamorous about getting up at two o'clock in the morning in the freezing cold, and searching all night to find somebody who's shacked up with his mistress at a motel! There ain't nothin' glamorous about that. There ain't nothin' glamorous about baggin' somebody's body that's been in the river for six weeks. There ain't nothin' glamorous about that. There ain't nothin' glamorous about . . . removing corpses out of an airplane. I mean, I've carried the remains of two human beings in my backpack. That's how little was left. There was no sense to even put it into a [body]bag, we just put it in a trash sack, basically, and put it in my pack, and I carried it out of there. And we got down to the bottom of the hill, and the coroner wanted to know where they were, and I handed her my pack. Ain't nothin' glamorous about that.
>
> Right now there seems to be this kind of feeling that if you show up, you get to be an ongoing member of mountain rescue. And you can at a certain level. But you're not gonna be picked to go out and do the more technically demanding situations. We're gonna use the people that we feel comfortable with and that we know. And is it hard to break into that level? Yes. And I've had people that have joined the group—been in the group two years—[and] never got a chance to work at that kind of a level. And [they] left. They said, "I never got to do it." What were they doin' it for? If they're doin' it for the *glory* of being able to jump out of that helicopter, they're in it for the wrong reason.

Many members readily adopted certain elements of this party line, especially the belief that emergency-rescue television shows like *Rescue 911* drove glory-prone, self-serving outsiders to join Peak in search of thrills and excitement.[5] All members, even those who joined solely because they thought Peak would be fun and exciting, were quickly exposed to the idea that glory seeking was an unacceptable motive, and consequently they either soon left the group or quickly revised their motives. In chapter 3, I discuss several varieties of this message as well as the process by which members conformed to it.

The second most common unacceptable reason for joining Peak was status seeking in the community. Indeed, the identity that a voluntary group can provide its members is often a powerful draw in recruitment.[6] Members were wary of outsiders who wanted to affiliate themselves with Peak to "be cool." Gary, who was one of the Ironmen, an EMT, and an eight-year, lead-status member when I interviewed him in 1995, said, "I think some people join the group to say, 'I'm mountain rescue, I'm cool, and maybe I'll get laid out of this.'" Roger was also one of the Ironmen and an eight-year, lead-status member. He held a similar view. He said, "I think people see the 911 shows or whatever, and they maybe join because of that. . . . [To] become a star, or a hero, or something to that effect."[7]

Thus, members said they were initially attracted to Peak for several different reasons, including meeting a certain type of person, providing and acquiring skills, and helping others in an exciting environment. Established members, however, were very cynical when speculating about what drew outsiders to Peak. They were convinced others were, in large part, seeking status and glory.

Triggers

Many members also mentioned a specific event that, when combined with their general interest in search and rescue, prompted them to join the group. The most common trigger was being invited. More than half of the rescuers I interviewed (12 of 23) said they were personally invited by one or more members to come to a business meeting, citing it as the main reason they decided to act on their general attraction to search and rescue. Although Peak was formally an open, voluntary organization, its informal acceptance processes were quite selective; thus, sponsorship from an established member helped prospective members earn recognition and gain approval.[8]

As I mentioned previously, Jim was single-handedly responsible for inviting many members to join the group, particularly in the early days. Maddie, a 10-year member in her mid-thirties, told me she was "recruited by Jim, for sure." She used to shop in an outdoor equipment store where

Jim worked, and after he got to know her, he began to pitch her the idea of becoming a member. Maddie said, "He was like, 'Oh, you should join mountain rescue, there's all these eligible guys!'"

Cyndi, a four-year member in her late twenties, also noted that being invited to attend a business meeting was the single most important event that led her to membership. She met a new member in the park while they were both walking their dogs. They began to talk about mountain rescue:

> I met Faith, and we started talking, and she's like, "Yeah, I do mountain rescue." ... And she mentioned that there was a meeting that night—Sunday night—she was like, "I'm going to the meeting, you wanna go?" So I went with her. I'd heard the group was around and I'd been meaning to go! But otherwise I'd probably never would've gone. So I was glad I went, and then I kept going.

Sponsorship was an important impetus for many members, but for women, especially those less experienced like Cyndi, joining the group with a "buddy" was very common. Search and rescue could be an intimidating atmosphere for women and inexperienced people, so the support of a friend who was in the same position helped new members to feel slightly more comfortable. This was certainly true for Barbara and me. Cyndi, who joined Peak about the same time as Barbara and I, told me that she felt quite out of place during trainings because she was unskilled in many areas. The one thing that kept her coming back, however, was that there were several other inexperienced women in the group:

> When we first started, there were a lot of girls that started then. It was you, me, Barbara, and Elena, and Nancy, so there was a whole group of other people who were all in the same boat. I had some background from being in the woods backpacking, but I was just like, "Well I don't know anything about ropes. This is kinda cool, and I'm just like everybody else. This is cool." And I was learning stuff, even if I did feel stupid. It's kind of like everything you do—it's gonna take you a while to catch on.

Thus, Peak's new members, especially the women, developed solidarity with one another because they felt like they were all "in the same boat" as they proceeded through training together.[9]

A second common event that prompted people to join the group was publicity. This took several forms. First, whenever the local newspaper covered Peak's more exciting, extensive missions, new volunteers always surfaced at the following meeting. Most members noticed this pattern, yet they were divided on whether the recruits were the "type" of members Peak wanted. Half of the rescuers cursed the press for "glorifying" search and rescue, suspected that the new recruits were glory seekers, and claimed that they themselves did not "need" the glamor of publicity (a pattern of heroic self-denial I discuss in chapter 3). The other half praised the press, welcomed the publicity, and claimed that it was a good way to recruit new members as well as to stimulate monetary donations from the community.

Besides media attention, Peak also received publicity through advertising. Peak occasionally placed ads in the local paper inviting prospective members to attend a business meeting, yet this method of recruitment was employed very sporadically, and it varied with the group's leadership as well as with its inner political conflicts. When I joined the group in 1994, none of these ads had appeared in the paper for a year, and they did not appear again until 1998. Several members I spoke with, however, cited these ads as their main impetus for joining the group.

A third method of publicity was the "Backcountry Safety Tips" pamphlets that Peak placed in local businesses such as outdoor equipment stores. Like the newspaper advertisements, this type of publicity was created and controlled by the group, but unlike the ads, it did not have member recruitment as its intended function. Although the main purpose of these pamphlets was to provide community members with backcountry safety tips, they also raised citizens' awareness about volunteer search and rescue services, which, in turn, attracted new members (as well as elicited donations from the community). Three members told me they joined after seeing this pamphlet.

A third impetus to join Peak was the occurrence of a major life event that either directly or indirectly involved search and rescue. For example, one woman joined because her family had been involved in a small plane crash when they lived in another state. She was so impressed by the rescue effort that she joined search and rescue when she moved to Peak County. In fact, some of the victims Peak rescued even asked how they could get involved with a rescue group in their hometown.

Roy told me that, although he had originally joined Peak in 1980, it wasn't until the death of a climbing friend before he got highly involved. He said, "I think when I really committed was in 1982 when Allison was killed. I kinda quit climbing after that. I quit climbing. She died April 21,

1982, and I didn't climb 'til 1985. But I did mountain rescue work. I could help people, but I wouldn't climb."[10]

Revised Motives

When some members told me about their motives for joining Peak, they specified that they had initially joined for particular reasons, but had since revised them or had developed others along the way.[11] Benny, the 36-year-old construction worker, told me how his motives changed shortly after he joined seven years earlier:

> I came in not as a community [service]-thing. I came in to meet [rock] climbers and mountain climbers. And help other people out, and to get to go out in the winter in that [weather] condition. . . . When you're a new member, it's kind of like, you know, giggly eyed, and bright eyed, and bushy tailed: "Wow, this is cool!" and "I get to do this!" There's just so much learning going on. . . . I moved from there into community. You know, that's what it is, it's community service. You also get to meet other people, and you get to do stuff that's active outside, but it's community service.

Benny still thought search and rescue was fun and exciting, but not as much as when he first joined. As the novelty of membership faded, he developed new, self-sacrificing motives for participating. As he performed altruistic acts, his motives became more altruistic in nature.[12]

Other members told me similar stories recalling how their motives had changed. Some identified a sharper change than Benny had, stating that they had experienced a revelation shortly after beginning with the group. They explained that they were initially lured to the group by some of the more seductive images of rescue work, such as excitement, danger, and status, but after a short time it dawned on them that "the point" of search and rescue was to help others. Cyndi, my cohort-peer, detailed how her original motives—to meet people, learn skills, and be involved in something status enhancing—were transformed after a few months:

> To begin with, I was like, "I'll meet new people, it'll be cool." And it was. We hung out at the bars, so it was fun. It was a way to meet new people—because my job [as an accountant] is kind of seclusional [*laughs*], so I was like, "This is cool." And you get to feel important because you

carry a pager. It was kind of cool. When my pager went off: "Gotta go. I get to go play with the toys [unique rescue gear], I get to ride in the helicopter, and ha ha ha, you're not." So you do it for a while, but after the first couple months you start to figure out that that's not the point. Well, I did, anyway [*laughs*]. It's going out and trying to help these people who are sick, or injured, or dying, or dead, or whatever. And that's not really the most pleasant thing to think about, but that's really why you're learning all this stuff. It's to help them, not because it's fun. (Even though it is [*laughs*]!) It's really easy to lose sight of the fact that there's somebody out there who's hurt. . . . So after a while, I was like, "You know, this is probably a good thing." And so then I was like, "Okay, *this* is why I'm doing it: I'm doing it because maybe I could try to help someone who came out here and doesn't know anything." So that's, I guess, why I stayed.

Cyndi's story demonstrated how she had to change her motives to remain in the group. She joined because of the status of membership and the type of people she would meet. After some experience with the group, however, she realized these motives would not sustain her membership, so she revised them, cognitively processing the change ("Okay, *this* is why I'm doing it").

Along with her own transformation in motives, Cyndi engaged in "anticipatory socialization" (Feldman 1976) with prospective members as well. She told me that when nonmembers asked her about search and rescue, she told them what to expect:

> If I'm talking to someone about coming in, I say, "No, no, it's not all fun and games. . . . Hey, this is really cool, and yeah, it's exciting, and yeah, we fly around in helicopters, and wow, you can tell your friends, and that's really fun. But that's not the point. You may never get to do that. You may be stuck in an office for hours, or you may be walking through the woods with a 20-pound, 30-pound, 40-pound pack on—for miles—and then have to turn around and come back and have done nothing. And you have to do that every single time, and you have to be happy about it. And if you can't do it, then there's no reason for you to join."

In this way, Cyndi not only screened potential recruits, but she also reinforced her own newly amended motives.

Elena also told me that once she finally found her niche in Peak, she enjoyed the status of being a member:

> You know, I think maybe when I first joined, it was more of a status thing, like to say, "Oh, I'm on mountain rescue." And now, I mean, people know, and I may tell some people, but it just isn't part of the conversation; it's not something I go out of my way [to tell people]. I don't even think half of my [coworkers] know that I am on mountain rescue. I don't have a reason to tell them. Whereas maybe a few years ago, [for] me personally, it was more of status thing. And I think that's maybe [the case] with people who join the group, it becomes sort of a status thing for a while. But then it kind of loses it glamor [*laughs*]!

Brooke, who joined because she wanted to meet "locals," told me that she thought it would be "exciting and fun." When she talked to outsiders, however, she downplayed the excitement-and-fun angle, emphasizing the serious nature of the work:

> I want people to realize that it's serious what we do. It's not all fun and games. We put ourselves in danger a lot, and I don't want people to join for the wrong reasons. I don't want it to be a self-glorification thing, I don't like people like that at all. If you feel like you have to belong in a group like this to make yourself look better to other people, you know, take it somewhere else.

The most striking thing about this statement, and many others especially from newer, less experienced members, is the dogmatic adoption of the group's rhetoric against glory- and status-seeking "wannabes." Many members developed these staunch convictions after only several months with the group. The complex process by which Peak socialized its members to adhere to these and other group norms is the topic of the next chapter.

Limitations to Role Fulfillment

Once they decided that Peak fit their needs, prospective members attended their first meeting, where the established members evaluated how well the recruits fit Peak's needs.[13] Occasionally, when prospective members looked particularly promising, rescuers would discuss them after the meeting. The conversation would often start with a comment on the recruit's physical appearance: "That guy looked strong, we could use him." The next concern would follow: "Yeah, but he works full time at the top of the [ski] mountain—he'll never be able to leave work for missions." Thus, members evaluated recruits' desirability with regard to two factors, or "inclusionary filters" (Van Maanen and Schein 1979): availability and strength. Generally, members needed to meet these prerequisites in order to participate in Peak.

Rescuers who were generally available—those with flexible and autonomous lifestyles—were an asset to Peak. As reports of injured or overdue parties were often delayed from the start, time was of the essence in responding to such emergencies. Rescuers had to be able to drop whatever they were doing at any time of the day or night to go on missions. Since Peak was a volunteer organization and no compensation was provided to its members, this requirement was an ideal—there were no members who could always go on missions—but those who could attend the most missions were considered the most dependable, gained the most experience, and rose in status the fastest.

Rescuers who were physically strong were also an asset to Peak because they were able to carry heavy equipment and injured victims over miles of mountainous terrain. Although members with specific rescue skills were also attractive to the group, these skills were useless if the rescuer who possessed them was physically incapable of reaching the accident scene. Thus, many members reasoned that skills could be learned along the way, but strength and physical fitness were essential prerequisites for membership.[14]

There were quite a few members who had trouble meeting one (or both) of these prerequisites. As such, these members tended to have less experience and status in the group. Demographic patterns explain some of this variation.

Parenthood

A common situation that limited members' participation was commitment to family, especially to children. Benny, the seven-year, lead-status member, was the divorced father of a 10-year-old son. He told me that when he had physical custody of his son (every other weekend), his role as father overrode his role as rescuer, saying, "When I have [my son], I don't go on missions." Benny speculated why so few members were parents and used Maddie, the 10-year lead-status member, as an example: "When you look at the people in the group, they're active people, and they don't see that having a kid is beneficial to being active. [Maddie] wants to have kids until she thinks about pregnancy, and then she's done [going on missions]." Children of dependent ages, especially preschoolers, were not conducive to the autonomous lifestyle that members needed in order to participate in Peak. Other rescuers recognized that the role of parent often took precedence over the role of rescuer and understood when the few parent-members could not go on missions.[15]

The incompatibility of the parent and rescuer roles was exemplified when Keith, a newly initiated lead-status member and father of a four-year-old, was taking one of his first turns as mission coordinator. An urgent call came in for Peak to assist the sheriff's department in the extrication of four severely injured victims from a van that had rolled off the side of a dirt road, down a treacherously steep 400-foot embankment. Keith's son was with him that day and, unable to find a babysitter on such short notice, Keith brought him to the mission, whereupon he felt overwhelmed while trying to watch his child and run the mission at the same time. To make matters worse, Keith's wife called on his cellular phone during the mission, wondering where their son was. She was livid to find out that the four-year-old was present at the scene of one of the county's worst accidents that year. Keith sharply curtailed his participation following that event.

Commitment to family appeared in other forms as well and drew rescuers away from missions. Bert, a helicopter pilot, had to have another pilot replace him on a search so that he could attend his son's birthday party. Drew, a longtime member and mission coordinator, cut his participation sharply when he began building his family's house, and another formerly active lead-status member, Roger, hardly came around at all right after getting married. Such outside commitments did not mesh with the spontaneity necessary to participate fully in Peak, and when these outside commitments increased, members had less discretionary time at their disposal.[16] Family commitments did not permanently detract from Drew's and Roger's participation, however: Drew resumed his active role once the house was finished, and Roger came back six months after his wedding. Rescuers with children, however, had a much harder time balancing both roles.

There was, moreover, a distinctly gendered aspect to the presence of parent-rescuers. There were 41 members on a typical membership list

(March 1997), and they were divided into two categories: "active" (28 members) and "inactive" (13 members). Of the 28 active members, 20 (approximately 68%) were men and 8 (approximately 32%) were women. Three of the 28 had children under the age of 18 (approximately 11%). All three of these members were men. Of the 13 inactive members, 10 (approximately 77%) were men and three (approximately 23%) were women. Four of the 13 had children under the age of 18 (approximately 31%). All four of these members were men. These percentages suggest several things. First, parents were less likely to be able to commit fully to the "active" rescuer role than nonparents. Second, fathers were more likely than mothers to participate in Peak. In fact, there was never a single mother of dependent-aged children on Peak's membership list during the entire course of this study.[17] Membership requirements were closely aligned with parental status: they greatly favored child-free members, substantially disadvantaged fathers, and functionally excluded mothers by demanding time and flexibility in individuals' daily schedules.[18]

Gender

Gender affected members' ability to participate because the women in the group were generally not as strong as the men in the group. As a result, men were more frequently chosen to do the more physically demanding tasks on missions. Often, these tasks were the urgent and exciting ones such as assessing the patient (because physically stronger people could get to the scene faster) or handling difficult extrications (because stronger rescuers could more easily maneuver the victims and the heavy rescue equipment).

On an individual level, however, there were some women who were physically stronger than some men, and in those cases, women were given an opportunity to perform. The need for efficiency required that members' ability, not their gender, be of primary consideration when tasking them with various duties on missions. Jim described his thought process when delegating responsibilities during missions: "In a technical rescue-type situation, I've found there to be absolutely no difference between the skill levels of a man and a woman. So in those type of situations, I look at who's available [and] who's got the skills; the gender factor doesn't fit in." Jim was proud of the group's ability to disregard "the gender factor" and to focus on completing the task at hand. By downplaying gender distinctions in this way, Jim not only increased the team's efficiency, but also provided individual women with opportunities to perform a variety of physical tasks. He further explained how he considered Peak's view of gender roles to be a progressive one, contrasting it with the traditional gender roles historically characteristic of the male-dominated search and rescue field:

> We're not bogged down into some of the old tried and true [ideas like] it's gotta be some male rock-jock that does this stuff. And that the women oughta be relegated to base camp—which kind of equates to "you gotta be barefoot and pregnant in the kitchen." . . . So we've had this kind of neat history of having an "open door"—to having women in any role.

Many of the other statewide search and rescue organizations I observed were highly male dominated, which anecdotally supported Jim's contention that Peak was less macho than other groups.[19] Brooke, the southern woman in her mid-twenties who wanted to meet locals, also felt that Peak was not dominated by men because, in her experience, the tasks she was asked to do were independent of gender:

> I never once have experienced *any* sort of discrimination in this group for being a woman. Never once. Which I'm very proud to say, because in a group like this, when physical tasks are expected of you, I have never once been discriminated against. Except for the obvious: they're not gonna pick me over a big, burly guy to be on a haul team. Which is completely understandable.

On the surface, then, individual members' gender was irrelevant; the most competent rescuer would be chosen to fulfill the role.

Yet, although members consciously tried to disregard stereotypes, they were not immune to them. Jim discussed an incident in which Peak was searching for a young man who had been missing for several weeks. The man had last been seen by his friends on a Friday night, fooling around by the edge of a rushing river. For several days, Peak's searchers scoured the river banks with no sign of the young man. When his coat was found in the water almost a week later, rescuers assumed that they were searching for a dead body. Peak sent several teams into the field to continue the search and, unexpectedly, was able to obtain a helicopter to help search from the air. Jim was in charge of the mission and only had one available member when the aircraft arrived. Jim explained to me what he was thinking when he decided to put Brooke (who was proud to say that she never experienced any type of gender discrimination) on the search helicopter:

> "Brooke, get up here." Because [I was thinking] I can give her an opportunity. I had no idea she was gonna be on the ship when they found the body. And then, do I protect her and say, "Well, bring her back here, and I'll fly in to go check out the body?" 'Cause that thought crossed my mind. No. She's signed up. "Land. Brooke, go check it." Now, she told me afterwards that she kinda, like, peeked around the bush and [confirmed that] "Yeah, it really was [the body]," and then scampered up the little river bank and waited for me to come. That's fine. That's absolutely, perfectly all right. . . . But she told me afterwards that it was a really big deal for her, and that she was really glad I let her do it.

Jim actively fought the urge to treat Brooke differently from other members when he suppressed the thought of protecting her from the sight of the dead body. He rationalized that she had willingly volunteered to take on a potentially upsetting task. Jim's actions then, were designed to disregard gender; however, Brooke's fulfillment of the task, as interpreted by Jim, was distinctly and stereotypically feminized: Brooke "peeked" at the body, "scampered" up a "little" embankment, and then dependently waited for someone else to take control of the situation. She did not "identify" the body, "trudge" up the hill to "direct" others to the scene. One could imagine this scenario as well, though it would be a distinctly more "masculinized" (and in this case, more appropriate) execution of the role.[20] Brooke did effectively complete the assignment she was given, but Jim's account of the incident illuminated the subtle ways gender stereotypes persisted.

When rescuers could not meet the physical demands of a mission, others became frustrated with them. Nick, the 33-year-old, risk-taking (and accident-prone) construction worker, told me about one time when he was on a mission with Cyndi and Elena. They had to wheel an empty stretcher (the "litter") two miles up a trail to reach Gary, the EMT, who was with an injured tourist who had fallen into a river. Nick told me that he got frustrated not so much because Elena and Cyndi were slow, but because he judged them to be out of shape. He blamed them for being physically unfit, and as a result, he set a fast pace for the three-person team. Cyndi remembered it clearly, and she happened to bring it up in our interview when I asked her if she saw any gender differences in the group:

Elena and I could've walked the litter up at a very nice little pace. And we would've gotten there. Maybe we would've stopped once. But [with Nick], um—I thought I was gonna throw up. I was so overworked. He had us pretty much *running* up the trail. There were points when we were going up hills, and I was like trotting—literally running—trying to keep up. And it was like "Why are you doing this?" . . . I was *gasping* for breath. [We stopped once, and] I put my head between my knees, and there was a couple times I was like, "I'm gonna either throw up or pass out!" And I was like, "I don't get it!" Elena and I could've gotten up there—maybe it would've taken us five or 10 minutes longer, but we would've been ready to turn right back around and go right back down the hill. And [when] I got up there. . . I was like "*Hzzzzzz!* [*heavy wheezing sound*]. Can't [*wheeze*] breathe [*wheeze*]!"

So I don't know what that [behavior] is. Maybe it's a male drive thing. Or maybe it's "I can push one step faster than you." Or maybe it's "I'm so much stronger than you, and I don't have a conception of the fact that you can't move as fast as I can." And they are! There are some guys on the team that are *a lot* stronger than I am. And they can move a ton faster than I can. But I'll get there. I just can't move that fast. And I'll turn around, and I'll go all the way out with them—doing a carry, doing whatever—I just might have to rest a lot.

Nick's treatment of Cyndi and Elena had some malicious undertones. I witnessed similar situations several times in my six years in Peak, and Nick was not the only member who engaged in such spiteful behavior, although it was often the Ironmen who did so. In this case, he was angry and frustrated because his teammates were out of shape and holding him back, so he pushed them. The result was that Cyndi felt degraded and subordinated by her inability to keep up. While there is no evidence that this incident was gender driven per se, it is interesting that Cyndi interpreted it as such, providing a clue as to how such instances made her feel with regard to gender.[21]

Age

Age was another factor that affected members' participation, mostly through their physical ability. Rescuers under 40 years old tended to be stronger, thus they were more often sent into physically demanding situations. As a mission coordinator, Kevin said, "If I want somebody to rip up a hill, I'm not gonna go for the 40-year-old guys, I'm gonna call the 20-year-olds, 'cause they've got something to prove. That's what they think, anyway."

Some members over 40 migrated toward coordinating the missions, especially those who had a great deal of experience. Jim related this process to me:

> We'd like to get Drew to run more missions. I really see that as a natural step for him and I see it for Kevin, too. We're getting a little older, we're getting a little longer in the tooth, [and] my beard's getting a little grayer, [so] Drew and Kevin and I—we all kid each other that we're the "over-40-mechanized-group."

In these cases rescuers who had experience did not lose much status when they aged because, as Mitch, the 23-year-old physically fit mountaineer, said, "You can make up for so much [lack of strength and stamina] with that knowledge and experience."

Members whose physical ability had declined due to age had mixed feelings about it, especially if they were less experienced because they had begun search and rescue later in life. Martin, the 53-year-old construction supervisor who joined Peak with my cohort, when he was 48, told me that he had been trying to accept that he was less able to enact the physical roles than he once was:

> *Martin:* I'm getting to the point where I ain't got many more years out in the field, and I know that. I can't beat the bush with the guys—or the girls! I mean, I can't keep up with *you* anymore!
> *Jen's Pride:* [Ouch.]
> *Jen:* It sounds like that makes you a little sad.
> *Martin:* Yeah, it does. 'Cause I like it. But each year I can feel it a little more. One of these days, I'm gonna have to stop pretending I'm 18 years old. The body can't take it anymore. . . . I've recognized the fact that each year it's a little harder for me to stay in shape, a little harder for me to keep up with the big boys. And I can't. I know I can't keep up with Gary or Nick when they go in the field up the trail. But I also know the pace I can use to get there, and I know that when I get there I'm still capable of helping and working. I've still got something in me. So I'm still useful in the field. Somebody's gotta be the slow one in the group. But I'm not the one who gets

there and can't do anything. I can still get there and still function as a member of the team and do something useful. It just takes me a little longer.

It is interesting that Martin justified his position in the group by saying he was slow, but he'd get there. This phrase was used by several women and by several men over 40, which suggests that it was a culturally learned rationalization. Less physically capable members felt the need to justify their worth, as Martin did by saying "I'm still useful," while simultaneously admitting they were slower than others. This is not surprising since people who were less strong (like Cyndi) could suffer severe sanctions from other rescuers (like Nick) if they overestimated their physical ability.

Finally, physical decline due to age may have been harder for male rescuers than female, perhaps because the men, like Martin implied for himself above, used to be able to keep up with the "big boys," or the Ironmen, whereas many women never could. When I talked to Kevin, who was in his mid-forties, he linked physical ability to masculinity:

Age is a humbling experience, that's all there is to it. You change. If manhood is measured by strength, I'm not the man I used to be. Things wear out. Bones are getting thinner, hair's getting thinner. Your body changes. . . . Although it doesn't mean I couldn't do it now. But now it means that I'm the turtle rather than the hare. But if I needed to, I would get there, and I'd get the job done. But I'm going to be more inclined to step aside or delegate somebody that has a little bit more spring to their step—even though I'm still springing—I don't have that same spring. I still have what it takes, but I just don't have as much of it [*laughs*]! . . . Why would you jeopardize an operation because of your ego? Stand back and let somebody else more qualified run with it. But that's kind of a "me" thing. I realize that isn't the norm. I think a lot of people have trouble accepting that they've changed. 'Cause your mind still feels like go-go-go, but the body does change.[22]

In the end, it was young, single men who were able to participate in missions fully, simply because they most often met the prerequisites for membership: they were strong and had flexible schedules. Furthermore, the men who joined the group tended to have more background experience and skills than women who joined, adding to the likelihood that they would be selected for exciting and challenging roles on missions.

3

Socializing Heroes

One thing that interests social psychologists is the cultural tension people feel to pursue both individual and collective interests. Bellah and his colleagues (1985) claimed that in America, people's rising sense of individualism is eclipsing their dedication to community. Hewitt (1989) also discussed this tension in detail, suggesting that most Americans construct a self through "pragmatic compromise": sometimes they place their own interests first, and at other times, they give priority to collective concerns. Heroes are an interesting example of this tension because, by most definitions, heroes are those people who gain recognition for prioritizing the group's interests over their own.[1] Thus, they can be considered an extreme example at one end of this continuum, as they often sacrifice a great deal personally to benefit others.

This tension between the self and the group can be seen in many organizations as well, because to achieve their goals, organizations must socialize individual members to conform to collective norms and values. Through various systems of rewards and punishments, they guide members' behavior to fit organizational needs. In some organizations, these sanctions may take the form of physical force, as when inmates in prisons or mental institutions are physically prevented from eating or sleeping at certain times of the day. Other organizations may control their members by offering material incentives, as when workers do their jobs and follow the company rules because they are paid a wage to do so. Still in other organizations, members may comply because they receive symbolic rewards, such as the acceptance they gain from a cult, or the prestige they receive from being associated with a local charity group.[2]

Peak was an organization that required its members to behave heroically. Rescuers had to sacrifice their own interests in order to help strangers in need. Because it could not offer material incentives, nor could it force its members to behave in certain ways, Peak gained members' compliance by using symbolic rewards. The group tightly guarded its only commodity, the status of "hero," and used it to entice aspiring members to conform to the group's norms. Members who did not conform closely enough were made well aware of their peripheral status in the group and thus were not granted the core membership that would allow them to claim the heroic identity of the group as their own. By making heroism an elusive and difficult goal to achieve, Peak ensured members' compliance as well as instilled in them a sense of group dedication.

Heroic Norms

Peak Search and Rescue included a core of dedicated individuals who were fully socialized to the group's norms, and several levels of members who were socialized to lesser degrees.[3] As a volunteer group, Peak had high membership turnover. To maintain a sense of permanency and stability, Peak kept members at the fringes until they had proved themselves by demonstrating their internalization of the group's most crucial norms and values.[4] These norms and values revolved around three dimensions of membership: consciousness, resources, and commitment. Within each of these dimensions, specific norms guided members' behavior to closely conform to the ideal of heroism. These behavior shifts moved rescuers through the stages of membership along the route to becoming a core member.[5]

Consciousness

As I have discussed, new members often joined Peak because it seemed very exciting. They envisioned themselves risking their lives in heroic rescue efforts such as hanging from rock ledges or flying into remote wilderness areas by helicopter. The reality of membership, however, was that each individual fulfilled a role in the larger system, and such death-defying scenarios were reserved for the highly experienced, seasoned members.

Peak's new members were encouraged to recognize their own unimportance early on and to demonstrate their understanding that membership was not a means to self-glorification. The group first socialized them to downplay arrogance and egoism and to display humility and respect. In this stage, the norms guided members to focus their attention on themselves in an effort to eliminate any attitudes of self-interest. Successful socialization in this stage moved them to peripheral status, where they were next socialized to orient themselves toward the group. Norms in the group-oriented stage encouraged members to focus on group goals by being team players and accepting any role assigned to them. Thus, socialization to group consciousness comprised two stages: first denying the self and then affirming the group.

Denying the Self In the stage of self-denial, members were required to set their egoistic interests aside and to realize that the self was secondary to the group.[6] Members who conformed to this norm demonstrated an awareness that the group did not exist to fulfill individuals' needs; members who deviated were suspected of being motivated by self-interest.

Martin, the member in his early fifties who joined Peak because he wanted to get involved in the community, thought his mountaineering and kayaking experience made him a perfect fit for Peak. Anxious to become involved and to apply his knowledge to a good cause, he asserted himself at many training sessions and business meetings early in his career. He told me that he became frustrated by other members' reluctance to recognize his skills and by the group's unwillingness to assign him any challenging or exciting roles.

After a year and a half of membership, Martin reflected on his original difficulty in breaking into the group, attributing it to his inadequate demonstration of the denial of self:

> When I first joined the group, all I wanted was to get involved. It was really frustrating because the more I tried to get involved, the more I was *prevented* from getting involved. I thought I knew a lot of stuff, and it seemed that no one gave me credit for it. With this group, it takes time to get respect. You have to learn the way things work around here—you can't just come in and be a part of it. I guess people thought that all I wanted was to show what I knew—and that was part of it—but I didn't know everything when I came in. Now I can see it really easily because I see the same thing happening with Wayne, now, too. He just doesn't understand that the more he tries to say what he knows, the more the group is going to shut him out. In fact, I told Wayne one day that he should ease up and back off a little. That was my advice to him, speaking from what I went through. I said, "Look Wayne, that's how the group is. They will not accept you until

they feel like accepting you; the more you push, the more they'll shove."

As Martin became socialized into Peak, he realized that he would have to undergo a "mortification of the self" (Goffman 1961a) and, as many group members put it, to "check his ego at the door." Once he began subscribing to the norm of self-denial, the group sanctioned him less harshly, and he felt more fully accepted. He also showed his conformity to the norm by socializing others, like Wayne, who had not yet demonstrated adequate self-denial. It was common for newcomers such as Martin and Wayne to experience "entry shock" (Cohen 1973), whereby the reality of the group's norms abruptly disconfirmed their initial expectations.

Members also demonstrated self-denial through actions or attitudes that not only downplayed but actively avoided self-glorification. To fade modestly into the background after a mission showed willingness to renounce self-serving reasons for participation in Peak. Conversely, members who talked to the press about their performance on a rescue without authorization from the group were sanctioned for using the group as a vehicle for self-aggrandizement. This type of grandstanding was one of the most basic infractions members could commit, and members who did so were formally reprimanded on several occasions: the board of directors suspended one violator from all group activity for one month, and threatened another with permanent expulsion.[7]

Our trainer, Roy, a core member with 15 years of rescue experience, told me that talking to the press was a form of self-promotion:

> A bad reason [to participate in the group] is self-gain, self-promotion. That's bad. 'Cause I think that's the worst thing you can do is to benefit from somebody else's misfortunes. . . . One of the biggest sins is talking to the press when you're instructed not to. 'Cause this is very sensitive stuff, . . . and if you're here to see your face on the front page of the *City Times* or *Western News*, maybe you might want to go someplace else.

Members felt that displays of excessive pride endangered the heroic identity of the group. To Roy, such hubris was a "sin." Indeed, our cultural conceptions, as informed by Greek mythology, show that hubris destroys heroes.[8]

Rescuers also demonstrated the norm of self-denial by resisting the urge to advertise their association with the group. Newer members who

overemphasized their affiliation with Peak were suspected of being motivated by a desire for a status boost in the community: taking advantage of
the group's heroic status so that they, as individuals, might be viewed as
heroes.[9] To avoid such suspicion, some of Peak's neophytes compensated
by purposely disguising their affiliation to outsiders. For instance, one
technique of self-denial was to wear pagers on a belt but to turn them in
toward the body so that the search and rescue emblem was not visible. By
downplaying their group affiliation, members signaled to others that they
were not motivated by self-gain.

Acknowledging mistakes also helped members to demonstrate humility, and thus conform to the norm of self-denial. Patrick was a support
member in his mid-twenties with a few years of experience in Peak. He
had some basic skills upon joining and worked diligently to refine them in
hopes of advancing to lead status. Patrick described an episode in which
he and an even newer member, Mitch (the young, awestruck climber)
were admonished for skiing, without authorization, into an avalanche-
prone area during a rescue. Nick and Gary were in a gully below them,
evacuating a snowboarder who had broken his leg. Patrick and Mitch endangered Nick and Gary when they skied above them by creating the possibility of triggering an avalanche.

Later in the rescue, Patrick broke a ski and then demonstrated poor
judgment when he chose to walk down the gully, without his skis, through
chest-deep snow. It took him four hours to get out of the area. He realized
later that it would have been both faster and safer to climb 30 minutes
back up to the top of the gully and ride down the mountain with the rest
of the team on the snowcat (a large, tractor-like vehicle designed for snow
travel). His decision risked not only his own safety but also Nick's, because
he had to accompany Patrick on his way out of the gully.

Because of the deep footprints that he made without his skis, this
episode earned Patrick the nickname "Posthole":

> I'm *slightly* embarrassed simply because it was a dumb thing to do, but
> that's the funniest thing. So many people like to think that they're above
> dumb things, you know, "God! He's so stupid, that was so dumb. I never
> do stuff like that!" I see a lot of that [in search and rescue]. They're more
> confident people; they're very confident in themselves. I'm sure they like
> to think that they never screw up, and that it's always someone else's fault,
> and they always know better than someone else. I think I have a little bit
> more humility than a lot of these guys. . . . [Humility is] having a very re-

alistic introspection to one's self. When I think about myself or I look in the mirror, I don't play myself short. I have certain faults, and I have certain things that I do well, and I don't think that I brush any of that under the carpet. If there's something I don't do well, I admit it to myself, and I try and do better the next time. . . . Some people like to think that they do some things well, so that's enough. I try to do everything well. I *don't*, but I try.

Patrick made an egregious error in the eyes of many group members because his actions, presumably motivated by self-glorification, had put others in danger. For him, this incident constituted a "debasement experience," in which newer members' self-concepts are broken down through a humbling group experience (Wanous 1992). In an effort to regain status with the group, Patrick acknowledged his mistake and took the blame for his rash actions and lack of thought. He framed the admission of his mistake within a "lesson learned" paradigm, which allowed him to isolate this aberrant act of perceived egoism and to override it with a more stable identity based on humility and self-denial.

Peak also displayed humility on a collective level. The group was often asked to assist search and rescue teams in other counties, and Roy told me that in the rescue community, Peak had gained the "reputation of the 'can-do' group" because its members always got the job done and rarely needed help. Yet despite their high level of skill and frequent participation in many rescues, Roy proudly told me that Peak was an "honorable" organization because the core members agreed that they never needed thanks for this work. For instance, Roy told me that when rescuers expected that the press would want to interview them after a mission, they would silently disappear:

We wouldn't have to say a word [to each other]. We'd look [at each other] and just nod our heads, get in the cars, and we'd go. They'd never hear from us. It was real honorable—we got in there, we did it, and we slipped out. Like commandos, almost. We were very proud of that. And many, many times, we would come out after missions, and all the doughnuts would be gone, all the coffee would be gone, and all the press would have their stories from the people that never left [the base]. And we'd get picked up, and we'd sleep on the way home, while somebody drove us home. That's honorable. And we never bitched, and we're not bitching now.

Roy's feelings reflected three heroic themes that are related to self-denial. First, heroes do not receive material rewards for their hardships, even if it's only in the form of coffee and doughnuts. Second, heroes must be willing to downplay their own exceptional abilities, almost to the point of keeping them secret, like commandos or other covert military operators. Third, heroes abide by norms of anonymity; they must avoid being recognized as heroes.[10] Popular culture reinforces this definition of the hero by romanticizing masked men who disappear before the crowd can thank them.

Accepting a Role To encourage members to learn that the self was secondary to the group, Peak required them to deny self-serving interests in the first stage of consciousness socialization. In the next stage, Peak stressed the group's primacy by encouraging members to actively affirm their role in the group. The shift to role acceptance indicated members' shift from self-oriented consciousness (self-denial) to group-oriented consciousness, which advanced them from peripheral to core status within this dimension of membership.

An example of role acceptance was the ability to be a team player. If a mission was to succeed, members had to realize that the whole team was greater than the sum of its parts. Benny, the seven-year, lead-status member and divorced father of the 10-year-old, explained to me that role acceptance was the crucial factor in a mission's success because it allowed a group of individuals to crystallize into a team. As an example, he recalled a mission in which the team had carried a 240-pound man with a broken ankle over three miles of steep, rocky, narrow trail at night:

> "Team" is very, very basic to the whole thing. There's a group of individuals that are *very* strong individuals. But they are all willing to work as a team. The group—it's like an ant farm. You can have ants fighting on each other [and] biting each other. But when they have a reason to build for the queen bee, or something, I mean, hell, they all seem to have some great master plan. And that's the same thing with mountain rescue. Well, we had a master plan: we wanna get this big guy from here down to there without killing ourselves.

Another aspect of role acceptance was that the members were willing to perform any task, regardless of how trivial or undesirable. When members explained this concept to me, they frequently used one of the least desirable jobs on a mission to emphasize their point by saying, "Somebody's got to get the coffee and doughnuts" for the other team members. That so many individuals referred to "coffee and doughnuts" showed how strongly Peak socialized its members to willingly accept even the most mundane, least glamorous role in a mission. Furthermore, in my first two years, this particular phrase was used far more than any other in the group culture, an indication of its power in socializing members to conform to the norm of role acceptance.[11]

Maddie, the lead-status rescuer and mission coordinator, had 10 years of search and rescue experience in Peak. She recognized the importance of an efficient division of labor, and told me that members' willingness to perform any task showed that they were transcending personal interest and putting the team's goals first. She cited Oliver, an experienced support-status member, as an example:

> I guess I have a lot of respect for [Oliver] because he'll come in, and he'll do whatever you ask him to do, no matter what. He'll never question, "Why is it you're doing that?" You can always count on him, and you can ask him to do absolutely *anything*. He'll go change the oil in the [rescue] truck if that's what you need to have done. I mean, he'll just do the grossest, dirtiest—and yet never question it. And yet he's put in a lot of time with the group, and probably would love to be ["lead-certified"], so to speak, but he's okay with not being there. . . . He's very happy where he is right now, doing the job he does, and he's okay with that.

Clearly, Oliver had been successfully socialized to the group consciousness. In Maddie's estimation, he had internalized the norms of both self-denial and role acceptance, as evidenced by his willingness to perform undesirable jobs and not expect anything in return.[12] This attitude granted him core status in the consciousness dimension of membership.

Rescuers also conformed to the norm of role acceptance by knowing when to be deferential and when to be assertive. In some instances, deference was a clear signal that a member had internalized the norm of self-denial and was willing to accept any role assigned. At other times, however, deference was not appropriate and could jeopardize the team's interests. Core members were able to negotiate these categories easily because they had adopted a group-oriented consciousness and used the group's best interests to guide their actions. Patrick ("Posthole") remarked that he struggled with situations in which he felt that self-denial was important, but in retrospect realized that he would have improved the mission's efficiency if he had asserted himself with his peers.

On one such mission, Gary, the lead-status, eight-year member who was in his late twenties at the time, needed assistance in carrying a cold, exhausted victim through the snow for several miles. Patrick was available for the helicopter trip into the remote area, as was Cyndi, who was neither as experienced, skilled, nor physically strong as he. However, there was only room for one person in the helicopter. The mission coordinator asked who wanted to go. Patrick recalled what he thought at the time: "You always wanna fly on the bird [*giggles*]. . . . If the helicopter's coming, you wanna be on it. But it actually went through my mind, 'It's not every day a helicopter comes in, and I've been on quite a few rides,' and I kind of stepped back a little bit and let Cyndi go." Patrick based his decision on the internalization of the norm of self-denial: he let the mission coordinator choose Cyndi for the mission. Later, however, he reasoned that because he was stronger than Cyndi, he would have been a better choice to help Gary haul the victim out of the woods on the sledlike stretcher called a "litter": "Gary needed someone to help carry the litter. And that's not what he got. He got Cyndi. . . . You know, nothing against Cyndi, she's a great help, but that's just not something she's very helpful with. Carrying a heavy litter through the snow, in comparison with me carrying something heavy through the snow. . . . Gary didn't get as much help as he wanted." Patrick explained what he had learned from this situation: "You hesitate to tell a mission coordinator that he's doing something wrong, 'cause you don't know what's going through his head. I've made it my policy *not* to [interfere], but I think I'm gonna change that. If I just absolutely, positively know everything is going to shit, and I can help, I'm going to."

Patrick was vacillating between self-oriented and group-oriented consciousness. He was beginning to realize that appearances could be deceiving. For example, some members' assertions might seem, on the surface, to represent a lack of self-denial. Once a member's consciousness had moved beyond self-orientation to group orientation, however, the motivation behind the action emerged as a more important factor. Because they were interested in the good of the group, rescuers who went beyond self-denial and accepted any role, even if it was controversial, showed that they had been fully socialized to the group consciousness.[13]

Resources

Managing rescuers' resources was a second key focus of group socialization. Experienced, knowledgeable members were highly valued in Peak because they were able to perform demanding roles that enabled the group to complete the missions. All rescuers, however, needed a minimal level of skill. They had to know how to survive in the wilderness for days at a time while they were in remote regions searching for lost victims, and they needed a certain amount of technical expertise in different environments so that they could help to rescue victims in such situations. These skills centered around the outdoor activities common to the county's residents, such as rock climbing, camping, hiking, rafting, kayaking, ice climbing, snowmobiling, and skiing in the backcountry where there was avalanche danger. Expertise in these areas was a very valuable commodity, and many wilderness enthusiasts actively sought such skill and training.

Many rescuers told me that several times in the past, people had approached Peak under the pretense of joining the group, had taken advantage of the free training that the group provided for its members, and had quit without ever serving on a mission. The members considered these people to be acquiring goods and services without any cost to themselves, or "free-riding" (Olson 1965). Yet it is possible that some people were not maliciously taking advantage of Peak; it is possible that they tried to join but soon quit because they realized that volunteering for Peak was not what they had in mind, or because the established members made them feel unwelcome (a likely scenario). So whether these transient members were truly free-riders was debatable, yet Peak's established rescuers invariably viewed them as such. As a result of this perception, members feared such predatory behavior from outsiders, and they spoke often about the phenomenon, referring to it as "getting burned."

Although Peak's experienced rescuers did not want to give away their knowledge to outsiders, the group needed to train its unskilled members. By openly and frequently denigrating the free-riders, Peak justified its refusal to train all members unconditionally. This "renunciation of outsiders" (Kanter 1968) set the stage for Peak to socialize its members to the norms surrounding resources. First, new members were responsible for developing their individual skill and becoming self-reliant on missions. After achieving this first, self-oriented step, they were granted peripheral status and were expected to use their skills to benefit the group. Members who demonstrated this shift from self-oriented to group-oriented resource management conformed fully to the group's resource norms and subsequently were granted core status within this dimension of membership.

Managing Individual Skill Peak's members had to be able to manage their own skills so that they could act responsibly on missions. Rescuers who were not self-sufficient endangered the team because they could sap the resources from a mission by creating a rescuer-turned-victim scenario. That is, if members entered the field and became lost or injured, the team would have to launch a separate rescue effort to help them. This effort, in turn, would reduce the energy that Peak otherwise could have devoted to rescuing the first victim. Therefore, acquiring and honing basic survival and rescue skills was crucial for less experienced rescuers, and the group strongly approved of this activity.

Patrick told me that the self-oriented goal of acquiring skill was one of his main reasons for joining the group. He also demonstrated his understanding of resource norms by explaining this self-oriented period as a necessary stage in reaching a longer-term goal that would benefit the group. Someday he would be a contributing member:

> I joined for selfish reasons. I want to learn things from these guys. They've been doing it for a long time, and they're good at it. And there's a lot of different ways to do things, and right now I'm kind of in the absorbing stage still. . . . I'm going out there and doing this, and I'm learning stuff every time around. And eventually I'm gonna absorb as much as I can handle, I mean, you're always learning things. And then I'm gonna be—I like to think—a competent rescue member.

Although members might possess the technical skills that were necessary to perform or assist in a rescue, it was important to demonstrate, as Patrick did, an understanding that their self-gain was only a step toward the larger goal of contributing resources to the team in return. Rescuers could gain the skills necessary to improve their own working knowledge and expertise; the group sanctioned members, however, when they used their newly acquired skills solely for personal gain.

Such a mismanagement of skills placed the offender in a precarious position with the other group members, as Patrick learned by skiing into the avalanche-prone area with Mitch. Although no one was hurt by their actions, many rescuers felt that they had used their skill (skiing into the area) in a way that detracted from the team's overall effort. In doing so, they diverted some of the resources from the team. Brooke, the young southern woman who was a support-status member, explained:

> Not only did [Patrick and Mitch] put Gary and Nick in danger as far as avalanche control went, but they also put themselves in danger. In any situation—any, *any* situation—you never, ever, ever send more people into the field than are needed. Because all that does is up the risk of them hurting themselves, and then us having to turn around and go save them. Patrick could've seriously hurt himself. He broke his ski and ended up having to posthole down in a blinding snowstorm. We then had another mission on top of that one, and Nick had to wait for Patrick to get down, then get him back and get him warmed up before Nick could go on the second mission. So not only did Patrick put himself in danger, he put two of our other members in danger, and he tied up one of our most experienced members for another mission.

Another aspect of members' individual skill management was knowing their own limitations in order to ensure that they did not exceed them. Maddie told me what she thought of one of my inexperienced cohort-peers: "I have a lot of respect for Nancy because she knows her limitations and she can speak up about them. And she's not afraid to do so." The group looked favorably upon rescuers who admitted when they were unsure because they could be trusted to carefully monitor their own skill level. They were regarded as valuable because they were predictably competent in certain roles.

Maddie also expressed her concern about members who were not aware of the limits on their abilities. One member in his early fifties, Jerry, had suffered a heart attack but was having trouble accepting a less strenuous role during the missions. Maddie explained to me that she had to be the one to tell Jerry that he could no longer go into the field:

> It's been really hard for him to learn what his limits really are. It came down to [me saying] "Jer, sorry, but this is the way it's gonna be. I know you wanna be right there with Gary, running up the trail, but he's afraid—and I'm afraid—you're gonna have a heart attack. And I can't believe you're *not* afraid you're gonna have a heart attack!" And yet, he wants to be put in the field with [the Ironmen]. And he doesn't see that there's a problem there.

Maddie also expressed concern about Cyndi in her early days, who once, when she had a badly injured leg, volunteered to ride a horse on a search that Maddie was coordinating:

> Cyndi still needs to learn about what her own limitations are. I don't think she knows that yet. When she was really injured this summer, she [said], "Horseback riding? I'll go horseback riding!" I [said], "Cyndi, your leg is still hugely black and blue. You're *limping* around here, and you're asking me if you can go horseback riding? No!" She told me she'd know if she could ride when she got on the horse. But [I said], "You have to tell me now. I can't just send you up there and see! It's either now or not at all." And she didn't want to be willing to make that choice then. . . . I don't play around with stuff like that. That bothers me. I don't know that she really understands what her limits are—or she may not understand what could be asked of her, and she doesn't realize that she might not be able to do what we ask of her, until it's too late.

Jerry and Cyndi had deviated from the norm of managing their own skill. In both cases, Maddie confronted them to keep them from over-stepping their abilities and sacrificing the goals of the mission. The sanctioning of this unacceptable behavior did not stop there, however. Maddie told me that after those missions she described Jerry's and Cyndi's transgressions to all the mission coordinators and to some lead-status members. Other members also heard about the incidents through informal conversations and gossip. By all these means, Jerry and Cyndi lost status within the group. These norm violations were fairly severe, in part because they threatened the group's ideal of heroism. Indeed, when heroes in stories meet their downfall, it is often because they ignore their limitations, a cultural theme that can be traced back to Greek mythology.[14]

Benny, the seven-year lead-status member, also stressed that Peak valued members who knew their limits:

> We want people pretty damn honest, and if you don't know [how to do something], we want you to *tell us*—anytime. Straight out, just say, "I don't know," and then we'll have you do something else if it's a really important task that needs to be done right away. We're not going to bite your head off for being honest.

According to Benny, one reason why rescuers might be inclined to overestimate their abilities was their fear of being negatively sanctioned for not knowing what to do. Another possible reason was members' desire to gain status by appearing more highly skilled and more competent than they actually were. Peak regarded these members as less valuable because their eagerness to be involved could override prudence and endanger others.

Managing Group Skill Possessing and applying individual skills was only part of the process of becoming fully socialized to Peak's resource norms. Once rescuers were able to manage their own skill, they achieved peripheral status. The group then assigned them to roles that required them to manage others' skills. In these roles, they taught the less experienced members and led groups of rescuers on missions. Peripheral members could advance to core status by conforming to this group-oriented norm.

Jim, the 20-year founding member, felt strongly that if the group was to function as a unit, team members needed to have confidence in one another's abilities. Other experienced rescuers shared this view and took an active part in training the less skilled members. This training not only fostered members' confidence in one another, but also benefited the group by increasing the overall depth of skill. Jim stated that our trainer, Roy, the mountaineering 15-year member, had taken on the bulk of this responsibility:

> Because Roy is more involved in the actual field operations [during a mission], he's still out there training these people. He's out there making sure [their skills are up to par]. I don't think you can *find* a more dedicated man than Roy. To go out there, year after year, month after month, and train these people in the basic skills necessary to be a functioning part of mountain rescue. It's an unbelievable commitment that he's made.

Roy was considered a core member because he was able to manage others' skills by teaching them what they needed to know to fulfill a role in the larger system.

Peripheral members were cautiously given the opportunity to conduct these training sessions by assisting a core member in an area they knew well. When Martin, the five-year member who had joined the group in his late forties, first joined Peak, he was asked to assist Roger in a white-water training in which Roger led a group on one side of the river, while Martin led a group on the other side. Before he crossed the river, Roger briefed Martin on the scenario they would perform: the two teams would work together to string a rope spanning the river about 10 feet above the water; then each side would use a specific system of pulleys and ropes to tighten the line enough so that a rescuer (in this case, Fred) could hang from it and use it to maneuver back and forth above the river.

Roger later told me, "Martin didn't do what I said. He tried to do his own thing and his team just didn't know how to do it. So they did it wrong and it was really dangerous—[the line] wasn't tight enough [it sagged], and Fred ended up in the water." Because the water was flowing so fast, it pulled Fred downstream, creating a "V" in the line with Fred at the point. The force of the water was so great that neither team was able to pull him to their side, and he was unable to release himself from the line immediately. Fortunately, he kept his head above the water long enough to free himself and swim through some rapids to the shore.

Roger viewed Martin's misjudgment of his team members' capabilities as a danger to the group. Subsequently, he recommended to the board of directors that Martin not be involved at that level without immediate supervision. This incident was so powerful that Martin was stigmatized, and he lost considerable standing with group members for a period of time following the event.

Individuals also managed group resources through leadership.[15] To coordinate a rescue in the field, team leaders had to assign individuals to tasks appropriate to their ability level. Knowledge of others' skill level, then, was crucial in the successful completion of missions. Nick, the five-year support member who was on the verge of attaining lead status at the time we talked, observed that Gary was a good team leader because of his ability to manage others' skills: "He'll let you do your capability, and if more needs to be added, he will [tell you]. But he'll let you wrangle the reins, basically. He will let you do your stuff until you screw up, and then he'll correct you." Nick saw that Gary had a fine awareness of others' limitations. He assigned members tasks that would challenge them individually, while carefully monitoring their activity so that they could learn without sacrificing the team's goal. This ability granted Gary core status within the resource dimension of membership.

Leading others also took the form of group coordination. Mission coordinators needed extensive knowledge of others' skills so they could utilize team members accordingly. This was crucial to the success of a rescue effort. On one mission, a problem arose because members were assigned to tasks that were beyond their ability. Roger blamed Joel, the mission co-ordinator: "Joel doesn't know half the people—the new members—and he sent people out there that shouldn't have been there. He's kinda out of touch with it. He didn't know the group really, the dynamics of the group. He doesn't know that kind of stuff 'cause he's not around the group enough to really know."

One way of improving efficiency was to conduct a formal session for disseminating information about rescuers' abilities. As a result of the problem that arose on Joel's mission, Roger explained, the team leaders were going to meet to "talk about group members and kind of bring everybody up to par on who should do what, and who's capable of doing what, and that type of thing." In this way the group socialized members to share information in order to enhance Peak's overall proficiency.

Commitment

Peak also socialized its members to commit themselves to the group. New members who participated intensely demonstrated a base level of commitment that advanced them to peripheral status. The more seasoned rescuers, however, viewed this self-oriented behavior with some suspicion because the peripheral members were reaping the rewards of group acceptance: friendship, skill, knowledge, excitement, and self-satisfaction. The core members were those who persisted beyond the realm of self-gain, and they were recognized as truly committed to the group. Proceeding through these stages represented an important distinction in members' commitment: a move from self-oriented participation to group-oriented persistence.

Participating It was difficult for unskilled, new rescuers to become accepted by the group because the established members feared that they were not committed to Peak's cause. Because new members sensed this lack of receptiveness, those who wanted to prove their commitment participated heavily in training sessions and missions during the initial stages of membership.

Many rescuers experienced this resistance in their first encounters with the group. Barbara and I certainly did; recall when, at our first meeting, Meg told us not to expect others to welcome us. Martin felt unwelcome during his first business meeting as well. He told me, "I kind of felt like I was a *spectator* when I first showed up. In other words, [they acted like] 'there's somebody there in the corner, we'll just let him sit in the corner.'" In this way, Peak was like other groups that require prospective members to invest substantial time and energy before they gain "anything at all from belonging to the system" (Kanter 1968:506).

New members were made to feel like outsiders. Peak tightly guarded the camaraderie and excitement from them until they had proved their willingness to participate. By creating such an inhospitable environment for newcomers, the group sent a powerful message about commitment expectations. Several members told me about their first few months with the group; Brooke's story was typical:

> My first impression was that they didn't really care if I was there or not, to tell you the truth. I came into a business meeting and no one said hello to me, no one said, "Welcome, thanks for coming," no one asked me to introduce myself. I just kinda sat through the meeting and then afterwards went up to this guy, who was supposed to be head of new member training, and said, "Hi, I'm new. Do I need to sign anything? How do I become part of this group?" And his reply to me was just, "Oh, just keep coming to the business meetings." And I was really serious about joining and becoming a member, and going through the training and doing what it took to be able to be called out to go on missions. And thank goodness I was determined enough to become a part of this group—to keep going to the business meetings. . . . At first I was kind of a loner; I would just go home [after the training sessions and meetings]. After people got to know my face and know my name, they'd say, "Hey, come to the Mineshaft" [for drinks] or whatever.

By the time I joined Peak, a year after Brooke, she had persevered and attended enough trainings and missions to eventually feel more comfortable in the group. But recall from chapter 1 that even though she had been a member for over a year and was dating Nick, one of the Ironmen, she still felt uncomfortable enough at the bar to ask me to sit at the "loser-table" with her. Established members were more receptive to newer members once they showed some dedication to participating in the short term, but they still held some reservations, which made newer members, like Brooke, uncomfortable, even a year later. The prevailing attitude was that the truly committed members would find a way to remain in the group, as

Brooke did, while those who were less serious would be weeded out, almost by a Darwinian process of natural selection.

Elena, the member in her early thirties who had experienced a few false starts in Peak, eventually committed to the group and became an active support-status member (and later a mission coordinator). When outsiders approached her about possible sponsorship in joining Peak, her responses were blunt and reflected the conviction that participation was a very self-oriented process:

> The way we have it set up now is that the people who really want to do it, and learn it, and do it for a good cause, will stick with it. And I think it's the people who don't really care enough about it that don't stick with it. And whenever people ask me about it, I always encourage them to come to meetings and I always tell them, "I'll go with you, but after that you're on your own. After that, it's up to you to get to the trainings. And after that, it's your decision as to what training to go to, when you attend, and how much you participate. And I won't be involved in that." Because you can't force someone to do it; they have to want to do it or not. And I think that's how I look at it for myself, too. When I first joined, maybe I wasn't that into it, maybe I wasn't working hard enough to achieve getting on the team. But once I put my mind to it, and once I realized it was something I was really gonna want, then I put the effort into it.

Elena detailed the amount of responsibility placed on the individual to prove commitment. She took the blame for her first few failed attempts at participation, citing her own insufficient levels of hard work and effort. She further clarified how participation was viewed as an individual process when she told me that she "achieved" peripheral membership only after she "put [her] mind to it" and "realized it was something [she] was really gonna want." She certainly held this philosophy—putting the onus of membership totally on the individual—when I joined the group, as evidenced by her refusal to talk to me, a new and unproven member.

Members' acceptance was enhanced not only by the quantity of their participation but by its quality as well. Benny, the divorced father and seven-year member, told me how his feelings of belonging intensified when, as a new member, he performed an important role during a crisis:

> They would give you a role, and then you would fulfill it or not fulfill it.
> . . . That's kind of how you proved yourself—to yourself and to the other

people—whether or not you could take on whatever they told you to do. And that also got you so that you were hooked, because when you're just sitting there, and you're just a doof, and then all of a sudden, you get to run this [rope and pulley] system, or you get to run this oxygen up [to a victim], you feel good, you feel like you're part of the group. And that felt great.

These feelings of "we-ness" or "communion" are an important mechanism in solidifying members' commitment to groups (Kanter 1968). Thus, group acceptance and member participation fed off each other: the more fully members participated, the more acceptance they gained, which led them to participate more.

Persisting Members who sustained their participation over a long period were greatly respected because their devotion to the group went beyond a commitment to themselves. Whatever their original goals were, persistence was regarded as anything that surpassed the achievement of those goals. For example, many members joined Peak because they sought skills, friends, or excitement. After extensive participation, however, their skills became second nature, their friendships with one another extended beyond group activities, and the thrill of the missions became less frequent. Rescuers who persisted beyond this point were group oriented in their commitment and had fully conformed to the group's commitment norms.

Mitch, the new member whose zeal caused him to ski into the avalanche-prone area with Patrick, observed that persistence had proved veterans' commitment and thus had won them core membership in the group. He used Roy and Jim, both longtime members, as examples:

I'd say it's a few-year commitment or so before you put in enough time and enough missions and enough trainings to really consider yourself a member. It's not that you're *not* contributing before that, but to be an integral part. Because otherwise, you came and you can leave. Until you get to that point, like Roy or Jim, I think that you have to put in a very significant portion of time and have an impact on the group over time to really be a part of it. Otherwise, you're just like a hired gun or something, for a short term. . . . I think that Roy is respected for his time, his effort, his sincerity, and the fact that he'll always be there at the stuff. As opposed to being someone who's—you know, there's so many "absentee" [lead-status] members.

Persistent members were highly respected by others because their commitment was group oriented; they were viewed as contributing to the whole. As Patrick said:

First off, [I respect] the people who've been in it for a while simply because they have length of commitment. They didn't try it and then not like it: "Oh, gosh, this isn't as much fun as I thought it would be." But obviously [Jim's] committed an incredible amount of time and effort [to] not what he does, but what *we* do. Which is help.

Patrick emphasized the idea that members who had devoted so much time to Peak were not gaining personally from their involvement. Jim's commitment was not to himself; it was to "what *we* do."

Rescuers joined Peak for various individual reasons, and for some these initial goals were replaced by group-oriented motivators. There was a saturation point beyond which self-gain became a diminishing return, and the group benefited from members' persistence. Mitch located this "point" by measuring "impact on the group over time"; Patrick defined it in terms of the amount of "time and effort" committed to the group. Maddie, the longtime rescuer and mission coordinator, reached her turning point when the adrenaline stopped rushing. She speculated that many members joined for the "rush" they received from the urgency of the missions, but for her, this rush had become routine:

I think to some degree, we're all a little bit of an adrenaline junkie in order to be in this group. I don't get an adrenaline rush out of mountain rescue. Not anymore. I definitely did at first, but [now] it's a lot more routine because there's not anything that surprises me anymore, in a victim and what happened to them and whatever. . . . [People] can still get an adrenaline rush, but they're not gonna get it the way they perceive they're gonna get it. For me, it's usually just getting out there [in the wilderness] on a mission. That's my favorite place to get energy.

Maddie had invested a great deal of time in Peak, and one of her initial rewards for joining was diminishing. Yet even though she no longer experienced the thrill of a rescue, she persisted with her group involvement.

Core membership in Peak was very time-consuming. Although many of the older members had less consistent rescue careers than Jim or Roy, others still generally felt that they were dependable. Elena, the support member and mission coordinator, spoke of Kevin and Meg, the married couple, who were longtime members but had been less actively involved in recent years: "You'll see [Kevin and Meg], except maybe not at training—but you'll see them when it counts. . . . Maybe not at the 5 A.M.s, but they'll be there. They'll let other people take a shot at it, but they'll be there when they need to be there." Meg and Kevin were group oriented in their persistence because their aim was to support their teammates on missions when it counted. This kind of sustained involvement in Peak's activities proved members' willingness to be committed not only to the group but to their teammates as well.

Mitch compared his own low level of commitment with Roy's persistence. In doing so, he revealed the idea that fully committed members were part of Peak's identity: "My leaving is not gonna affect the group at all. If Roy left, there'd be a big hole in this thing, so he's much more a part of the group's identity than I could be." This rationale appears paradoxical: members who committed fully to Peak were viewed as having achieved a group-oriented commitment that surpassed individual fulfillment. Yet at the same time these members were so crucial, *as individuals*, that they were viewed as constituting the group's very identity.

In these ways, Peak used the symbolic reward of heroic status to socialize new members to group norms in three key areas: consciousness, resources, and commitment. Within each of these three dimensions, rescuers moved through two stages of membership, first mastering the self-oriented norms, and next mastering the group-oriented norms. Once they achieved group orientation within all three dimensions, they were considered core members of this heroic group.

4

Dealing with Crisis
Rescuers' Emotions

Rescuers' experiences on dangerous, difficult, or gruesome missions called for them to engage in "edgework." Recall that high-risk takers, or edgeworkers, push themselves to the edge—to their physical and mental limits—because there they encounter an intense sensory experience that gives them a feeling of control over impending chaos. For most edgeworkers, this feeling is addictive and compels them to pursue high-risk activities repeatedly. Yet the intense feelings they experience at one level of risk may quickly become routine and unexciting, largely because once they accomplish a feat, they are not at the "edge" anymore. Thus, in order to recapture the same "rush," they are driven to pursue even higher risk and to push their limits farther each time.[1] I found that Peak's rescuers often engaged in edgework on missions. They had to be able to complete their task under intense stress, and members who could remain in control—those whose edge was farther out—were more often sent on challenging rescues because they were considered better suited to handle them.

Although it was important for rescuers to have the skills to accomplish the missions, it was more important that they were able to regulate the intense feelings that arose from such dangerous or gruesome experiences; they believed that uncontrolled feelings rendered them useless. As I discussed previously, any social group may create its own unique belief system about emotions, or "emotional culture."[2] Peak's emotional culture, like many others, contained beliefs about how certain emotions operated, when it was appropriate to feel and to express them, and how inappropriate feelings should be handled. These beliefs helped group members to structure their own behavior and interactions with others.

One important aspect of Peak's particular emotional culture was rescuers' belief that there were certain feelings that threatened to push them over the "edge," preventing them from maintaining control over the situation, and thus hampering their ability to perform edgework. Rescuers who lost their composure were not considered reliable and were thought to be threats to themselves, other team members, and the victims because they acted without thinking; emotions, as Gary told me, "got in the way." In addition to their beliefs about how emotions operated, the group members also held beliefs about how to control or "manage" these feelings. I found that some of these "emotion management" (Hochschild 1983) techniques prevailed over others in the group's emotional culture.[3] The rescuers' emotional culture—their beliefs about emotions and the emotion management techniques they used to achieve desired emotional states—was a crucial feature in their ability to engage in edgework, to perform physically during high-risk situations.[4]

Furthermore, beliefs about gender also figured prominently into these patterns of emotion management, which is not surprising since certain emotions and management techniques are highly gendered in mainstream American culture.[5] In Peak, there were different "feeling rules" and emotional "display rules" (Hochschild 1983) for women and men, which greatly influenced how rescuers understood and enacted edgework.

The Gendered Emotional Culture of Edgework

The levels of difficulty, danger, and stress varied greatly among Peak's missions. At times, members were asked to perform only slightly demanding, low-urgency tasks such as hiking a short distance up a trail to carry a hiker with a twisted ankle out to the parking lot. Other times they were asked to perform very difficult, dangerous, or gruesome tasks such as entering a potential avalanche zone to search for a missing skier, negotiating the rapids of a rushing river to reach the body of a drowned rafter, being lowered down a cliff face to rescue an injured rock climber, or extracting mutilated bodies from a plane crash. It was these physically and emotionally demanding situations that most threatened rescuers' sense of control, requiring them to engage in edgework—to negotiate the boundary between order and chaos—not only during the missions but before and after as well.

Four stages of edgework emerged as I talked to rescuers about their participation in missions. These stages were distinctly marked not only by the flow of rescue events, but also by the feelings members experienced in each stage. Women and men experienced edgework differently, interpreting and managing feeling in gender-specific ways while they prepared for missions, performed high-risk activities, reflected on their participation, and made sense of their actions.

Preparing for the Edge: Anticipating the Unknown

Missions were unpredictable events, and members were often required to use whatever resources they had to accomplish their task. Many of Peak's members, like other edgeworkers, found it exciting not to know what to expect from a rescue, and they felt challenged by the prospect of relying on their cognitive and technical skills to quickly solve any puzzle that suddenly presented itself. Yet other rescuers viewed the missions' unpredictability as stressful, and they worried in anticipation about performing under certain conditions.

One common worry was that they might be physically unable to perform a task either because they would not be strong enough, or because they would not know what to do. Elena, the five year member in her early thirties, expressed uncertainty about knowing how to help an injured victim:

> I'm always wondering if I'm going to hurt somebody more than help them. I'm always wondering if I'm doing the right thing. "Do I move [the victim's] head, or could it break her back?" You know? I mean, I always second-guess myself in the field. I guess my problem is that I'm always unsure of myself. Like, I'd be afraid that I would do more damage than good, in a way. . . . And that's where my hesitation always comes in. I mean, it's a big problem too because I know what's right, and I don't speak up about it because I'm unsure of myself. You know?

Not only did Elena worry about her preparedness to help victims, she also saw this apprehension as problematic; importantly, she felt that her lack of confidence in her ability was the source of the problem, not her ability level itself.

Cyndi, my cohort-peer who was in her late twenties, told me of her reaction while driving to the scene of the van rollover, the mission with four critically injured passengers that Keith had tried to run while watching his four-year-old. Search and rescue was called because the accident was inaccessible to the paramedics, who needed ropes to get down to the victims and a hauling system to get them out. Cyndi was at home when she got the page to respond, and knew that she might be one of the first members on the scene because it was close to her house. She reported feeling "panicked" as she drove up there:

> From my house [to the scene], I was in a moderate or higher state of anxiety! Because everybody else [on the radio] sounded like they were panicking, so I was like, "Something really bad has happened." And I thought I was gonna be one of the first people on the scene. So at that point, I was panicked. I wouldn't know where to start, you know? I didn't have a clue. And when I got up there Gary was on the scene, so I was just like, "Thank God. I don't have to do anything [take charge]. Okay, tell me what to do."

Cyndi felt highly anxious and worried that she would not know what to do. Her "panic" subsided, however, once she realized the victims' lives would not depend on her decisions.

Members also worried about their ability to maintain emotional control, realizing that they could encounter a particularly upsetting scene on a mission. For example, Maddie, the 10-year member and mission coordinator, told me that one situation she dreaded was encountering a dead victim whom she knew. She expected that this situation would be one that most threatened her emotional control, the one in which she would be most likely to go over the edge:

> I think my biggest fear has always been that [the victim] is gonna be, eventually, somebody I know. And eventually it was. With Arnie [who was killed] in an avalanche. And yet, I was okay with that. I was more okay than I thought I might be. I always *think* I'm gonna lose it, but I guess you expect for the worst, and then you usually do better. Or, expect that "What would you do if you lost it?" or "How would you get it back?" And so I've planned ahead.

Worrying about what could arise on a future mission led rescuers to make a plan of action ahead of time, speculating about their potential reactions to stressful events. Preparing for edgework by imagining numerous different scenarios gave them some sense of control over the unpredictable future, and through such planning, they were able to manage their uncomfortable anticipatory feelings about the unknown.[6]

Maddie's statement also typified another technique rescuers used in conjunction with planning and rehearsing future scenarios: they set low expectations for themselves. Part of their planning process was to prepare for the most demanding possible situations, the ones in which they were most likely to fail. This emotion management strategy served two functions. First, it made members acutely aware of their progress toward the edge on missions. For example, expecting that she might not be able to remain in control if she encountered someone she knew, Maddie told me that she approached dead-body recoveries cautiously, prepared to hand off her task to someone else. When she began to feel she was nearing the edge, she was ready to say, "Hey, I can't do this." The second function of setting low expectations was that rescuers would probably perform beyond them. In this way, they set themselves up for success, remaining within their limits on a mission while feeling good about surpassing their expectations.

Brooke also used this strategy of underestimating her ability; specifically, she reduced her anxiety by overemphasizing safety practices. She told me that if she was extra safety-conscious, she could anticipate better control in dangerous or risky situations:

I'm Miss Safety. I am *Miss Safety*. I mean, I get two people to check my knots [that tie me into the lowering rope], and I check everybody else's knots. 'Cause I'm scared to death of heights! And [to other members] I'm like, "Wear your helmet, wear your helmet! Don't get too close to the river without a PFD [personal floatation device]!" I mean, I am Miss Safety. So hopefully [getting into a dangerous situation] won't happen to me because of my attitude towards it.

By practicing safety, Brooke felt that she had better control over what might happen to her (or others) during a rescue, yet it is clear from her statement that she still did not feel overly confident; "hopefully" she would stay safe.

Anticipating a poor performance and uncontrollable conditions were common ways the women on the team prepared for the variety of situations they could encounter on a mission. Underestimating their ability was not a very common practice among the men in the group, however. Most of the men in Peak used the opposite technique—sheer confidence—to prepare for emergency action. Brooke told me that overconfidence was effective for two of the Ironmen, Gary and Nick. She claimed they were able to perform at very high levels *because* of their high expectations of themselves:

> I think that both of those guys see themselves as Superman, which is not necessarily a good thing. They sort of see themselves as being invincible, [and] I think that they might test their physical limits more than I would. They might go into a situation that I would stand back and say, "I don't think that's safe." But they're convinced that nothing's going to happen to them. . . . But then again, I think that has a lot to do with the mental aspect of it. You know, they see themselves as being more capable of doing something than I would. Therefore, as long as they see themselves being capable of it, they are capable of it—if that makes any sense.

According to Brooke, extreme confidence was effective for Gary and Nick, yet she did not think that it was a viable emotion management technique for her to employ. She felt safer being wary of an uncertain situation, but acknowledged that Gary and Nick were safer charging into the same situation. She saw their confidence as enabling them to perform at high levels.

When I asked Gary himself about his experience in extreme situations, he responded with strong certainty in his ability, supporting Brooke's perception of him:

> *Gary:* I like being thrown knee-deep [into challenging situations]. I like it when the shit hits the fan, and having to get my way out of it.
> *Jen:* Don't you get nervous that you might not be able to do that?
> *Gary:* Nope.
> *Jen:* Do you think you'll always be able to do that?
> *Gary:* Yup. I am a cocky, young, think-I-can-do-it-all kid. I can get out of a situation. Probably because I have never *not* done it. I perform tremendously under pressure. That's when I shine at my absolute, top of my game. And I love being put in the hot seat. That's one of the reasons I do mountain rescue.

Gary highlighted an interdependent relationship between confidence and ability: not only did confidence enhance performance, but past performance enhanced confidence.

Other men were extremely confident too, even when others accused them of overestimating their own ability. Roger, another one of the Ironmen, was a very experienced, lead-status member. He described his ability to assess avalanche danger, a highly unpredictable phenomenon, as better than most other members'. On one occasion when the team was practicing avalanche skills, Roger walked out to the edge of a "cornice" (a windblown pile of snow overhanging a steep hill or cliff, which can break off and cause an avalanche). Another highly experienced rescuer, Shorty (also an Ironman), questioned Roger's safety judgment because if he broke the cornice and caused an avalanche, he could easily have been swept up in it, carried down the mountain, and buried under several feet of heavy snow. Roger was angered because he was very confident in his ability to assess how far out he could walk on any cornice without breaking it, reasoning that his past experience gave him this knowledge. He had spent much recreational time in the backcountry, examining cornices and, through trial and error, learning where they typically break:

> I could probably tell a lot more [about avalanche potential than other members], and I can usually say, "Well this is where it's gonna break and this is where it's gonna slide." And sure as shit, when I get out there on my skis and I jump around, that's right where it breaks and that's right where it slides. You know, if you're just a normal person walking out there you're an *idiot*, but I don't think I am because I know what I'm doing. Shorty even questioned me, like, "Do you think it's really safe to be doing that?" And it's like, "Well, I wouldn't be doing it if it wasn't safe. It's not safe for you to be doing it, no, but it's safe for me to be doing it because I know what I'm doing." You know, I have a respect for it.

Roger's confidence helped him prepare for edgework in the event of a real mission. By stating where he thought cornices would break, he was quite literally reaffirming his ability to assess the edge—the boundary between safety and danger—which allowed him to feel in control of the situation. One way to view his activity was to consider it objectively dangerous: Roger had crossed the safety boundary, as evidenced by the many avalanches he had caused. Yet he considered his actions safe: even though he had caused many avalanches, each time he proved he was right, demonstrating his fine awareness and superior control of the edge, which signaled to himself and to others that he could approach it and work there without going over it.

By relying on "successful" (i.e., survived) past experiences, the men in the group became confident about almost any future performance. Patrick explained why, using this same circular rationale. He described Jim, the

founding member: "Jim is very confident in what he does. For good reason, because he does a good job. . . . But I think that's one of the big reasons why he does things well, 'cause he has a lot of confidence in himself."[7]
This form of ex post facto validation helped Peak's male rescuers interpret
the relationship between their confidence and skill.

There are several explanations for this gendered difference in preparation strategies. First, in general, men were more experienced than women.
Through their own recreation and group-related activities, men's exposure
to risk was both more frequent and more hazardous than women's.[8] Yet
this gendered confidence pattern was not totally explained by differential
risk exposure. When I talked to equally experienced men and women, apprehension and lack of confidence still dominated women's anticipatory
feelings, and men still tended to feel confident. Furthermore, even when
women performed well on missions, it did not seem to boost their confidence for future situations, while conversely, men's poor performances did
not erode theirs.

A second factor in explaining this pattern was that the masculine nature of rescue work made men feel more at ease in the setting, and thus
they tended to display unwavering certainty that they could handle any
situation in which they might find themselves. Peak's women felt disadvantaged in this masculine environment and, taking this into account, set
low expectations for themselves.[9] In one way, their feelings were based in
reality: they were aware that, on the whole, the men in the group were
physically stronger, and thus able to perform harder tasks than they.

In another way, though, women's insecurities were due to cultural and
group stereotypes about men's superior rescue ability. For example, the
prevailing belief that men are emotionally stronger than women made
women question whether they would be able to perform edgework in potentially upsetting situations, while the same stereotype enabled men to
have confidence that they would maintain control in those situations. Yet,
my observations (discussed later in this chapter) yielded no gendered pattern of emotional control. Another stereotype that made women worry
about their rescue ability was the belief that men were more mechanically
and technically inclined than they were. This stereotype came into play
during trainings and missions when the group used any kind of mecha-
nization, such as rope and pulley systems, helicopters, snowmobiles, or
white-water rafting equipment. Cyndi told me she felt "hugely" intimi-
dated in her first year by the technical training, yet she later became quite
adept in setting up and operating rope and pulley systems. Elena told me

that during her first training she looked around at "all the guys" and thought, "What am I doing here? I'm not even qualified for any of this." Cyndi and Elena's feelings of inferiority acted as "place markers" where "the emotion conveys information about the state of the social ranking system" (Clark 1990:308).

Because women were often marginalized in this way, both their own and others' expectations of them were lower than they were for the men in the group. By remaining trepidacious and maintaining low expectations that they would often exceed, the women reaffirmed their place in the group as useful. Although they feared admitting when they would be unable to complete a task, because as Cyndi said, it meant "you're admitting to everyone else that you're not as good as them," the women in the group felt that bowing out early was preferable to failing. Cyndi said others would think, "At least they didn't fuck the mission up. They stayed, and they helped, and they did something." Thus, trepidation and confidence emerged as gendered emotional strategies used in preparing for edgework.

Performing on the Edge: Suppressing Feelings

During Peak's urgent missions, clear thinking and rational action, core features of edgework, were seen as especially crucial.[10] However, in such demanding situations, members' capacity for emotional and physical control was seen as more tenuous: emotions threatened to push them over the edge, preventing them from physically performing at all. Rescuers who were easily scared, excited, or upset by a mission's events were considered undependable. Members employed several strategies to control these feelings during missions, which allowed them to perform under pressure.

Rescuers were particularly leery of the onset of adrenaline rushes because such potent physiological reactions threatened their composure; they felt that the emotions they experienced as a result of adrenaline rushes could "get in the way" of their performance. Although an adrenaline rush is a physiological and chemical reaction, not an emotion, Peak's members used the term "adrenaline rush" to refer to two distinct (and potentially problematic) emotional states: fear and urgency.[11] Yet adrenaline was not totally undesirable; in fact, at lower levels rescuers welcomed it because it helped them focus and heightened their awareness. Mostly, though, rescuers were encouraged to see adrenaline rushes as an important situational cue, one they should heed as a warning that they were at risk of losing control.

One way rescuers talked about adrenaline impeding performance was when they experienced paralyzing fear, which rendered them ineffective, increasing risk for their teammates and for the victim.[12] Cyndi expressed a typical perspective when she explained the difference between helpful and harmful adrenaline rushes. She described a time when she was trying to cross a river on a series of slippery rocks, each of which was just beyond her comfortable step, requiring her to jump from one to the next. Other rescuers were waiting for her to cross, and she knew that they would be able to reach her if she slipped and fell into the rushing water. Nonetheless, she could not do it:

> I mean, I knew that I was perfectly safe. And I was trembling like a leaf, and my heart was racing, and there wasn't a damn thing I could do about it! I could sit there all day long [saying to myself], "You're gonna be fine, you're gonna be fine, you're gonna be fine," and I just sat there shaking. I was just kind of like in one of these sort of states: huge adrenaline rush. . . . There's a point where some fear is a good thing—adrenaline—and it helps you focus, because you know that you need to be careful. If you're in a situation where there is some fear, maybe an avalanche or a river, you want to get whatever it is you're doing done quickly because the faster you get out of it, the safer you are. But then there's a point where it stops being an aid and it becomes a hindrance: fear outweighs your ability to act. I think that's the worst thing in the world you could do for a mission, just freeze and panic, where you spend more time combating your fear than thinking about the situation you're in.

Interestingly, Cyndi equated adrenaline with fear. She used these terms interchangeably, noting the edge between a useful and a detrimental physiological reaction that she experienced as fear. Her description highlighted both sides of the edge. She described the controllable side, where "some fear is a good thing" because rescuers could use their aroused feelings to create order and perform at higher levels. She also explained the other side, the chaotic side, where too much fear impeded rescuers' ability to act rationally and efficiently. They would become overwhelmed with emotion, a phenomenon that strips individuals of their ability to make self-indications and thus monitor and control their actions.[13]

In addition to telling me that emotions "got in the way" on missions, Gary also told me that emotions were dangerous because they caused rescuers to lose control. He pointed to an instance in which Brooke, who was a relatively new member at the time, began to cry during a mock rock-climbing rescue. She and another member were each tied to one end of a basketlike stretcher called a "litter." The rest of the team lowered them over the side of a cliff to reach the stranded "victim" halfway down. Gary explained:

> An example of emotions being dangerous was Brooke. Her not telling anyone she's afraid of heights, and then being put on the litter team and going over the edge and bawling her eyes out. She didn't tell anyone she's afraid of heights. To her, that was a weakness so she didn't tell anyone. . . . And all of a sudden I look over and she's a quarter way down the wall, and she's bawling her eyes out! And to me, that's unsafe. That is a total and complete loss of control. And that's what I mean: losing control of your emotions can be unsafe.

Another problem Peak's members attributed to adrenaline was that it could cause them to misinterpret routine situations as urgent. Maddie explained how feelings of urgency and excitement were problematic and had to be suppressed:

> [Rescuers need to] realize the urgency, and manage that urgency. And that really is the big part [of participating in a mission]. I know I still get it every now and again, that adrenaline rush is really going as you're walking in to the [victim], and that can really get in the way, big time, out there. Because most of the time we're not in a rush to get that person out. We can't be, or we're gonna injure them.

When Patrick and Mitch skied without authorization into the avalanche gully, group members accused them of letting their adrenaline override rational, controlled action: they skied into the gully because it was exciting and risky, not because they were needed on the scene. Brooke said, "It was just poor judgment, they jumped the gun, they had the adrenaline running. I can't imagine what they were thinking." When I asked Patrick about this, he accounted for his actions by interpreting his adrenaline as urgency. He said, "The reason I went is because I wanted to get down to the victim. I wanted to help." It seemed that overestimating urgency was a common problem for newer members, who tended to overreact to low levels of urgency. Jim told me that many newer, inexperienced members "think that every mission is this life-saving, oh-my-God, adrenaline-pumping deal. It's not. That's not what it's about."[14]

While excessive fear and urgency were seen as potentially dangerous overreactions to adrenaline, loss of control due to fear was more often associated with women's reactions, while becoming too "excitable" was more of a male phenomenon. One reason men and women might have experienced adrenaline rushes differently was because men were confident at the prospect of undertaking risk, which may have caused them to interpret their adrenaline during missions as pleasurable and exciting. Since women, on the other hand, reported more cautious mindsets in preparing for missions, worrying about their ability to exercise emotional and physical control in risky situations, perhaps they were more likely to define their adrenaline rushes as fear.

Men and women, however, managed their feelings of urgency and fear similarly: they suppressed them. For example, Martin, the construction supervisor in his early fifties who had been in the group for five years, explained his experience on the four-victim van-rollover mission. He was one of the few rescuers sent down the embankment to the accident scene, and he told me that his strategy was to concentrate on his assignment, ignoring everything else that was not directly related to his task:

> I was [attending to] that woman, getting her in the litter, being in charge of that litter, and getting that litter up the hillside. I was wrapped up in what I was doing. I mean that was one [mission] where we really had to work. There were really bad, hurt people. [I thought], "Let's do what we can and get them back up that hill." . . . We were so exhausted, so by then it was just a technical problem, you know? I didn't have time to get involved with the victims.

Martin kept his cool by prioritizing his actions in the situation, taking one step at a time to achieve his goal of evacuating the victims. The demands of the mission forced him to focus his attention on his task and pour all of his time and energy into completing it. This narrowing of focus is a common process during risky situations, and those who engage in high-risk activities frequently report losing awareness of factors extraneous to the risk activity itself.[15] It is interesting that Martin had narrowed his focus so much that he considered the victims themselves to be incidental to his actions on that particular rescue.

Cyndi told me that while on the same mission, she was in control of her emotions, successfully suppressing them because she was working the rope systems up on the road, unable to see beyond the drop-off down to the accident site. She felt differently, however, when one of the accident victims reached the top of the hill in a panicked state. The victim, who had a broken arm, had managed to climb up the 400-foot embankment in an effort to catch up to the rescue team who was evacuating her critically injured mother. Cyndi was thrown off-kilter by this sight:

> Because I was up at the top, it wasn't real. You know, I could sort of disassociate, it's like, "Okay, let's just get the job done and not think about it." But then you're meeting this person [climbing out of the accident scene] who is just out of it. I mean, she was panicked and [she had] adrenaline [rushing], and I was just kind of like, "Okay, there really are real people down there, but I'm not gonna get panicked. I need to calm this person down, because she's not gonna help rushing up to the scene, and getting in the way of the paramedics [while] trying to get to her mother."

Cyndi's emotional control was threatened when the victim emerged from the trauma scene. The sight forced her to the edge, where her ordered, controlled action was threatened by her feeling of chaotic, uncontrolled panic. She quickly narrowed her focus further, successfully managing her impending panic by monitoring the victim's behavior. In this way she was able to keep her feelings at bay while she continued working.

Another way emotions interfered with performance was when members were disturbed by the graphic sight of the accidents they encountered. Recovering the body of a dead victim, for example, held great potential for upset feelings, especially if the death was violent or gruesome, leaving the body in pieces, excessively bloody, or positioned unnaturally (such as having the legs bent backwards or a limb missing). Such situations could cause extreme reactions in rescuers, possibly preventing them from doing the job they were assigned. On the whole, men were assumed to be better suited for these gruesome or graphic jobs because they were perceived to be emotionally stronger than women. For example, Brooke made a statement that reflected the idea that emotional strength and masculinity were intertwined when she said that, under such extreme conditions, Peak's members had to "have the balls to go in and do what needs to be done. . . . I think you have to be [emotionally] strong to see what you see and to deal with what you deal with in this group."

Other members stated these gendered expectations more blatantly. Maddie told me she had noticed a common pattern in the 10 years she had been in the group:

> I think there's an emotional consideration [to being in this group], because our society says men need to hold their emotions in check more so than women. It's expected. It's an expectation from our society. And so, in any kind of situation where emotions could come into play, you know, something that's really gruesome, [the mission coordinators] aren't gonna ask us [the women], they'll ask the guys first.

Jim confirmed Maddie's suspicions when he told me that, as a mission coordinator, he tried to utilize members for jobs according to their ability, regardless of gender, except in one situation:

> I do, however, hesitate to use women in body recovery-type situations. . . . I want to protect 'em from the exposure to that type of an incident. I can't tell you why I wanna protect 'em, but that's what it is. And I wanna protect the new members too. 'Cause I think it's a horrible deal. And, you know, my wife asks me all the time, "Why do *you* have to go do the body?" Been there. Done that. I can do that. Why subject somebody else to it?

Jim reasoned that those with less emotional strength—women and inexperienced members—should be protected from the trauma of recovering dead bodies. Women, however, tended to be the less experienced members, so perhaps choosing experienced members also meant choosing men over women. In this way, stereotypes and experience interacted to create a strong pattern where men were much more likely than women to recover dead bodies.

Yet men, experienced or not, were not immune to the potentially disturbing effects of gruesome rescues. In fact, Martin told me that when he came upon a particularly gruesome plane crash, "I barfed my guts out." Meg, the 10-year member in her mid-forties who was married to Kevin, told me that despite stereotypes of masculine emotional strength, she had seen experienced men who had trouble dealing with dead bodies, even though they were willing to assist in the recovery task:

> I've seen people that are very, very macho and strong and opinionated become very sheepish in those situations. . . . [They] march right in, and as

soon as they get a visual on it [the body], they're off doing something else. [They] walk away. Can't look, can't touch. . . . And for me, a body recovery is just like recovering a living person. You know, it's just a body of who was there, and the "who" part is gone. . . . So body recoveries are not so difficult for me, but for some people it's a real struggle.

Thus, even for members who were expected to be emotionally tough, emotions also "got in the way" in dead-body situations because they could cause some rescuers to go over the edge, losing their ability to perform under stressful circumstances.

One emotion management strategy rescuers used to combat these upset feelings was to depersonalize the victims, which Meg alluded to by saying a body is not a person because the "who" part is gone. Her husband, Kevin, the 10-year, lead-status member, told me exactly how he maintained emotional distance from the victims on a rescue, in particular, from dead bodies he had helped recover:

[Recovering a dead body] brings out a shield or a protective type barrier. I go in knowing it's a fatality, that the spirit is gone, this is merely the vehicle in which he or she traveled around this planet. . . . I try not to get emotionally attached. I feel very mechanical. It's just something that has to be done, and if I'm there, I'm part of that effort to take care of it. . . . I have put myself in a mission mode. I'm mission-ready, I'm focused, we're doing something here. So sometimes [in my mission mode] I become linear [and] cold. . . . Another interesting thing—I cannot tell you any of the names of the people I've bagged. It's my way of coping with it. I'll know the name going in, and within several days, that name is no longer accessible in my memory bank. . . . I have no idea where or why or how I came up with—I'm going to say—that "ability." But that's the way I do it. I know some of these guys will remember names years down the road. I don't. I've taken care of it, and there is no need to store it away. In a way, it wasn't my problem.

Such detachment is a common way people maintain instrumental control in emotionally threatening situations.[16] Tyler, an eight-year rescuer in his late twenties, told me of another way rescuers detached when recovering dead bodies:

Some people don't look at a dead person's face. And the reason is that a face is someone's identity. Someone's body—I mean, pretty much a body is the same on everyone. But a headless body lacks an identity. You know, you need to put a face with a person, you don't put feet with a person. And by not looking at someone's face, you really can take some of the identity out of it. And it almost can seem more surreal, and that what you're dealing with really isn't even a body. So it can be easier for some people. It really helps them control how they feel about it.

Jim also felt very strongly that emotions not be a part of recovering a dead body. He described one occasion when the team was extracting a drowned victim from a river:

> There is nothin' glamorous about taking somebody's human remains, stuffing 'em in a black bag, hauling 'em up the hill, and throwing 'em in the back of the sheriff's van. There is *nothin'* glamorous about that. And when I'm in those types of situations, there's a space that I have to go to in my head. And it's real no-nonsense; it's time to say, "Let's get the job done. Let's roll up our sleeves," if you will. You know, that is not the time to re-flect on "What's it all about?" or "Why we're all here." It's a time to roll this *carcass* into a bag and drag it up the hill. And people on our team started with that [being philosophical during the extrication]. [So I said], "I don't wanna hear it! I want the guy *off* the log, *in* the bag, to the *top* of the hill. Are we ready to go?" And we should be, [*snaps*], ready to go.

Jim's "space" in his head helped him perform because it allowed him to depersonalize the victim (the "carcass"). In his view, the other members' choice to reflect on larger philosophical questions was poorly timed, inter-fering not only with the mission's efficiency, but with his own strategy of suppressing emotions as well. He asserted himself, chastising other mem-bers for their violation of the norm of emotional detachment.

Meg, Kevin, Tyler, and Jim all had their own way of depersonalizing their actions on missions—acts of bravery and heroism that would seem to be logically motivated by a deep concern for other human beings. Yet, in these intense incidents, rescuers emphasized the need to depersonalize the victims, to think of their bodies as inanimate "vehicles" that someone once used.

Fear, urgency, and emotional upset were some of the powerful feelings that threatened rescuers' control during missions. As a result, members ac-tively worked to suppress them, maintaining a demeanor of "affective neutrality" (Parsons 1951) by focusing on their task and by depersonalizing the victims. This group norm of displaying affective neutrality signified a cool-headedness that was considered safe and effective, and the group considered those who could achieve it in the most critical of circumstances—those who could push the edge the farthest—to be their most valuable members. Roy, the mountaineering 15-year member, told me that the best way he could describe search and rescue was "decision making under duress." This idea clearly conveyed that the ability to engage in edgework was the most important quality in a rescuer, and that the key to edgework was emotion management.

Going over the Edge: Releasing Feelings

Immediately after the mission, rescuers' suppressed feelings began to surface. They viewed the sensations they got from successful mission outcomes, like reuniting victims with their family, as the ultimate reward, and I often witnessed them expressing these positive feelings upon hearing the news of a saved victim. They instantly discarded their objective demeanors and became jovial, slap-happy, and chatty. They released the pent-up stress that they had tightly managed throughout the missions by shouting, high-fiving each other, making jokes, and talking about what they had been thinking and feeling throughout the mission.[17]

Occasionally, rescuers would realize that they had just been in a risky situation that could have gone awry. Reflecting back on the hazards they had undertaken and overcome made them feel ambivalent. On the one hand, they felt energized, which they generally regarded as a positive feeling of control and competence.[18] Yet, on the other hand, these positive feelings were infused with unsettled feelings of doubt when rescuers realized how dangerous the situation had been. Kevin told me how he felt when looking back:

> I think while you're in the situation, the risk or the apparent danger isn't as highlighted—it's not quite as strong or acute as it is after you've had time to reflect through hindsight what exactly transpired. . . . When you're in the situation, you are doing, you are operating, you are moving, you are trying to accomplish something. You're fixated to an extent. But after the mission, you get back and you go, "Wow! That was—" you know, "What if, what if, what if?"

I asked Kevin how he felt after one particular mission where he was in a helicopter during a risky maneuver to reach an injured hiker. He said, "It was that night when I was sitting around the house going, 'That was insane where that helicopter was!' . . . [I felt] lucky. [And] a *big* adrenaline rush." As Kevin thought about the rescue, the feelings he had been suppressing had a chance to rush forward, taking him to the edge emotionally; his ordered experience became somewhat chaotic in retrospect. He described a pattern that many rescuers experienced. While on the mission, they had maintained composure and objectivity by engaging in strategies to suppress their emotions. However, once the danger was over, they let down this tight control and confronted feelings that challenged their interpretation of what just happened. During this stage of edgework, members tried to make sense of the myriad emotions that bombarded them, wondering if perhaps there was some luck involved in their success.

Alex was a British botanist in her early thirties. Although she had only been a member of Peak for five years, she was a highly experienced mountaineer and had been on several search and rescue teams in the U.K. She told me of a time when she and Roy had a brush with death while they were on a team together. They were ice climbing up an avalanche-prone gully to reach some stranded hot-air balloonists whose balloon had crashed at the top of a cliff. The mission coordinator was able to contact a helicopter, which was going to be able to reach the stranded victims sooner than Roy and Alex, who were still only halfway up the gully. The mission coordinator radioed Alex and Roy and told them to get to a stable, safe place because the helicopter was coming in, and the wind it would create above them could stir up the snow and cause an avalanche in their gully. They assessed their location at the base of a 75-foot frozen waterfall and thought they might be safe if they positioned themselves close to the ice (the momentum of an avalanche would propel the snow in an arc, providing a safety zone between it and the vertical icefall). At the last minute, Alex saw an ice cave twenty feet up, behind the frozen waterfall. They decided they would be safer there, so she climbed up and then pulled Roy up to her. She told me what happened next:

> The two of us landed in this snow cave, and just then we hear this *roar*, and we're like "Oh my God, an avalanche!" And we like, peer out from behind the ice fall, and the *balloon*, with the basket and all of the fuel tanks and everything, just came thundering down the gully, [and the basket] just *exploded* [broke into hundreds of pieces] at the bottom where we'd

been standing, and just carried on down the gully. And we were just like [*shocked expression: jaw dropped, eyes wide, speechless*]. I mean, we just sort of lay there, like "Oh my God." I mean, we were expecting an avalanche, not the *balloon*. . . . If we had not moved out of that position and got out of the gully, I mean, we'd've just gotten smack-a-roonied by the balloon. We were both pretty shaken by that one. I don't know, maybe we felt more vulnerable or something, but we were definitely shaken up. . . . Roy kept grabbing me and saying [*yelling*], "I can't believe that happened!" and "Oh my God!" I'd say it was definitely the closest I've come in a rescue to getting snookered.

Even when rescuers emerged from missions safely, these types of close calls could disturb them for days or weeks afterward, bringing their mortality into sharp relief.

Missions with negative outcomes frequently left rescuers with stronger and more unpleasant feelings than rescues that ended successfully, and members often reported being at home alone when they first encountered these feelings. One source of upset feelings was recurring memories of emotionally disturbing scenes.[19] Cyndi described to me how the visual images of her first dead-body recovery—a victim with a severed arm—bothered her:

I got home [from the mission], and I had to get up [in a couple of hours] and go to work. So I did the work thing, and then I got home, and I was by myself, and that night sitting at home I got this mental image and, um—I don't know. It was unpleasant. For the next couple or three days you get, like, these images. If I think about it, I can still see it. Yeah, so it was not pretty.

Recurring visual memories are common when emergency workers first see dead bodies as part of their occupational duties.[20] But for Peak's rescuers, these recurring memories were not always just visual. One member told me that he once assisted in the body recovery of a fallen rock climber after which he did not sleep for three weeks. He had many upsetting flashbacks of both the sights and sounds from the scene: seeing the victim's legs broken backwards from the fall, and hearing them crack as rescuers straightened them to fit him in the body bag. Alex, the British rescuer, remembered feeling the weight of one dead body she helped carry out from the four-passenger van rollover: "I just remember how *heavy* it was. You know, they say 'dead weight'? That was one of the most memorable [missions]. That one lived with me for a while."

These upsetting flashbacks could be compounded by knowing personal information about the victim. When the rescue hit too close to home, members' confrontation with the stressful emotions was more intense. For example, on one mission, Tyler, Nick, and Shorty volunteered to travel to another county to extract the dead body of a kayaker, which was stuck in the middle of a rushing river. The kayaker was killed when the front of his kayak got sucked under the water and pinned between two rocks in the river. The force of the water behind him pushed the back of his kayak up into the air and then folded it over on top of him, snapping both of his legs backwards and trapping him in his kayak. The victims' friends were unable to reach him, and he drowned. Shorty, who was also a kayaker, knew the victim and felt compelled to help retrieve his body. Tyler explained that even though Shorty was able to remain controlled during the mission, the emotions he was likely to experience afterward were threatening for two reasons:

> Shorty wouldn't want to see that [accident] because he's a kayaker. He doesn't want to see the face of a drowned kayaker, with their eyes open or a terrified look on their face, or a mutilated face or whatever. This guy's face had been sitting there beating against rocks in a kayak for 20-some hours. Shorty doesn't need to see that. Especially in that situation, because he knew the guy.

Because Shorty knew the victim, and because he was a fellow kayaker, he was much more vulnerable to the negative effects of this body recovery than either Tyler or Nick. Yet even Nick found that particular mission more difficult to deal with than other missions, causing him several disturbing flashbacks. He told me that for days afterward he had strong, negative feelings:

> *Nick:* It was really messing with my head. I mean, every time I looked at a river or just thought about rafting or kayaking or whatever, I would just focus on the way the body looked. . . . I didn't think it was gonna be that beat up. It was only in the river for a day before we got to it, but it was pretty beat up.
> *Jen:* How do you feel when you see stuff like that?

Nick: A little nauseous. Nervous about getting hurt in that situation, you know, dying in that same situation that the person was in. Especially since the week before I checked into kayaking lessons [*laughs*]!
Jen: And did you follow up on that?
Nick: No.

Nick was unable to control these intrusive images, and they bothered him because he felt vulnerable.[21] Such feelings of vulnerability diluted the emotional charge rescuers got from edgework, and as a result, they tried to manage the uncontrolled flow of conflicting emotions in the immediate postmission period. In the most intense cases, rescuers reported feeling overwhelmed with emotion, unable to control it, and needing to release it in some way.[22]

There were several ways members released these feelings. One way was by crying. I talked to Elena, the support-status mission coordinator, shortly after her first (and only) dead body recovery. She told me that she thought she was "okay" until she got home and was in the shower, where she started to cry. She said this was effective in releasing some of her feelings, stating that she never cried about it again, yet it did bother her for days afterward. She felt that this initial release was enough to reduce the backlog of feelings that had piled up while she was suppressing them during the mission. It allowed her to regain her composure, reducing her stress and anxiety to manageable levels. In essence, she lost and regained her self-reflexivity.[23] This pattern of releasing emotions by crying, however, was gendered: men never reported crying as a means of dealing with the emotional turmoil of missions, while women occasionally did. Although it is possible that men and women did cry with equal frequency and masculinity norms prevented men from reporting it, it was more likely that women saw this as a more acceptable emotion management technique and coped in this way more often than men.

Releasing pent-up emotions was not always the direct result of a death. Maddie told me that she was under a great deal of stress while in charge of one mission where she sent three rescuers into a highly avalanche-prone area to search for a lost skier. Although the rescuers took precautions to keep themselves safe, Maddie's high level of anxiety at the base was noticeable, at least to a local newspaper reporter who interviewed her while the other rescuers were in the field. The reporter ran a story about the mission the next day and described Maddie's "very emotional" state during the operation:

Maddie Smith, who was in charge of the command post at the rescue headquarters, got very emotional when she discussed the dangers faced by her co-workers, and the precautions they were taking. "They all have tons of avalanche training, but there are no avalanche experts—they're all dead. You can never learn enough, that's why my ear is glued to this thing (radio), because they're my buddies," she said, in a slightly choked voice.

By this account, it appeared that Maddie was trying hard to control her emotions during the mission, though she let them go soon afterward when she and several other rescuers went to a local bar to unwind. She told me that she began sobbing on the five-minute walk from the parking lot to the bar, but by the time she arrived she had regained her composure, attributing her tears to the "pent-up stress" from being in charge of the mission. As when members felt vulnerable by retrospectively realizing the danger they had been in, Maddie was confronted with a feeling of her teammates' vulnerability, compounded by the feeling of responsibility for putting them there.

After the most traumatic missions, such as one occasion when members extricated the charred remains of several forest fire fighters caught in a "fire storm" (an extremely hot, quick-moving, and dangerous type of forest fire), the group provided a professionally run "critical incident debriefing" session where rescuers could talk about their feelings after the mission. While these sessions encouraged men (who were the ones most often involved in such intense missions) to express their feelings, there were only two of these sessions offered in my six years with Peak. As a general rule, Peak's culture did not encourage men to express their feelings after emotionally taxing rescues, a phenomenon that is common to American culture in general: women tend to cope with emotionally threatening feelings by crying, while men tend to cope with stress by withdrawing, becoming angry, and using drugs and alcohol.[24]

It was common for Peak's members to drink alcohol after both positive- and negative-outcome missions; however, rescuers generally consumed more after negative outcomes, such as dead-body recoveries, as a way of coping with anxiety and unpleasant feelings. After Tyler, Nick, and Shorty recovered the trapped kayaker's body in another county, Tyler told me that they bought a twelve-pack of beer for Nick and Shorty to drink while Tyler drove them home. In the three-hour drive Shorty drank two of the beers, and Nick drank the remaining 10. When I asked Nick about this, he told me that he drank beer after missions to try to "calm down, to relax

. . . [I was tense] because I didn't think the body was gonna be that beat up. It's kinda like if you had a rough day at work, you drink a couple beers. . . . I think [it's] just part of releasing any tension, even if it's just adrenaline that you have stored up." In this way members used "bodily deep acting" (Hochschild 1990)—manipulating their physiological state to change their emotional state—by relaxing themselves with alcohol in an effort to dampen the chaos of their surfacing feelings.

Maddie also talked about members' alcohol use after emotionally stressful missions. In her 10 years with Peak, she noticed that more men than women used alcohol to release their emotions, attributing this difference to gender socialization:

> I think the guys hide [their upset] a lot better [than the women]. And deal with it by going and drinking beers. I mean, that has always been the way they deal with it—for years. And I don't think that's good. Because this post-traumatic stress—I mean, you can see it in a lot of our guys after a big, heavy-duty mission. You know, just going to the bar and drinking beers doesn't release it always. And then it starts to come out in their personal lives, and I don't think that's healthy at all.

Maddie explained men's higher alcohol consumption rate over women's with cultural expectations for them to hide their feelings and to appear emotionally unaffected, an observation supported by social research.[25] Maddie also believed alcohol use to be a dysfunctional, ineffective strategy for some of the men she knew, an observation that has received inconclusive support in coping research.[26]

Rescuers often reported feeling more easily overwhelmed in the period after a mission, and they attributed these feelings to their failure to release all of their pent-up emotions.[27] Thus, another way they dealt with their feelings was to leave the group temporarily or quit altogether. After recovering the trapped kayaker, Nick turned off his pager so that he did not hear any calls for missions, saying that during the several weeks that followed, "I didn't go on any rescues. . . . I just wanted a break." And Roy explained the experience of another member, Walter, who had been in the group several years before I joined. He told me that one summer, in the span of only a few weeks, Walter had been on several stressful missions:

> He had been on a suicide, and he'd been on a couple of plane crashes. And what broke his spirit was [on the second plane crash] a tree branch

caught, and it threw maggots in his face. You know, into his nose and stuff. And that was it for him. He said, "This is fuckin' bullshit! This is it!" A suicide, a plane crash, another plane crash, and then you have maggots in your face? I mean, are people trying to kill him?

Walter removed himself from the emotional stress of Peak's missions by quitting the group. Roy saw this as a reasonable solution; to him, these incidents were so emotionally charged that they were not only "spirit breaking," but were also life-threatening.

Thus, rescuers understood their emotions through what Stearns (1994) has called the "ventilation" model of emotions. During missions, they experienced an intense emotional buildup, which when released afterward, often took them over the edge into emotional disorder and chaos.

Extending the Edge: Redefining Feelings

The fourth stage of edgework was marked by members' ability to regain control of their feelings and cognitively process them, retrospectively redefining and shaping their experiences, a process Kitsuse (1962) termed "retrospective interpretation." Often this involved neutralizing their post-mission negative feelings, which was important to edgework because, if left unresolved, negative emotions could shake members' confidence and impede their performance on future missions. In the long term, positive-outcome missions allowed rescuers to extend the edge; members' success served as evidence that they could push their limits further next time. Negative outcomes, however, threatened to compress the edge, leaving members wondering if they were capable and unsure of the risk they were willing to assume in the future. In this way, rescuers employed another type of "deep acting" where they "visualiz[ed] a substantial portion of reality in a different way" (Hochschild 1990:121). They aimed their emotion management techniques at cognitively changing the meaning of what happened, which transformed their feelings about it. This helped them to maximize their future edgework ability.

Guilt was a stressful emotion for rescuers in the wake of unsuccessful missions. Peak's members could feel personally responsible for the outcome, for example, if they failed to save a victim. On one occasion, rescuers felt bothered by a mission where a kayaker died in a river race. Many members were at the race, volunteering to act as safety agents on the river banks, throwing lines to any kayakers in trouble. One racer's kayak flipped upside down, and he was unable to right himself. Although many tried to reach him—fellow racers chased him down, people standing on the banks threw safety lines—no one could get to him until he floated through the finish line four minutes later. Many bystanders speculated that he was knocked unconscious while he was inverted and subsequently drowned. Jim told me that he repeatedly went over the incident in his mind that night, trying to think of something he and the team could have done to reach the boater more quickly. He could find no flaws in the team's response, yet found it difficult to accept that the boater died. Kevin echoed Jim's feelings when he told me that he felt compelled to return to the scene in search of an answer: "It bothered me that I wasn't able to do *something*. And I went back that night to stand by the river, to look at it, to reevaluate, and I came to the same conclusion: there was nothing I could've done, other than create a worse situation." This incident was particularly troublesome for group members because they saw the accident and were so close; standing there on the river bank they felt helpless while the kayaker drowned. Two days later the local newspaper reported that the kayaker had died when, due to a genetic defect, his heart "exploded." Many members were relieved by this news because it confirmed the conclusions they had come to through their careful reanalysis: they could not have saved him.[28]

One way members neutralized their guilt was by redefining their part in missions. One technique was "denying responsibility" (Sykes and Matza 1957) for the victim's fate. Members were often reminded that their first concern on a mission was to protect themselves; second, their teammates; and third, the victim. The rationale was that if rescuers hurt themselves on a mission, they could not be any help to anybody else. In fact, they increased the burden on their team members who would then have to divert rescue resources to help them. Brooke demonstrated her understanding of this protocol when she told me, "The safety of the group comes first. We're volunteers, and there's no reason in the world that we should put ourselves in danger to save somebody else. There is *no reason*. And it is our choice [if we decide] to do so [to put ourselves in danger]." It was therefore irrational for rescuers to endanger themselves to help someone else, especially since they bore no responsibility for putting them there in the first place. By encouraging members to define their part in the missions as above and beyond the normal duties of average citizens, this perspective helped members avoid feeling a sense of personal failure in the event of "failed" missions.

Another way members avoided feeling responsible for not saving people was by attributing control to a higher power. Meg told me that she relied on her "personal philosophical beliefs" to help her deal with the potentially negative feelings that could result from recovering a dead body. She used this technique to accept the reality that people die, as well as to deny any responsibility for it:

> I realize that, in what we're doing, the reality is that there are gonna be the dead bodies. That's part of what we're doing. So that part doesn't bother me. I mean, I always feel sad, and I feel bad—and there are still the situations, the really horrific things, you still can visualize, after years, you know—but that doesn't mean I dwell on that. . . . I guess I deal with it by saying, "Shit happens." To good people too! . . . You say, "God, that was awful," and move on. That's part of life. When it's your time, it's your time. Sometimes you go out nice and easy, and sometimes you go out pretty gory. That's the reality of it. You know, I was born and raised Catholic, I believe in God, and I think that helps. I mean, I believe that that's just a body. The spirit's gone. That's not who the person is.

Rescuers also denied responsibility by blaming the victims themselves. Cyndi told me how she reconciled her conflicting feelings about the dead victim with the severed arm she helped recover. He had taken his brand new pickup truck up a narrow, steep hiking trail to see how well the four-wheel drive worked and was killed when he rolled it off the trail into a ravine. Cyndi said she kept trying to remember that he did something stupid: "Maybe it was easier because what he was doing was really stupid. I mean, it's not like he did everything right and he was killed by a drunk driver. You know, he was doing something really stupid." Gary told me that he often said to himself, "'God, I'm glad that's not me.' It sounds selfish but it's really not. . . . If they're dead, they might have done something stupid to get there. That's not our fault. It's not your fault that that person out there is dead." And Alex noted that, "It's just easier to rationalize it when [you know that] he was doing something where he knew the risks." Not only did members dodge guilt using these rationalizations, but they sidestepped vulnerability too. The victim's stupidity was the cause of death, and rescuers, who considered themselves much smarter, could avoid such a fate.[29] Through these methods, rescuers were able to temper their feelings of guilt and vulnerability which, in turn, helped them to maintain a positive self-image and reassure themselves about their own ability to survive edgework.

Members also redefined their part in "failed" missions through emphasizing the positive side of negative events. For instance, although dead-body recoveries were very unpleasant experiences for everyone in the group, most members were prepared to voluntarily assist in them, pointing out how their part in retrieving bodies helped the grieving families. Many reasoned that it was better for the victims' families to have "closure" to the incidents so that they could move on, as opposed to never knowing whether their loved ones were alive or dead. Nick demonstrated this positive spin when he justified his general willingness to recover dead bodies, saying that he felt good when he could "help out the family by getting the body back [to them]." In this way, group members imputed important meaning to this unpleasant but routine activity, defining body recoveries instead as good deeds.

Another technique members used to counter the stress of emotionally taxing missions was to weight the successes more than the failures. Although they took great pains to separate themselves personally from failed missions, denying responsibility and downplaying meaning in those situations, members actively sought a personal connection with the successful missions, acknowledging their role in them, and allowing their participation to be meaningful and important reflections of their selves. Personally accepting credit for successes protected rescuers by bolstering their confidence and making them feel like they had control over risky conditions.[30]

Several members reported that saving someone's life was the ultimate reward of search and rescue and was unlike any other feeling they had ever had.[31] One search for a 68-year-old hiker, Polly, lasted five days. The team scoured the mountainside where she had last been seen, finding no clues, and becoming less optimistic that she would be found alive, if she were found at all. On day five, the mission coordinator sent Martin, Kevin, and one other member up in a search helicopter for one last sweep of the area before permanently calling off the search. Martin told me that it was by "a miracle" that he spotted something red peeking out from underneath a boulder and directed the helicopter closer to investigate it. There they found Polly, severely dehydrated and weak, but alive. Martin told me how his part in the mission made him feel:

> The whole experience of finding her was the kind of feeling you want to get out of mountain rescue. I mean, we saved somebody. There's no

question in my mind, that really meant the difference between her being dead or alive. And it was so good a feeling. . . . I feel good when we help people, but this was just so *different* because I honestly think we saved somebody's life. You know, we made a huge difference, and *I* made a big difference. I was the one that saw her. I was very involved in it. In my mind, "I found her." I can't deny it. I really felt good about myself. I felt that the time that I've put into the group—for all the good times we have and the bad times we have—it was worth it for that one thing. . . . That was probably the biggest kick I ever got in my life! I can't tell you how good I felt about that!

Clearly, Martin's experience was an emotionally rewarding one. He welcomed these feelings and openly expressed them. He noted that he did not want to deny his personal part in the mission—he couldn't deny it—he needed to identify personally with such a life-saving event, which allowed these feelings to significantly enhance how he felt about himself. When I asked him how long these feelings lasted, he said, "I was high for days! I still felt good, I was still floating on a high. Just from saving her." Martin drew on this experience to retrospectively reinterpret his unresolved negative feelings, steadfastly holding to the idea that all his rescue experiences were "worth it for that one thing."

Meg told me about a time when she and Kevin (her husband) were on a winter search for a missing woman. They trudged through the deep snow all night before they finally found her at four o'clock in the morning. She was huddled under a rock outcropping, disoriented, hypothermic, dehydrated, and having trouble breathing (they later found out she had a collapsed lung). They got her warmed up and hydrated, and then helped her walk out of the field:

We pulled her out, and we hiked her down having her step across the top of our snowshoes [so she didn't sink in the snow]. I mean, we went side-by-side for *miles* letting her walk on [top of] our snowshoes to get down. . . . She still sends us a card at the holidays. You know, "You saved my life." That one was really rewarding. It was successful, it was a good ending. They're not always that way, which leaves you feeling kind of empty. But that was one of those happy-ending ones.

When I asked Meg how long she felt good about that rescue, she said:

I *still* feel good about that. I mean, it's [been] eight years, and I still feel good that at some point I made a difference in one person's life. If you can make a difference in one person's life, that should be enough reward. I mean, I still think about her, and I still think back on missions that have been very successful, you know, and I try and dwell on those.

By "dwelling" on the good, Meg was able to evoke and sustain her good feelings in the long run. Many members used this technique: They defined their overall participation in search and rescue as valuable, and thus were able to extend the edge—risk more emotionally and physically—because the rewards outweighed the costs.

5

Dealing with Others in Crisis
Managing Victims' and Families' Emotions

One of the rescuers' most important activities during missions was to manage other people's emotions, specifically, those of the victims they rescued and their awaiting family members. Rescuers paid close attention to others' feelings because such intense emotions (for example, fear of an evacuation procedure) could potentially disrupt the smooth functioning of the missions. Thus, rescuers were frequently involved in helping others to direct, shape, transform, or evoke their own emotions, a process sociologists refer to as "interpersonal emotion management" (Francis 1994).[1] At times, interpersonal emotion management can be adversarial, such as when detectives try to manipulate criminals' emotions to elicit trust or fear, and thus, their confessions.[2] Other times, interpersonal emotion management can be a cooperative process, such as when therapists and clients work together to interpret and make emotional sense of the events in the clients' lives.[3]

The process of interpersonal emotion management has implications for individuals' sense of self as well as for their relationships with others. When people manage their own emotions, they understand where they fit in the world, in part, based on how close they can come to the social rules governing emotions. Similarly, when people help others to manage their own emotions, the relationship may become a central feature in their understanding of who they are. For example, the manner in which interpersonal emotion management is accomplished (e.g., cooperatively or coercively) may reveal important information about the status and power of each person as well as about the level of intimacy between them.[4]

Rescuers became interpersonal emotion managers for the victims they rescued as well as for the family members awaiting news of their lost loved ones. In the process of managing others' emotions during crises, rescuers formed very close relationships with victims and their families—much

114

closer than would normally develop between strangers in routine situations. Such compressed intimacy development is an unusual dynamic for everyday stranger encounters, yet in times of disaster, the rules of stranger encounters change: people are obliged to be open and accessible to strangers in crisis situations.[5]

After the missions were over, victims and family members often thanked rescuers for their help, citing interpersonal emotion management as one of the things for which they were most thankful. Additionally, victims and families tended to cast their thanks as emotional "repayment" and pursued their newly formed intimate relationships with rescuers to different degrees. This suggested that both the interpersonal emotion management rescuers provided as well as the level of intimacy they achieved in this compressed period of time played a role in the normative exchange of emotions, which Clark (1997) called the "socioemotional economy."

Compressed Intimacy Development

Rescuers developed close relationships with victims and families by managing their emotions in two situations. First, during rescues, group members had to manage victims' emotions, and second, during searches they had to deal with awaiting family members' emotions. In both cases, rescuers took the lead in redefining the crisis for others in an effort to get their emotions under control.[6] Sociologists have shown that since emotions have such a strong social component, changing people's interpretation of a situation can influence their felt emotions.[7] Thus, rescuers changed victims' and families' emotions from problematic to useful by doing just this: controlling their definition of reality. However, they did this differently for victims than they did for families. The principal difference was the degree of authority with which rescuers demanded that victims and families accept the definition of reality they were imposing. To demonstrate this difference, I use the terms "tight" and "loose" to describe the two ways rescuers defined reality for victims and for families.[8]

"Tightness" in Managing Victims' Emotions

I use the term "tightness" in interpersonal emotion management to refer to situations in which emotion-managers (in this case, rescuers) require emoters (in this case, victims) to conform to specific emotional directives. Tight emotion managers wield a great deal of authority in defining the situation and, thus, the norms and roles that correspond to it. They establish power by taking control and demanding specific emotional reactions from others, from whom they allow little input.

When Peak's rescuers arrived on accident scenes, victims were often feeling one of three ways, depending on the situation: embarrassed, anxious, or traumatized. These emotions could impede rescuers' ability to accomplish their task because they could keep victims from cooperating with the team. In order to elicit victims' cooperation, rescuers tightly managed their emotions by requiring them to conform to only one definition of reality—a reality that was inconsistent with their "problematic" emotions, as I will illustrate below. Victims contributed very little in defining the situation and subsequently had very little say in what emotions they were to experience. In this way, tight interpersonal emotion managers unilaterally direct others' emotions and, by extension, others' situational roles and selves. However, tight interpersonal emotion management does not have to be coercive; in fact, Peak's victims willingly and gladly ceded control to rescuers because they knew rescuers were there to help them. As a result, victims immediately trusted rescuers, quickly adopted their definition of reality, and tried to fulfill the roles rescuers gave them.

Neutralizing Embarrassment One common feeling victims had was embarrassment. For the most part, embarrassment occurred when the rescue situation was not serious. For example, in the summer of 1998, Shirley and her husband, hikers in their early fifties from Minneapolis, got off a main trail and followed a "game trail"—a path made by deer and other animals that can be intermittently passable, and usually leads nowhere. After realizing they had made a wrong turn and backtracking toward the main trail, Shirley twisted her ankle so badly she was unable to walk. Her husband had to leave her while he hiked out to get help. He called 911 and the sheriff dispatched Peak.

Gary and I were the first rescuers at the trailhead, so we set out to find Shirley, who was about an hour up the trail. By the time we reached her, she had been sitting alone for two and a half hours. We introduced ourselves, and Gary, an EMT, began his medical assessment of her, making sure she was hydrated and warm. As he asked her medical questions, she not only answered them but also immediately followed her answers with extraneous information. For example, when Gary asked her if she had any medical conditions, she said no, and then began to tell us how she had gotten off the trail. When he asked how many days she had been at altitude, she said two, then told us she knew she was wearing the wrong kind of shoes (instead of high-cut hiking boots she wore low-cut sneakers, which may have caused her to twist her ankle).

Shirley was clearly embarrassed about making the wrong turn and wearing the wrong shoes. So much of her commentary focused on excusing and justifying her actions that it was difficult for Gary to get the information he needed to assess her medically, a common problem other rescuers reported as well. As a result, Gary and I found ourselves validating her reasoning and readily accepting her excuses. We even offered excuses for her, saying that the trail was poorly marked, and that the place where she had gone off it was a common place for hikers to get "turned around," even though it wasn't. In these ways, we pretended not to recognize Shirley's embarrassment, hoping it would make it easier for her to regain her poise.[9] By helping her manage her spoiled identity, Gary and I were able to neutralize her embarrassment and elicit her cooperation in the rescue process.[10]

After we had spent some time with Shirley and Gary had splinted her ankle, she apologetically told us that she had drunk so much water while she had been waiting, that she really needed to urinate, but because she could not use her leg, she had been unable to do so. Gary suggested that he wait about twenty yards away while I help Shirley with the task at hand. I recorded the experience in my field notes:

> I readily agreed as though I had done this a thousand times before, even though I hadn't. I commended her for drinking the water and stressed the importance of hydration at these elevations. I helped her stand on her good leg and steadied her while she unfastened her shorts. I then got behind her, hooking my elbows under her armpits, and we both squatted together; with her bad leg sticking straight out, she balanced on her good leg and me, and that way she was able to go. She made some apologetic remarks about weighing 140 pounds, and although my legs began to burn from holding her in that position, I told her she wasn't heavy at all. It became almost funny when she was still peeing after a long time, so I tried to lighten the mood a little by saying "Boy, you really are hydrated!"

In order to urinate, Shirley had to allow me, a stranger, to become intimately involved in her private affairs. Although she had no way of knowing it, it was common for rescuers to see victims in these unflattering, backstage conditions; rescuers often had to help victims with physically intimate things such as urinating, vomiting, and even on one occasion, changing a tampon.[11]

It can be embarrassing when anyone needs assistance performing the most basic functions, and both Shirley and I were aware of the potential awkwardness of the moment.[12] By joking with her, I tried to ease the tension by downplaying the seriousness of the situation, a common technique used by both the embarrassed and their audience to facilitate the flow of social interaction.[13]

Victims also used self-deprecation to manage their embarrassment. Unsure of how rescuers would treat them and fearing rescuers would think they were stupid, victims usually took the lead in disparaging their own actions in nonserious rescues. Like Shirley, they often explained that they knew they had done something stupid. Rescuers listened to victims' stories, but then tacitly rejected their definitions of themselves as stupid by telling them all the things they did right, as Gary and I did for Shirley, which neutralized her embarrassment. In this way, we engaged in "protective practices" (Goffman 1959) to redefine Shirley's identity by redefining the situation: she was a rational, intelligent person who had experienced some bad luck.

Listening to victims tell about their personal experiences also helped rescuers form a stronger social bond with them than would normally be formed in an interaction between strangers. Making oneself open to others, for example, by listening to them, is one main way of forming social bonds and a sense of shared obligation to each other.[14] Some sociologists have suggested that friendship bonds are based almost solely on the willingness to be each other's audience and "listen with interest to one's . . . tale of joy or woe, victory or setback, hope or despair" (Kemper and Reid 1997:60). Thus, rescuers' willingness to listen accelerated intimacy development.

Alex, the British botanist who was an experienced mountaineer, was also concerned about neutralizing patients' embarrassment. She told me how she wanted them to feel on a noncritical rescue: "They're feeling pretty bad about what's happened and also feeling pretty embarrassed sometimes about having to be rescued and things. And I guess to a certain extent, I'd like people to feel comfortable and not feel badly about what's happened . . . and [know] that it's not a big deal, they're not causing a lot of trouble." Rescuers worked hard to control the definition of the situation when victims were embarrassed: they emphasized that the rescue was no big deal and that they did this all the time. One way they made patients feel like they were "not causing a lot a trouble" was with a preemptive strike: before victims could say anything, rescuers might arrive on the scene and say something like, "What a beautiful day for a hike!" thus setting the tone for the interaction so that others would interpret their experiences accordingly.[15] These types of comments were subtle suggestions that the rescuers used to help the victims save face.[16] If victims did not take the hint and began to apologize or avow their stupidity, rescuers would take a more direct approach and respond with something like, "Hey, I'm happy to be here. I got to get out of work!" to show that they were not inconvenienced, in fact, they were enjoying themselves. In this way, rescuers tightly managed victims' emotions: they consistently denied the victims' definitions of the situation as embarrassing and replaced it with their own version of reality, establishing a working definitional consensus of the rescue as "fun."

Gary sustained the "fun" definition of the rescue by fostering a joking relationship with Shirley throughout the entire event, even after it seemed we had successfully neutralized her embarrassment. For example, after I helped Shirley urinate, I left her with Gary and headed back down the trail to intercept the team bringing up the stretcher and to direct them to the place where she had gone off the trail. By the time I returned with the team, Gary and Shirley had developed quite a rapport. As we loaded Shirley in the stretcher, Gary jokingly informed us that our first priority was to get Shirley out in time for her dinner reservations at Del Mar, a fancy restaurant she had been looking forward to all week. She could go to the hospital and X-ray her broken ankle afterward. Apparently, they had been joking about it since I left. It appeared as though Gary had transformed her embarrassment into a good time. This observation was confirmed a month later in a thank-you letter she wrote to the group. Shirley said, "I consider the rescue on [that trail] to have been one of the best memories of my life."

Alleviating Anxiety A second common feeling victims had was anxiety. Many injured people did not know how they would get out of the woods or who would come to get them. If victims sat alone for an extended period, they could work themselves into a frenzy. Having no idea what to expect, they became apprehensive while imagining how they might be evacuated. For example, some people thought they would have to walk on a broken ankle, others worried that a helicopter would not be able to get to them. Still others thought that the evacuation would take days, which it almost never did. The longer they sat waiting for help, the more fears they could develop. Shirley thought she actually might die from her broken ankle. In the thank-you letter she said, "It's hard to believe you can die from a broken ankle until you slip and fall and hear the sickening crack of your own bone and realize that you're three miles up a rugged trail . . . Neither [my husband nor I] could imagine how I was going to get to the trailhead."

When rescuers did arrive, sometimes victims were surprised to find out that they would be lowered down a sheer cliff face or tied into a stretcher and wheeled out over the steep, rocky trail they had come up. If victims were stranded on an island after a frightening swim through the rapids, they might be quite anxious knowing that they would have to get back in the water to reach the shore.[17] Anxiety, like embarrassment, could impede the rescue efforts by making the victims unfocused and uncomfortable. Yet unlike embarrassment, anxiety caused more than just a disruption in the social interaction: it could directly impede the instrumental functioning of the mission, for example, if a victim refused to get into the stretcher to be lowered down a cliff face.

In these cases, rescuers alleviated patients' anxiety by inspiring confidence. They were able to abate the victims' trepidation by appearing competent and making the situation seem routine. One way they did this was by appearing "professional."[18] Kevin, the 10-year, lead-status member married to Meg, told me how rescuers tried to instill confidence in the patient:

You wanna act professional. . . . I don't want 'em to think they're in the hands of some bozos. You wanna be careful around the patient that you don't [say], "I've never seen a carabiner like *this*." And I can see the patient laying there going, "Huh. I wonder what *that one's* all about." So I think that's how you handle yourself. You don't let 'em know [if] you don't know what you're doing. If you don't know what you're doing, that's fine! Get over and ask somebody. But be careful where you ask the question. . . . I think in the patient's mind you could definitely affect how they're feeling with their rescue or their safety. *Definitely*. It doesn't help 'em mentally or physically.

Kevin, like many rescuers, thought that a victim's emotional state was an important part of their physical well-being during an evacuation. He emphasized that rescuers should have a great deal of sensitivity to victims' feelings during the rescues, because anxiety could have detrimental effects on the patients' condition. Research has generally found this to be true: emotional state can affect physical well-being, and increasing a sense of control over a situation can lower stress.[19] Furthermore, Kevin suggested that rescuers reserve their questioning for "backstage" (Goffman 1959) behavior only in the presence of other rescuers, maintaining a purely competent impression in front of the victims.

Another way rescuers alleviated anxiety was by comforting victims: using sympathy and empathy to reassure them and calm their nerves. Relying heavily on gender stereotypes, many rescuers saw women as better able to perform this role, a belief that permeates popular thought and appears in other social settings as well.[20] For example, when I asked Jim, the 20-year, founding member, what kind of steps he took as a mission coordinator to manage victims' anxiety, he told me:

> [On] long evacuations, if the people [rescuers] are available, I will tend to split [the team] up between male and female so that we have a good balance on the evacuation teams. And one of the reasons I like to do this is because, for the *most* part, females have a better ability to empathize with the patient. And it seems, almost instinctively, that they'll take a position at the head of the patient and be close to the patient. Whether the patient is male or female doesn't seem to make any difference. I think it has something to do with the traditional role of the female nurse, or the mother—whatever all that stuff is—it works. And the patients will *look* to the females within the team for comfort and reassurance. And so I do that. I've *seen* it. I've seen it happen. Having been an EMT for several years, [I've] gone in there, you know, technically able to fix the problem, [but] find myself lacking in the ability to give a victim the comfort, reassurance, and empathy that they need to sustain a prolonged evacuation. Because that [the victim's emotional state] is a whole 'nother factor that has to be involved in there.

Jim subscribed to the idea that women were better at providing victims with emotional support, while he, as a man, found himself only able to provide instrumental support. Yet empirical research on differences in how women and men communicate social support has resulted in inconclusive findings.[21] Furthermore, it seemed as though women, by virtue of their "superior" emotional capabilities, were considered better than men at achieving intimacy with victims. This idea has also received inconclusive support in the literature on gender and intimacy.[22]

Finally, victims could feel relieved once rescuers arrived. Rescuers encouraged this feeling in all nonemergency cases; they wanted victims to feel confident and secure. Some victims evidenced this relief by talking constantly. Since their anxiety was already alleviated, rescuers maintained this relaxed state in victims by just listening to them. Vince, the three-year member who dropped out of college to become a paramedic, found that at times he had developed surprisingly close relationships with some of the victims he had helped, and attributed this to the intimate stories that victims told him and to his role as listener. On one occasion, Vince camped out with Smitty, a victim who had been lost for several days and had accepted that he was going to die when, through a series of inadvertent circumstances that I will detail in chapter 7, Vince found him. Smitty was so elated that he talked Vince's ear off all night. Vince could tell that Smitty was relieved and comforted, so he just listened. The next afternoon, the evacuation team reached Vince and Smitty, and they began their seven-mile, six-hour carry-out. Smitty was still talking, this time to all the rescuers on the team. I asked Vince how well he thought he knew Smitty after listening to his stories all night:

> It was strange because on the carry-out, he would repeat those same stories to the new team members that were there. And I found myself feeling like, "Well, I already know this stuff. I know Smitty, he's my friend. I've known him for years." It was like I'd been there forever. The new tales, the new stories, and the new experiences that he was sharing with all these other people, you know, I was already privy to.

By presenting themselves as professional, by comforting, sympathizing with, and listening to them, rescuers tightly managed the victims' anxiety by sustaining a particular definition of the situation that did not fit their feelings of anxiety. By accepting their rescuers' definition of the situation, victims were forced to transform their detrimental feelings into ones that benefited the rescue effort as well as their own physical state.

Preventing a Psychosomatic "Crash" A third way rescuers managed victims' emotions occurred during critical incidents. When victims were seriously injured, rescuers paid special attention to how their feelings could affect their physiological well-being. Alex, the British rescuer and EMT, told me how, during critical incidents, downplaying a serious injury could be harmful to the victims:

> You shouldn't always be saying to the patient, "Everything's going to be fine." . . . That can take down the natural defenses that a person has, and if you take more of the approach, you know, "You hang in there and we'll get you out of here as soon as we can . . . ," their bodies sort of think, "There is something wrong, I've got to keep fighting here." Instead of like "Oh, okay, I'll just relax [*sigh*]," and then their own body's defenses are not really working for them.

The reverse was also true: rescuers were not to focus too much on the severity of the injuries by letting the victims know how bad their situation was. This could also send them into shock. Alex explained one occasion when she was recreationally rock climbing with a group of people and one became injured:

> I remember once, to cut a very long story short, a rock fell on somebody's head and from the front he looked fine, but the back of his head was just half gone. And I remember sitting on the ground with this guy and the helicopter was coming in. . . . And I was saying, "This is serious, but you've got to keep fighting it. We've got the helicopter on the way," . . . and he was doing okay. And then the girl who'd knocked the rock off comes running over and went, "Oh my God! Look at the back of his head!" And I remember him just: *pppt* [passing out]. That was it. He was out. He just, like, panicked and got all shaky and just lay down on the ground. And then the helicopter came. But I remember just thinking how foolish that was. And some other people told her how foolish it was and took her away.

Alex's comments demonstrated the need for rescuers to maintain a consistent performance during serious situations. Goffman (1959:216) termed this ability "dramaturgical discipline," identifying an individual with this ability as someone who "does not commit unmeant gestures or faux pas . . . [and] does not give the show away by involuntarily disclosing its secrets." The woman who let the victim know that he was seriously injured not only ruined the team's performance, but also caused him to have a physiologically adverse reaction to the news. Disciplined performers also have the ability to "suppress [their] spontaneous feelings in order to give the appearance of sticking to the affective line" (Goffman 1959:217), which suggests that rescuers' own emotion management was required for them to manage victims' emotions effectively. The woman who knocked the rock off was unsuccessful at this as well, as she "broke frame" (Goffman 1961b) by openly expressing her horror at the victim's injury.

Alex's experience also demonstrated another dynamic: managing the victims' emotions in severe situations required their cooperation. Rescuers tightly defined situations for victims by saying things like "this is serious," and likewise demanded specific emotional reactions from victims in order to protect them physically. Whether or not rescuers believed it themselves, they always strove to construct one particular definition of the situation for victims: they tried to make victims believe, and thus feel, as though they were going to survive.

Kevin also discussed this process of "symptom management" (Strauss [1973] 1998) when he told me about an air force cadet who had fallen 100 feet while rock climbing. He had broken some bones in the fall, so the team was worried about possible internal and spinal injuries. Despite the severe nature of the victim's injuries, Kevin focused on his emotions:

> His mental picture—his internal well-being—was based on him having the *feeling* that he was gonna survive, that people were there helping him, that they were working to get him out of a situation [emphasis added]. . . . He had been able to sustain himself through the efforts of the group [members] that were there, [and] his [own] determination to get out of the situation. . . . I think that [ability] was part of the individual, but it was also part of the team: "Come on pal, we're gonna need your help to get through this. This is what we're doing, here's what it looks like," and that helps them get through to the next stage in their [rescue] events. . . . And he was *fine* until we got him into the medical ship [helicopter] with the doctors, and that chapter was over, he kind of went "Aaaahhhhh" [*big sigh*], and his system just went into shock. And they started working him [medically tending to the shock]. So you gotta keep the mind going, you've gotta keep the spirits up, you've gotta keep working along. He went into shock in the right place: with trained medical people on a medical evac ship.

Kevin highlighted the idea that a victim's well-being was a cooperative effort in interpersonal emotion management. The rescuers' job was to be the "control agents" (Glaser and Strauss 1965) for patients, managing their potential shock symptoms by maintaining secrecy with regard to the most serious aspects of their medical condition.

Sometimes victims' feelings could impede the rescue efforts because they were too petrified or traumatized to cooperate physically. For example, in early July 1996, Lorna, a tourist in her forties, was hiking up a trail that ran parallel to a rushing river with many waterfalls. While her dog was taking a drink from the riverbank, he began to slip into the river. Lorna ran to his aid, but in her effort to reach him, she too fell into the river, which was icy cold and running swiftly with fresh snow-melt runoff. She was carried downstream about 350 yards over several small waterfalls before she was able to grab a rock and pull herself up onto a small island in the middle of the river. She waited there while her husband went for help. Two years later, on the anniversary of the accident, she wrote a letter to the local TV news station (and copied it to the group) nominating the group for the station's "Hometown Hero" award. In that letter she described her experience while she waited on the rock: "I was pretty beat up! There was not an inch of me that did not have cuts and bruises. I had two broken ribs, a cracked rib, a broken tooth, a bad laceration on my knee, swellings all up and down my shin, and my knee was already swollen and painful to where I could not bear any weight on it."

When Tyler, an eight-year rescuer in his late twenties, and one of the Ironmen, reached the scene with a team an hour later, he briefly entertained the idea of setting up a clothes-line-type of system so that they could slide Lorna along it above the water. After realizing that Lorna was near hypothermia, he discarded that idea and decided that the fastest, and thus safest, way to evacuate her was to swim her back to shore, using a human chain made of rescuers. However, Lorna did not want to get back in the water. She was petrified. In her letter, she expressed how the group members managed her emotions during her ordeal to effect her evacuation:

> They tossed a life jacket out to me on the end of a rope. They also sent a helmet out too. They shouted encouragement from the shore and kept me talking to them the whole time. I tried to wrap myself up in the blanket [that her husband had been able to throw out to her] and when I was quiet for too long, they would shout for me to answer them. They kept me going, they kept me alive. I was very weak and hypothermic by this time. . . . One of the rescuers, [Tyler, swam out and] sat in the middle of

the river with me and talked to me. He accessed [*sic*] my condition and made sure I understood their plans to get me out of there. When I began to cry, he gently took me by the shoulders and told me I could not do that right now, he needed me there with him. There would be time for that later, when I was safe. . . . They were very clear with their directions on how they wanted me to achieve this. They had to put me back in the river and pass me from one [rescuer] to the other until they reached the shore. I was not exactly cooperative initially! The thought of being dunked in that cold water again was not what I had in mind. They held me tight and made me feel safe, I knew they would not let anything happen to me.

It is clear in Lorna's letter that she felt that the rescuers deeply cared about her well-being. Yet the way they ensured that she survived was by not allowing her to feel the severity of her situation and by demanding specific emotional responses from her. For example, as she was about to lose control of her emotions, or "flood out" (Goffman 1961b), Tyler re-asserted control over her feelings by forbidding her to cry. Tyler told me that, in trying to convince her to get in the water, he said, "I *promise* I won't let anything happen to you." In these few minutes of interaction, rescuers were able to develop such an intimate connection with her that she trusted them with her life: she "knew" these strangers would protect her.

Lorna's letter also demonstrated the lasting effect the event had on her life. She marked the two-year anniversary by writing the nomination letter and by sending a copy to the group. Furthermore, even though she was fully recovered physically, the letter stated that her experience "changed my life forever. . . . My husband and I . . . are still healing from this trauma. It has impacted both our lives tremendously."

"Looseness" in Managing Families' Emotions

Quite a different dynamic occurred during searches when rescuers spent a great deal of time with the family members of lost victims. Searches could last a couple of hours, several days, or, in some cases, a week or more. The longer a search lasted and the closer the proximity of the family, the more likely the family members were to come down to the group's base building and hang around. They wanted be there and often flew in from other states if their loved one was missing for more than a day or two.

Not knowing the fate of their lost loved ones could make this time pass unbearably slowly for many family members. They often wanted to be helpful and stay occupied to keep their minds off the seemingly futile search, and this took several forms. Some family members and friends joined the search teams in the field. Others went to the local deli to buy sandwiches and refreshments for the returning searchers. One adult son, whose 68-year-old mother, Polly, was lost for five days, swept out the base building's entire garage in his effort to keep busy and be useful. If the family members were from out-of-state, they spent a great deal of time on the phone to friends and relatives back home, keeping them abreast of the situation.

For the most part, family members tried to stay out of the way so the mission coordinators could do their jobs, but when their anxiety overtook them, they began to hound the coordinators with questions. They wanted to know what every radio transmission meant when field teams reported back to base. Often these messages were relaying information about where the teams were and what terrain they had covered, or perhaps that there was inclement weather moving in. Rarely was any single radio transmission reporting anything substantial, such as clues or sightings; more commonly, the mission coordinators used the information they received as pieces in a large puzzle. They plotted the field teams' progress on maps, slowly eliminating the area covered, and prioritizing the likelihood of uncovered terrain.

Rescuers were generally sympathetic to the difficult emotional position the families were in, but they did not have time to express their sympathies or discuss their grief; they had a job to do. Mission coordinators often assigned one rescuer to stay with the family and be the liaison between the family and the group. The job served two functions: first, it kept the family out of the coordinators' way; and second, it provided the family with up-to-the-minute information, which was seen as the decent thing to do in helping them through this emotionally rough time.[23]

In dealing with family members, much of the liaison's emotional energy was spent on "emotion-focused coping" (Lazarus and Folkman 1984): encouraging others to discuss their feelings and to deal mainly with their emotional responses to the crisis, which in this case were the variety of emotions that accompanied families' grief and pain. Liaisons spent a great deal of time talking to family members about their feelings and openly avowing their sympathy for them. Coping commonly takes on this type of solely emotional focus when there appears "that nothing that can be done to modify harmful, threatening, or challenging environmental conditions" (Lazarus and Folkman 1984:150). In addition to discussing their grief, liaisons also frankly discussed the potential outcomes with the family members, forcing them to confront the possibilities that their loved one could be found alive, dead, or not at all.

In these ways, rescuers managed family members' emotions much more "loosely" than they managed those of victims, guiding families through the many different feelings that corresponded with the various definitions of reality the rescuers imposed on them. Although rescuers wanted families, like victims, to arrive at particularly "healthy" and useful emotions for their situation, they permitted families a much wider variety of paths to get there than they did for victims. This type of interpersonal emotion management was a collaborative process: rescuers and family members worked together to construct several possible definitions of reality as well as to identify and analyze their feelings.

Validating Grief Many rescuers did not want the job of family liaison; in fact, many did not want any interaction with the family members at all, although at times it was unavoidable. For the most part, rescuers feared they would say something that would hurt the family members, and they wanted to avoid the discomfort of witnessing the family's grief. For example, Alex, the British rescuer, told me of her experience on one mission where a high-school-aged girl had disappeared, leaving a suicide note in her car parked at a hiking trailhead. Alex was put on a field team with the girl's father and discovered that being so close to a family member during a search produced some difficult personal feelings that she had to handle. She told me what she was thinking as they hiked along the trail together:

> He kept saying to me over and over again, "What usually happens in situations like this? What usually happens?" I just remember that question over and over again. . . . I didn't want to say to him, "Shit, I don't know! I've never been on a mission where somebody'd left a suicide note before!" You know, I didn't want to be overdramatic about the whole thing and get him wound up into a frenzy. But I didn't want him to think it was routine either. . . . I was like, "I don't know, I can't tell you what the outcome is, we've just got to keep looking. We've just got to keep looking." . . . I wanted him to feel that I was just as concerned as he was to find her . . . [and] at the time I really was, *because* of him. . . . I certainly wouldn't've been as closely attached to it if I had been in a group with [other team members]. We'd have been worried and concerned, but to be with *him,*

you know, I was like walking along the whole time thinking, "Oh my God, this is his *daughter* that we're looking for. What's going through his mind?.". . . And he had a cell phone with him, and her mother kept phoning him. And he was very calm about the whole thing and he kept saying, "We're still looking, we'll let you know if anything happens." And then, you know, he was being polite to me, too: "Oh, what do you do for a living?" That kind of thing. . . . And we searched all through the night until the early hours of the morning and we hadn't found her by then. And I remember how nice he was then, too, you know, "Thank you so much for looking, we'll see you later." . . . But that really affected me, mostly because he was so nice and calm about the whole thing, and he must've been absolutely torn apart inside. And that totally horrified me.

Alex was uncomfortable being with the victim's father. Like me, when I felt sympathy for the avalanche victim's wife, Alex felt great sympathy for the father and sensed that he needed emotional support, but she did not know how to express it, or what the result might be, a common predicament faced by people trying to offer sympathy.[24] Not knowing quite what to say and fearing she would say something that would upset him more, she took her cue from him: she tried be polite yet show that she was concerned. If rescuers had had some training in this area, they might have felt more comfortable in the role.[25]

Oliver, a seven-year, support-status member in his late forties, was a seasonal resort worker in Peak County. As an ex-police officer, he had much experience with grieving family members, yet he was still uncomfortable around them. He said: "You don't stand there and pat 'em on the back and say, 'Oh, I know how you feel.' You don't know how they feel. You really don't know what to say. But you don't want to be completely stonewall-silent either because that could be very uncomfortable, too. But then, what do you say?"

Because most rescuers did not know how to cope with emotionally distraught family members, they avoided being assigned to them. Yet, all rescuers felt that the family members needed someone who could help them deal with their emotions, thus they all agreed that the liaison role was a very important one that needed to be filled. This assumption is supported in the literature on coping and social support: people fare better on measures of emotional health when they have contact with someone who can keep them apprised of their loved one's condition as well as with someone who they believe can understand what they are experiencing.[26]

Women were more often appointed to fulfill the liaison role because they were considered better suited to talk with others about their emotions than men. When I spoke with Martin, he told me that he was not good in the role of dealing with the family members because he was "not a super people-person." I asked him what qualities would make a rescuer good at dealing with families:

> Incredibly even-tempered. Quiet, calm—you know, you have to be a quiet, calming type of personality. I'm just the opposite. I'm a go-get-it, let's-do-it [type of personality]. I think you have to have a calming effect on the family. Somebody that can get the information to 'em but keep them calm. And can empathize with them. You said, Do I feel their pain or do I understand it? You have to feel their pain. I think that person works best. I think some of the sheriff's girls that work for the victims' assistance [program] are really good. I've watched them a couple times, and they are really good.

It seemed that women (like the "sheriff's girls") were better at sympathizing and empathizing, which Martin considered to be critical elements in managing family members' emotions. It is not surprising that many rescuers relied on the "nurturing woman" stereotype when justifying why women were so often assigned to stay with the families, although, again, this assumption has met with inconclusive empirical support in the coping and social support literature. It is interesting, however, that Martin stereotyped women as even-tempered, quiet, and calm in these situations, which was a common sentiment among many group members. As I have discussed previously, such emotional control did not characterize Peak's women when it came to performing dangerous tasks during missions; women were often considered emotionally unpredictable and less rational than men during crisis situations. Such risky roles were best performed by men, who were, in Martin's words, "go-get-it, let's-do-it" types of people and had the market cornered on the emotional stoicism required to take risks.

Even though many women were also uncomfortable interacting with family members, they were generally more willing to take on the role than men. I asked Cyndi, the five-year member in her late twenties, if she thought that spending time with the families might actually be harder for women, if they were indeed better empathizers, than for men, who were considered better able to distance themselves from others' emotional pain. She responded citing women's superior comforting ability as the most important provision for the family:

> Maybe it's harder for you, but I think it's better for them. If they had somebody who was just standing there who was just kind of like, "Oh everything's gonna be fine," rather than somebody who could actually touch their shoulder, or give 'em a hug, or hold their hand, or just sit beside them and be with them, I think a girl is probably better at that than a guy. I don't know [*laughing*], but don't you think? I mean, I just don't think it would do me a whole lot of good to have Nick standing beside me going [*claps hands together and shrugs*] "Gosh, we did all we could." Any of [the guys]. I don't know . . . I can't see 'em going over to someone and being able to empathize. And maybe a lot of people [families] don't want that; maybe they want to be by themselves. But I would hope, on some level, that it helps. You know, we're not feeling their pain, but at least they know somebody cares.

Cyndi thought that families needed to connect emotionally, possibly in the form of a hug or a touch, to help them through their emotionally difficult time. Like Martin, she also considered the women in the group to be better suited to forging these intimate connections than the men; yet unlike Martin, she did not think it was possible to feel the families' pain.

Validating family members' grief in this way was important. During the search, family members could express a variety of emotions related to their grief, such as guilt or joy about the past, uncertainty or faith about the present, and fear or hope about the future. Rescuers felt it was important to allow family members to interpret the situation almost any way they needed to, and thus they validated many different feelings family members expressed.[27] These assumptions—that many different emotions are valid during the grief process, and that emotions will change as the griever proceeds through different stages of the process—are crucial elements in some forms of grief counseling.[28] Furthermore, popular cultural beliefs about psychology reassert the view that the griever will experience many different and valid emotions.[29] Thus, the liaisons, expecting that the family members' emotions would run the gamut as they defined the past, present, and future differently, loosely guided families' emotions in response to the diverse realities families experienced.

Meg, the 10-year member, had a great deal of experience in discussing family members' feelings with them. I asked her if the role was stressful for her:

> For me? No it isn't for me at all. That's a good position for me in mountain rescue, because I find it very easy to talk to people and let people talk to me. And I'm empathetic to the feeling part of it too. Which isn't always the case, I mean, some rescuers have trouble with that. . . . I think I'm good at talking to the family.

She told me of one occasion when she had stayed with the adult son of a hunter who was lost for three days. The situation was not looking good. The victim had been out in the rain for two nights without his heart condition medication. The son was assisting in the search, and Meg was charged with the duty of being the liaison between him and the group. She told me how the experience was emotionally draining on him:

> There were a couple times [during debriefings or strategy-planning sessions] that he needed to cry, and he was a macho hunter and all these macho rescuers were around, and so it was a good role for me to grab him by the hand and say, "Let's go for a walk." And kind of get him away from the people that he felt uncomfortable crying around. . . . Because I think sometimes, particularly guys, have trouble with that. . . . He was an outdoorsman, he knew what the chances of survival for his father were. And at that point it had only been a short time since I had lost my dad, and we shared that, I talked to him about it. It's a horrible feeling to lose a parent. So I kinda really empathized with where he was.

As when they spent time with victims, the rescuers who spent the most time with family members developed quite a strong relationship with them. Two of the key emotions that allowed this connection to take place were the empathy and sympathy that group members openly displayed with families. Other research has also found that providing a sufferer with empathy and sympathy during a crisis may lead to a quicker, more intense, and trusting relationship between strangers.[30] This may be because sympathy acts as a bridge in social interaction, allowing people to care about each other's problems.[31] This was certainly true in Peak's case. I noted this phenomenon to Meg, asking her if she felt that the family liaison role facilitated a uniquely intimate relationship between her and those she helped:

Uh-huh, because it's hard to get close to people in their very deepest emotional times. And maybe the thought of losing a loved one is probably the most difficult time in anyone's life. Ever. And when you get close to someone and touch their soul, and they let you in, that's probably one of the closest times you can get connected with people, I think. And the hardest time! Because people usually don't let you get close to their emotions like that. But they bare 'em when the situations are the most difficult. I like that part [of rescue work].

She continued, noting that it took a specialized skill to read someone else's emotions. She contrasted this emotional skill with other skills the group needed, most of which were physical in nature:

There are people in our group that I wouldn't want near the family members! 'Cause they'd have 'em hysterical and in tears. Maybe they're too forthright or too blunt or maybe too nonlistening. . . . It doesn't take a lot of physical strength to sit with the family and talk with them, or to grab that son and make sure you get him out of the group environment and alone to where you can talk a little bit and maybe cry a little bit. That doesn't take a lot of physical strength, but it takes some real sensitivity to people's emotions. And there are a lot of people [rescuers] that don't see it! I mean [in that case] they didn't even see the fact that the guy [the son] was ready to bust out *bawling*! You know, they didn't even *see* it!

Meg was able to read others' emotions and validate what they were feeling. She typically managed family members' feelings by letting them set the tone and define the situation. Other members, she commented, were less adept at managing families' feelings in these ways.

Balancing Hope and Reality A second way rescuers dealt with families' emotions during a search was by helping them maintain hope while preparing them for the grim possibility that the mission might turn out badly. Rescuers believed that it was important to be honest with family members to help them emotionally prepare for either outcome, and for this reason, they strove to make sure they fully understood several possible versions of reality. Oliver, the ex-police officer, told me of one search for a woman who had not returned after going hiking to collect mushrooms. Her adult daughter wanted to be part of the search, and ended up on Oliver's team. He assessed her emotional state: "Her daughter came out with us. So that was a very precarious situation, to have her actually out searching with us. We had to kind of handle her with kid gloves, you know, not say what we suspected; everybody was thinking that she was probably dead. But we did find her alive." Oliver emphasized the "precariousness" of the emotional situation, evoking an image of the daughter hanging in the balancing between two emotional states. The team members were very aware of maintaining this balance, so as not to push the daughter too far to one side or the other. This was exactly what many rescuers feared: saying the wrong thing and upsetting the family member. Yet those rescuers who were not afraid to deal overtly with the family members' emotions made sure to weight both sides equally, evoking diverse emotions in response to the possible outcomes.

Kevin, for example, told me that when he talked to families, he focused equally on hope and reality, acknowledging the real possibility of either outcome instead of avoiding it, as other rescuers, like Oliver, did. Kevin conceptualized a continuum between pessimism and optimism and tried to help family members come to an emotional "balance" somewhere in the middle:

> I find that a lot of people that I talk to in these situations want the facts. They *think* they want the information—that comes into play, too. Some people really don't want to hear it, but they need to hear it. Because it's real. This isn't imagined, it's real. . . . I think it's my responsibility to answer their questions, be sensitive to their concerns, and not be doom-and-gloomish. But not, yet, on the other hand, be so euphoric, like, "Oh, don't worry about it, everything's gonna be just fine." . . . I think you've got to come to a balance, and either one of those are emotionally unbalanced. I think if you're too doom-and-gloom, you've weighted the scale in one direction too far. And if you're too euphoric, you've tipped the scale in an opposite direction that I don't think is quite healthy. . . . I don't like to weight it entirely one way or the other. . . . I think it helps them keep things in perspective. . . . So I find that it's best to deal with those people in a balanced perspective, trying to find a center point, but yet with extreme realism that this could turn out great, and this could turn out bad. But I don't dwell in either extreme.

Meg echoed Kevin's sentiments, saying that she tried to spend time with families to prepare them emotionally for the possibility of their loved one's death. I asked her what kind of things she actually said to them, and she used the missing hunter's son as an example:

[I said] "I've been at this a long time. There are some missions that are very successful and bring us the outcome that we want to hear. There are some missions that I've been on that haven't been so successful, and those are the outcomes we never want to hear. And it happens both ways. We're gonna hope for the best here, but the reality is [that] your father has dementia, he has been without his [heart condition] medication for three days now, and he's been out in the rain two nights in a row. This is not a good situation. You realize, this is not a good situation. But it's not hopeless. So let's hope for the best, and let's go out there and get to work, and hope that the outcome is the one that we'd like it to be." Those kind of conversations. . . . There's a fine line there, you don't want to defeat them while they're searching, but you also don't wanna make them believe that everything is okay. Because sometimes it's not.

Meg and Kevin believed their strategies to be the most beneficial way to handle family members' emotions while their loved ones were lost. Research supports this strategy, finding that when in crisis, those who maintain realistic expectations but who think positively show lower levels of stress than those who do not.[32] Kevin and Meg were also trying to reduce family members' use of denial about the missions' potential negative outcomes. Kevin stated that they needed to hear the truth. Some social workers and doctors promote this view as well, contending that denial is less likely if the families of injured or dying people are kept constantly informed with the straight truth about their loved one's condition.[33] Although rescuers could appear emotionally detached when providing families with the straight truth, they also signaled that they were concerned. In the example above, Meg used the pluralized forms "we" and "us" in referring to herself and the son, showing her solidarity with him and indicating that they were united in their desire to find the hunter alive. This was one way she forged an intimate bond with him. Other research has shown that sharing intense emotions may contribute to this feeling of solidarity.[34]

It was hard for rescuers to deal with family members when they knew that the odds were overwhelmingly against the survival of the lost victim. It was even harder, however, when rescuers knew the victim was found dead but had to wait to tell the family members. For example, Meg also told me that on one occasion she was acting as the liaison between Peak's coordinators and the family of a victim buried in an avalanche. The rescuers had found the victim, and by all accounts, he appeared dead. However, due to Peak's protocols, in the absence of obvious signs of death (such as decapitation or rigor mortis), only a doctor or the coroner could pronounce a victim dead. Part of the reason for this policy was that there was a slim possibility of reviving victims, especially if they were in a situation that lowered their body temperature so much that they appeared dead (such as a cold-water drowning or an avalanche burial). In these cases, the rescuers were informed of the victims' death, but had to wait to tell the family members until the body could be pulled out of the field and transported to a hospital. Depending on the location of a victim, this could take hours. Thus, in the case of the avalanche burial, Meg was unable to inform the family, even though she already knew the outcome:

> I think the hard part for me was that I knew he was dead, and we were waiting until that was confirmed at the hospital to tell the family. So I was actually there for what I think is almost the harder part: knowing and not being able to say, initially. That was very difficult for me. Because you could see that they were still hopeful, and I knew in my heart that it was futile. That hour or so of getting that body out of there and into the hospital was real hard.

Jim told me how, in his 20 years of experience, he had learned how to prepare families for bad news by giving them bits of information slowly. He used the example of a six-day search for a missing 22-year-old hiker in the Mount Alpine area. On the last and final day, the group was ready to give up the search when Jim tried one last, dangerous helicopter maneuver to get a glimpse into a giant crevice at the foot of Mount Alpine. He spotted something and knew it was the missing hiker. He had fallen 1400 feet to his death. Jim could not tell the family, however, because he first had to get a team into the remote area to recover the hiker's body. He told me how he handled it:

> And then you get to play this little game of, you know [*casually whistling and looking around*], we'll land the helicopter, you know, pick up Roy, Gary, and Patrick, [and] fly them in. [And tell the family], "Well, we *think* maybe we found the [back]pack." I mean, I knew exactly what it was.

Yeah, it was his pack. And the pink stuff splattered all around it was what was left of this kid.

Meg's and Jim's stories indicated that not only were the rescuers managing the victims' emotions by maintaining a balance between hope and reality, but on some level, they were doing the same for themselves. Thus, the "emotional dissonance" (Hochschild 1983) created by not being able to update the family immediately caused a great deal of emotional strain for the rescuers themselves, yet they continued to work in the best emotional interests of the family. Once rescuers knew the victim was dead, they scaled back their efforts to encourage the family to accept multiple realities, and they started guiding them more tightly toward one single definition of reality so that they would be more emotionally prepared for it. In general, the range of emotions rescuers shared with families made their relationships quite intimate in a compressed period of time.

The Fate of Compressed Intimacy

After the crisis was over and the victims were either safe or found dead, the rescuers' work was done. Whatever the outcome, the end of the mission transformed the intimate relationship between the rescuers and the victims or their families. The rapport that rescuers and victims had developed was interrupted as the latter were carted away in ambulances; the emotional connection rescuers had with family members was cast aside as families embraced their loved one or collapsed in grief. Sometimes these intimate relationships were terminated completely; other times victims and families felt obliged to pursue them in some form.

Accepting Sympathy for the Loss: Terminating the Intimate Relationship

In the event that victims were found dead, rescuers expressed their sympathies to the families. The type of sympathy they had expressed during the unknown period was for the emotional turmoil families experienced while not knowing the fate of their loved ones, which helped them maintain and develop deep relationships with family members as they connected with them on profound emotional levels. The sympathy that rescuers offered after the mission was over, however, was of a different sort because it was used to express sorrow for the family's loss. Rescuers offered their sympathies in saying good-bye to families, and used it to signify a relationship-closing interaction. Thus the two types of sympathy employed during missions yielded two different results for social interaction: one facilitated relationships, the other terminated them.[35]

Sometimes rescuers became the bearers of bad news. Jim told me how he informed the family of the fallen 22-year-old hiker once they recovered his body:

> I got to take the family up on the porch of the log cabin in the drizzling rain, and huddle 'em all together and say, "He ain't comin' back." And then hear all the denial. . . . Mom didn't wanna hear the fact that her only son, who she didn't want to leave home, has come to [this state] and now died. Of course not. You never want to hear that stuff.

As he was informing the family, Jim began to cry with them, which was very uncharacteristic for him in such situations. Gary read this emotional display as one of genuine sympathy, saying, "Jim was showing his emotion with them, that he did deeply care, that he was trying his best. And that we were all trying our best."

Meg told me what she said to the family of the avalanche victim, once they got him to the hospital and pronounced him dead:

> I guess it comes from the heart. I just said it was a very sad thing, the rescuers tried very hard, but unfortunately he had been buried a long time and, you know, they couldn't save him. . . . Once they know, they no longer need you for that hopeful support. It's a different role. They move on to another phase. . . . The good-byes then [in that situation] were actually very short. . . . I expressed my sympathies, you know, "You're in my thoughts and prayers. I'll remember your son in my thoughts and in my prayers. I hope everything works out well for you," and you move on. 'Cause it's time for them to move on too. The relationship then becomes different, I think. They move on to a reality of death, but when you're working with them, you're in that gray area still. So it's different.

Meg highlighted the change in her role and the change in her use of sympathy. Although she had spent hours with this family, sharing some of their deepest thoughts and feelings, the relationship ended as abruptly as it had started.[36] Meg never heard from the family again.

Other rescuers expressed their sympathies by giving the family a comforting touch or a hug before they left. Cyndi was on the scene with some family members when their son's drowned body was found. She told me she did not quite know how to react: "I walked over and just gave [the parents] a hug and said 'Sorry,' and I just started crying. Because, I mean, what do you say? It's just like, oh my God, this is the most awful thing!" As she told me this story, Cyndi's eyes welled up with tears. She paused for a moment, then continued. "I mean, your kid just died. And it's not that— um—It's just a very uncomfortable situation. You just don't want to be there. There's nothing else that you can say. You know, 'I'm really sorry.'" Goffman ([1955] 1982:41) suggested that "farewells sum up the effect of the encounter upon the relationship," and this certainly seemed true in Cyndi's case, as she hugged the family, expressing fairly intimate sentiments for stranger interaction. Rescuers often expressed such heartfelt sympathies to those with whom they had connected so closely during the unknown period. They felt they at least owed families that, although at times they felt as though they should do more, given the level of emotional closeness they had attained.

Alex was unsure about the end of her relationship with the father of the young girl who had left the suicide note. A few hours after Alex was called back into the base, other rescuers found the girl dead. Alex never saw the father again, although she recalled feeling her relationship with him was somehow unfinished: "But I remember when they had a memorial service for her, I really wanted to go, but I felt like I'd be an impostor or something. I remember thinking about that. You know, I really wanted to go to the service and see *him* again, but I just felt that I didn't belong there or something. I didn't go." Many rescuers felt this way. They were confused about the relationship's status and their role after the missions. Torn by the lack of norms governing intense, intimate relationships with strangers, they reacted in varying ways to the news of a death, yet, in the end, they all terminated the relationship.

Families of the deceased did not pursue their relationships with rescuers either. It was rare for Peak to hear from them again. Two of these families wrote the group a letter thanking them for their efforts, but contact from families of the deceased was much less frequent than from families of survivors (my data contained 44 letters from survivors and only two from dead victims' families). This dynamic suggested that the outcome of the missions determined the direction of sentiment flow: if the victim was found dead, the family's misfortune outweighed most of the effort the rescuers had contributed to the mission, and thus, the rescuers owed the family sympathy (which the family accepted). Although families usually thanked the group, their own emotional matters concerned them more. If, on the other hand, the victims came out of the mission alive, the flow of sentiment was reversed: families and victims paid immense gratitude to rescuers, often sustaining the intimate bond.

Offering Gratitude for the "Save": Extending the Intimate Relationship

The fate of the intimate relationships developed during missions varied substantially when the missions ended favorably. Having built a strong rapport with families during the missions, rescuers rejoiced with them when the victims were found alive. Meg was with the hunter's son when they found his dad alive, despite being without his heart medication for two rainy nights:

> We were ready to give up, and I was working side-by-side with his son, and then we got the radio call that they found him [alive], and . . . the tears welled up in both of our faces, and I mean, I felt wonderful for him. . . . He had resigned himself to the fact that his dad was dead. I mean, he and I talked about it. . . . And so it was a *wonderful* feeling when they found him, I mean, he was just so elated, and I was so elated *for* him, I was like, "Oh what a wonderful thing to get your dad back after you think that he was gone." I was so happy for him. And he walked up to me and put his arms around me and said, "My God, thank you." And then he was gone. I never saw him again, and I never will! But I feel good about the time that I spent with him, 'cause I felt that I really helped him in that very difficult "what's-going-on?"-time. But I also felt that I was realistic and made sure that he was realistic. You know, that he understood. And he did.

Families paid rescuers immense gratitude for their help. The son sincerely thanked Meg, and then their relationship was over; she never saw him again. Yet their interaction did have a lasting effect, at least for Meg. Even though it had been years since she had seen the son, she still displayed strong emotions as she told me the story. In Rubin's (1985) terms, Meg's relationship with the son constituted a "bond," a lasting emotional connection between two people. Intimacy, according to Rubin, is the "sharing of thoughts and feelings," which requires an emotional bond, but an emotional bond does not require intimacy. Thus, it appeared that Meg's relationship with the son was intimate during the search, as they talked about their most personal thoughts and feelings, yet it became merely a bond afterward (at least for Meg), since they did not continue to interact on this level, but she still felt emotionally connected to him.

Other victims thanked rescuers and also continued the relationship somehow. After we got Shirley down to the trailhead with her broken ankle, but before she went to the hospital, she insisted on having us pose with her while her husband snapped several pictures to commemorate the experience. She later sent us copies of the photos along with a donation and a note thanking the group for its efforts, and specifically thanking Gary for "our brief, but very close relationship." The note also said to look her up next time any of us were in Minneapolis, and she enclosed a $75 gift certificate for the team to have drinks at Del Mar, the fancy restaurant she never got to visit. Shirley's letter demonstrated a second function of "farewells": they not only "sum up the effect of the encounter upon the relationship," but they also "show what the participants may expect of one another when they next meet" (Goffman [1955] 1982:41). Shirley suggested that we continue contact with her by getting in touch if we came to her hometown—a distinctly intimate offer for the few hours the team members spent with her. In this way, she made a bid to extend the intimate relationships that had developed on the rescue.

Still another woman, Polly, the 68-year-old hiker who was lost on a mountain for five days (while her son swept out the group's base building), was so grateful to the group that she wanted to give back something special. She asked Kevin, Peak's treasurer, what the group needed and how much it would cost, and shortly thereafter, she launched her own private fund-raising campaign to raise $9000 for new team jackets. She went on a small "inspirational speaking" tour, presenting her spiritual experience during those five days alone on the mountain to churches and junior high schools. In lieu of payment, each forum she spoke to sent the group a $50 donation. Periodically, she wrote to Kevin (who was also one of three rescuers who had found her) to update him on the progress of her fund-raising efforts. Her letters were always written on stationery that said, "Desire and Determination Bring Any Goal Within Reach." She felt this phrase summed up her experience, as her first letter specifically referred to it: "Dear Kevin, Hey, how about this letterhead?!" Her letters to Kevin became more and more friendly as their relationship sustained itself beyond the actual rescue. For example, one letter, written a year and a half later, during ski season, started out by saying, "Dear Kevin, How's the powder?," an enthusiastic greeting that may have operated to reestablish the relationship's intimacy that faded since the last interaction.[37] She continued by detailing how she was chipping away at the ice on her own driveway in North Dakota and talking about her daughter's wedding plans. She devoted one small paragraph (of four) to the donation checks she was including. This letter ended, as all her letters did, with "My very best, and thanks forever to all the team at Peak. With love and gratitude to all, Polly."

Once Peak bought the jackets with her donation money, she requested that we send her a picture of the team wearing them, standing in front of a "Huey" helicopter—the type of helicopter that was used in evacuating her from the mountainside. She also sent postcards to the group from several stops on her European vacation, just to say hi. Kevin reciprocated, writing back and calling to keep tabs on the fund-raising. He also organized the members to have their photo taken with the helicopter and made sure Polly got a copy, two and a half years after she was rescued. Clearly, the event had a tremendous impact on her life. Polly's reaction to her rescue was more pronounced than most victims', in that it was marked by a great deal of mutual obligation, warm feelings, and reciprocity, which are common features in friendships.[38] Kevin agreed when I asked him about it. He said they had become "pen pals."

Other victims and families also expressed their gratitude with letters as well as monetary donations, which usually ranged between $75 and $300. Some felt that the debt of gratitude could never be repaid, and they often noted the disparity between the dollar amount and their appreciation, saying, as one man did, "The enclosed check [for $100] is not in any way a valuation of your service, which was priceless to me, but a token contribution that may help your group pay for some needed item or maintenance."

Victims and families were grateful for the work the rescuers did, but many thank-you letters revealed exactly what that invaluable work was. Coincidentally, almost one year to the day after 68-year-old Polly was lost for five days, Hilda, a 67-year-old hiker from California, got lost for four days on the same mountain. (This coincidence later led rescuers to start calling the mountain "Blue Hair Hill," in honor of the two older women.) A week after her rescue, her husband, Earl, expressed his and Hilda's deepest gratitude in a letter to the group. His letter highlighted the two ways rescuers controlled families' emotions on missions. First, families realized that, even though many rescuers never verbalized their sympathy, it was a deep concern for others that drove them to help a stranger, and this concern had invaluable consequences in their lives. Second, Earl thanked rescuers for the special attention they gave in managing his family's emotions as they waited for news about Hilda. In these ways, the letter illustrated that gratitude was the normative repayment for such a large outpouring of sympathetically motivated actions, as well as for performing interpersonal emotion management:[39]

> Hilda and I want to express our very deepest thanks and gratitude for all of your tireless efforts in effecting the search and rescue of Hilda last week. . . . The care that you gave to the family, informing us regularly of your intricate plans, and updating us on the progress . . . did much to lift our heavy hearts when we feared the worst. . . . The realization that you were sparing no resources, time or talent to find Hilda brought tears to our eyes. . . . We cannot overestimate the value of what you have done and will be continuing to do for others. THANK YOU!!!

The letter was accompanied by a check for $15,000.

6

Labeling Heroes
Letters from Survivors and Families

In my six years with Peak, I collected 46 letters that thanked the rescuers for their work on missions. A few of these notes (four letters, approximately 9%) came from other counties' emergency service agencies, thanking Peak for traveling there and assisting them in a search or rescue. Most of the letters, however, came from rescued victims and their families (42 letters, approximately 91%). I have already mentioned that victims and families sometimes explicitly expressed their gratitude, and that sending thank-you letters was one way they did so. By taking a closer look at the content of the letters themselves, we can learn more about the kinds of things for which the victims and families were grateful.

There were three general gratitude themes in the letters, and each theme revolved around the idea of heroism. As I have suggested, because heroes are humble and self-effacing, they cannot self-identify as heroes; the title must be granted by others. Furthermore, scholars have asserted that heroism must be socially recognized; a hero's existence is completely dependent on others' reactions.[1] Thus, these letters were important in constructing the members' heroic identities because they provided one of the means through which others could recognize rescuers' heroic acts and label them heroes.

In thanking the rescuers for their help, victims and families identified three aspects of rescuers' heroism: their willingness to intervene in urgent situations; the acts they performed during the missions; and their exceptional individual characters.

Heroic Intervention

The first heroic theme was intervention. Scholars have suggested that heroes are individuals who intervene in situations to change or influence the course of events. Heroes challenge and transform the status quo and bring about solutions to seemingly futile circumstances.[2] When Peak's members were willing to participate in another county's mission, and the rescuers themselves emerged safely from it, the sheriffs and mission coordinators considered it a "successful" mission, regardless of whether the victim was found alive or dead. When Peak received thank-you letters in such instances (approximately 9% of the letters), the out-of-county agencies were apt to thank the members for their willingness to participate; for them, members' participation itself was heroic. For the families and victims themselves, however, the victims' status at the end of the mission was, understandably, much more important. If the victims survived, their families and the victims themselves (for obvious reasons) were much more likely to send thank-you notes (40 letters, approximately 95% of letters from families) than if the victims were killed (two letters, approximately 5% of letters from families).[3] Thus, it was extremely rare, as these numbers show, that group members received gratitude for trying, but failing, to save a victim.[4]

Furthermore, since one of the prevailing themes in these letters was labeling the group members and their efforts heroic, this predominant pattern of only receiving thank-you letters when victims survived suggested that the members' "successful" intervention—saving the victims—was the most important factor in labeling them heroes. Even when rescuers performed incredibly heroic deeds during a mission in their attempts to intervene on a victim's behalf, if the victim did not live, the family would usually not send a thank-you letter, and consequently, they did not label the rescuers as heroes. Sociologists have suggested similar things about heroes in other settings, for example, in the military; failed attempts to save others' lives are accorded substantially less honor than successful attempts and thus are less likely to be considered heroic.[5]

Not all the letters referred to dramatic, life-saving efforts. Victims and families usually thanked the group for its part in affecting a mission's outcome in some important way, even if it was a modest contribution. For instance, one man who had injured his knee while climbing Mount Alpine specified how Peak provided him a safe trip home: "It could have been an entirely different outcome if it wasn't for you and your volunteer group. . . . Again, thanks a million for your efforts in getting me safely off the mountain." This man was grateful for Peak's successful intervention: getting and keeping him out of danger.

Another man was caught in a similar situation and explained the different outcome that could have occurred if it were not for the rescuers. He had torn two ligaments in his knee while skiing in the backcountry, called 911 on his cell phone, and two rescuers snowmobiled in to evacuate him. Although his injury was not life threatening, he wrote a letter to the group members thanking them for their assistance. He said, "Getting out [of the woods] easily probably saved my knee from a lot more damage." In both these cases, the victims noted that their alternative courses of action could have been more dangerous or caused more damage, and they thanked the group members for their contributions—making a difference in their lives—even though they were not actual life-saving contributions.

Another example of rescuers' modest intervention occurred one spring when several of Peak's members took a week-long mountaineering trip to a national park. One day, the park rangers asked them to assist in evacuating a woman who had broken her ankle high up on the glaciated mountain. The superintendent of the park later wrote a letter thanking Peak's members for the difference they made in the rescue: "With the assistance of the Peak Search and Rescue Group, the operation went smoothly and safely. Without their help, the operation would have been much more difficult and time consuming for our rangers to perform." Like other letter writers, the superintendent was grateful for the group members' willingness to intervene. He noted that without Peak's help, the situation could have been much worse. In these letters noting rescuers' modest contributions, the letter writers thanked Peak for helping them avert a larger, more difficult, and dangerous problem.

Another theme in thanking members for their heroic intervention was the emphasis on the long-lasting or far-reaching effects the successful rescue efforts had. For example, when Polly, the 68-year-old hiker who had been lost on Blue Hair Hill for five days, was on her fund-raising tour speaking to churches and middle schools about her spiritual mountain experience, Peak received a letter from a sixth-grade teacher, along with her class's $50 donation. The letter said, "Thanks to your rescue efforts, my students were able to enjoy her presentation of mountain climbing experiences. . . . Your work benefits more people than just those whom you rescue. Thank you."

Other letters were more dramatic in stressing the lasting effects of rescuers' intervention. In these letters, victims often thanked Peak for saving their lives. At times, victims would punctuate this message by marking important life events that they were able to enjoy, thanks to Peak's life-saving efforts. One snowshoer, who spent a night lost in the woods with her husband, said, "Thanks to you, I'm celebrating another birthday." The passage of life events seemed to give people the opportunity to reflect on their near-death experiences and show rescuers that their efforts were long lasting. Recall that Meg and Kevin still received an annual Christmas card from the lost hiker with a collapsed lung, whom they rescued in 1986. Each year, according to Meg, the victim reminded them that they saved her life and thanked them for doing so.

Earl's letter thanking Peak for finding his wife, Hilda, after she was lost on Blue Hair Hill for four days, epitomized this tendency to express the most gratitude around special celebrations:

> In a few days, Hilda and I will be celebrating our 35th wedding anniversary. This will truly be a celebration that each of you has made possible. When we consider the joy that you have contributed to us as a couple, and to our family, and a very large number of friends, we are overwhelmed! We thank God and we thank each of you for your sharing so freely of your own selves in so many ways to allow us to have a joyous celebration rather than a funeral.

When the obstacles to be overcome were overwhelming, victims and family members viewed Peak's intervention as more valuable. As the sense of futility increased, so did victims' and families' gratitude for the rescuers' successful efforts. Indeed, one of the core components of heroism is overcoming great odds.[6] On one occasion, five of Peak's rescuers traveled to a nearby county to assist in a search for five lost backcountry skiers. (This particular search garnered national attention and instigated a debate over whether the skiers should be charged for the multi-thousand-dollar effort put into finding them.) The skiers were missing for several days while blizzard snows fell and temperatures dropped below zero. There was little hope of finding them alive when Jim, Peak's 20-year veteran, was asked by the statewide search and rescue board to run the operation. He brought four of Peak's members with him and took over the command. The next day the skiers were found alive. The media dubbed the event "Miracle in the Mountains," and the family of one of the rescued victims wrote a letter about Peak to the local newspaper's editor: "We would like to express our warmest appreciation and gratitude to the five members of Peak Search and Rescue who risked their own lives in very adverse conditions to bring to safety individuals whom they did not even know. This type of heroism too often goes unheralded." This letter demonstrated another tenet of heroism: the more individuals risk (in this case, rescuers risked their lives), and the less they are invested personally (in this case, the victims were strangers), the more likely the effort is to be characterized as heroic.[7] Furthermore, when the heroism label was combined with the media's classification of the mission as a "miracle," it reinforced the idea that heroes are the ones who perform them.

In fact, if victims' and families' letters were accurate, it was fairly common for Peak to bring about miracles—far more common than the definition of "miracle" implies. Polly's family thought she was dead after the fifth day of searching, and the mission coordinators were ready to give up the search when, from the helicopter, Martin spotted her red jacket during the final sweep of the area. Polly's family wrote to the group:

> [We] would like to thank . . . all the . . . wonderful volunteers who helped pull off that miracle. That is the only name we can give it, a miracle, because life was snatched from death. I think you have some sense now that the lady you saved is very special to a lot of people. Her continued presence in the world will make it a better place for many people.

This letter exemplified two themes related to heroic intervention: first, the group surmounted what seemed to be impossibly large obstacles, so much so that the family labeled the event a "miracle"; second, the letter conveyed that Peak's success made a difference not only in the victim's life, but also in the lives of all those to whom she was important; thus a ripple effect significantly amplified the consequences of the heroic intervention.

Peak produced another miracle after Lorna, the hiker pursuing her dog, slipped into the river, was carried down several waterfalls, and landed on a rock in the middle of the rushing water. Recall that she was so grateful for her safe evacuation that she nominated the group for the local TV station's Hometown Hero award. In her nomination letter, she explained the impact the event had on her life:

> I know you [the TV station] have reported on their acts of heroism and bravery in the past. I am hoping to touch you with the story of how they touched my life so intensely two years ago today. July 5th is the anniversary date of an experience I had that changed my life forever. . . . They saved my life that day. . . . [My husband and I] both know what a miracle it is that I survived this [type of accident]. Not many do!

Like many other letters, several themes arose in this section of Lorna's note that highlighted the heroic intervention for which she wanted Peak to be recognized. First, the rescue not only saved her life, but changed it forever, which supports the notion that heroes transform the status quo. Second, like Polly's family, Lorna also termed her rescue "a miracle," which suggests that, as heroes do, Peak's rescuers overcame great odds to ensure her survival. Third, because of these things, she considered Peak's work heroic and wanted the group to be recognized for it.

In the event that the members did not accomplish their desired task, that is, when they recovered a dead body rather than finding someone still alive, they became demoralized.[8] The process was even more demoralizing, however, when the families paid rescuers very little gratitude for their efforts. One winter there were several avalanche victims within a two-month period. One of the victims, Arnie, a well-known local skier, was the friend of a woman who was an ex-member of Peak. She wrote the group a letter, expressing her thanks, and acknowledging the hardships of "failing":

> Now I realize, more than I ever did as a member, how important the group's work is. All the training hours, . . . the frustration and seeming futility of the missions with unhappy endings—I want you all to know that it's all vital and it all matters to those who find themselves or their loved ones in need in the backcountry. Despite this difficult winter, please don't lose faith and keep up the good work. As individuals and as a group, you are a true asset to this community.

Knowing, from her own experience, that rescuers would be demoralized, this woman wrote to them emphasizing the importance of their work. She stressed the transformational power Peak had in the community saying that its work "mattered," suggesting that it was heroic, even if it did not feel that way at the time.

Heroic Acts

A second gratitude theme in the letters was for the heroic acts rescuers performed while on missions. Victims and families thanked rescuers for the specific things they did during the searches and rescues. The most prominent of these acts was that of sacrifice, which has been shown to be a core element of heroism in other settings.[9] Victims noted several things that rescuers sacrificed when they went on missions at a moment's notice and stayed for days at a time: sleep, time with their families, and even money when missions took them away from work, which they frequently did. For example, the snowshoers who were lost overnight remarked that rescuers' sacrifice of time was the most important element in their eventual rescue: "We can't give enough thanks to Louie who spent many hours coordinating the rescue effort and [to] the two snowmobile rescuers, Shorty and Nick, who spent extraordinarily long hours trying to find us overnight and [who] were back out very early Wednesday morning and eventually did find us." Earl and Hilda's letter also expressed their gratitude for rescuers' willingness to sacrifice not only their time (four full weekdays), but also their own safety to find Hilda: "Certainly the time that you gave with no previous notice must have ripped apart your usual schedules in ways we don't understand. Thank you! This was volunteer help at its very finest. We know that some of you were placed at considerable risk for your own personal safety and we want to thank you."

Victims and families, like Earl and Hilda, recognized that risk was an important factor in accomplishing the rescues. When Arnie, the well-known local skier, was found dead in the avalanche, his family wrote the group, specifically mentioning the risk rescuers undertook to recover his body as soon as possible. They said of the group members, "We will be forever grateful for their efforts [in locating Arnie] and placing their own lives in peril to do so."

On another occasion, Peak's members assisted a neighboring county's team on an avalanche rescue. The victim was found dead, but the other team's mission coordinator thanked Peak in a letter, expressly referring to the members' willingness to risk their personal safety for the rescue effort:

> Even though the weather conditions were not the best and the slope conditions may not have been the safest to work on, there was not one complaint or refusal to assist. Those of us who direct avalanche rescue operations feel very fortunate to be able to call upon people like you for your valuable assistance in time of great need. . . . The cooperation shown by all rescue members in order to get the job done in the best possible manner was outstanding.

In these ways, families, victims, and even other organizations thanked rescuers for the specific acts of sacrifice they made during missions. Sociologists have contended that voluntarily risking one's life to help others is often an important feature in defining heroism.[10]

Another heroic act that appeared in victims' and families' thank-you letters was the help Peak provided. The ability and willingness to help others, especially when combined with the element of sacrifice, was the essence of heroism and the basis for the gratitude found in the letters. One woman, after throwing out her back on a hiking trail, said, "It was a great comfort to know you were there to deal with the situation." Another person, a man whose backcountry skiing partner had gotten lost, said, "It was a great comfort to know that your crew was mobilizing for what I feared would be a rescue of a seriously injured and hypothermic friend." Coincidentally, both these (and other) letter writers used the same phrase ("It was a great comfort to know") to express their relief when they realized that there was a group of people willing to help them and take charge of the situation. The manifest goal of physically helping someone seemed to have the latent function of helping them emotionally as well. It gave victims and families the feeling that they were not alone, and that they would be saved, an idea that coincides with those I have presented previously: that rescuers worked to control victims' and families' emotions, and that victims and families thanked rescuers for such interpersonal emotion management. The letters further illuminate this dynamic, suggesting that interpersonal emotion management may be a key feature of the heroic act.

Many letters also referred to the members' competence and skill. Because the victims and families of survivors were more inclined to write these letters than those whose family members were killed, it makes sense that the skill and competence the rescuers displayed while saving someone would be considered very important. Thus, they were prominent features of the gratitude members received for their successful efforts. The literature on heroism has contended that specialized skill and competence are important in defining heroism because they help heroes successfully intervene in situations where unskilled others might fail.[11] In fact, Peak's culture itself, as I have described, considered rescuers' skills to be integral to the idea of heroism. For instance, when the neighboring county's sheriff thanked Peak for assisting in locating the body of a tourist caught in an avalanche, he drew attention to the group's exceptional skills: "All of us, citizens and visitors alike, are indeed fortunate to have resources of your caliber available." Likewise, the hiker who had injured his knee and was evacuated from Mount Alpine said that his rescue "was as professional and smooth as I could have ever expected. I can't thank you enough for the way you handled this possible *dangerous* situation." The rescuers' skill shone through in these situations, directly affecting the outcome of the missions and thus precipitating grateful responses.

Other acts for which victims and families thanked rescuers were those that required a great deal of strength or power. Victims tended to remember these acts, perhaps because they themselves were physically incapacitated to some degree and unable to perform them on their own. For example, one woman who twisted her ankle on a hiking trail was piggybacked out by one of the Ironmen, Tyler. She described her experience in a thank-you letter:

> For the next three hours Tyler carried me down the mountain. It was and remains an astonishing experience. When the others [rescuers] met us we had already established that since I was in little pain, and since Tyler still felt energetic, we would continue the "piggyback rescue mode." . . . Near the end of our ordeal I could tell that Tyler was close to complete exhaustion. The trail we were on was merciless and ascended as often as it descended. Nick, another Peak member, carried me a short way and gave Tyler a break. He, too, was amazingly strong.

Of course, feats of strength and power are key in some definitions of heroism. Popular culture reinforces this definition of heroism in its creation of fictional superheroes such as Superman (who is "faster than a speeding bullet, stronger than a locomotive, able to leap tall buildings in a single bound") and other comic book characters whose superior strength helps them physically triumph in adverse situations.[12]

The last act victims appreciated was the care rescuers gave them throughout the ordeal: medical care, physical care, and emotional care. When Lorna, the hiker who fell into the river while going after her drowning dog, was finally evacuated from the water, she was placed on her back and strapped into the stretcher ("litter") to be wheeled down the trail. In her nomination letter to the TV station, she described the care and compassion rescuers gave her after her harrowing experience in the river:

> They made sure they caused me the least amount of discomfort possible. The ambulance team was there too and showed just as much compassion and concern [as Peak]. The rescue team even took the time to try and find our dog, to no avail. It took some time getting down the trail, again, I am

not sure how long. They all made comments on how pretty the flowers were and when I said I wished I could see them, they picked a few and gave them to me. Our Mountain Rescue team has to be one of the very best in the country.

Lorna's letter demonstrated how the care rescuers showed went beyond simply providing help. She called it "compassion and concern," and other letters used similar terminology; for example, another said: "Thanks to everyone in your organization for their very professional but caring efforts that they showed us." Lorna viewed the acts of looking for her lost dog and picking her flowers as ones of compassion. These acts made her feel as though the rescuers really cared about her, which was one of the reasons she nominated the group for the Hometown Hero award. Thus, compassionate acts appear to be core elements of heroism, an observation often overlooked in the scholarly literature on heroism, but integral to many formulations of altruism.[13]

The acts for which victims and families thanked rescuers—sacrificing themselves, taking risks, providing help, demonstrating competence, skill, and strength, and showing compassion—led them to label these actions as heroic because they were the key behaviors that enabled rescuers to intervene successfully in their lives.

Heroic Identities

In addition to characterizing the rescuers' heroic intervention and heroic acts, the thank-you letters also emphasized the heroic identities of the rescuers. Basing their evaluation on these two particular features of the rescues—the successful outcome of the missions and the rescuers' actions during the missions—victims, families, and other emergency service agencies imputed heroic identities to the rescuers, making statements about who they were as people. For example, the piggybacked victim described Tyler and the rest of the team members: "Several times during our trek Tyler stopped, balanced me on his back and pointed out the spectacular views he didn't want me to miss. (Is this an amazing guy, or what???) . . . I remember the rescue as beautiful: the beautiful wilderness and even more, the beautiful spirits of every one who helped me." The victim attributed "beautiful spirits" to every rescuer involved in the mission and labeled Tyler an "amazing guy." She logically induced these conclusions about the rescuers' identities—their inner selves—from the evidence she observed: the rescuers' strong and compassionate acts and their ability to help her.[14]

Lorna, in her letter to the TV station, also surmised that the group members were exceptional people who possessed certain heroic qualities. Two years after her rescue, she still felt so strongly that she nominated them for the award. She said that the rescuers themselves possessed these heroic characteristics: "I can not imagine a group of people as compassionate, dedicated and competent. There are not enough words to relay to you their abilities! They are truly an extraordinary group. . . . Not many [victims of this type of accident] have the opportunity to thank these wonderful people as we do."

It was common for victims and families to impute specific emotional qualities to the rescuers, as Lorna did when she called them "compassionate." She based her judgment on certain compassionate actions the rescuers engaged in while on the mission, for instance, when they looked for her dog and gave her flowers. She first labeled the actions as compassionate, and then the rescuers themselves as such. Earl and Hilda's letter also extrapolated from the rescuers' actions to make declarations about their identities. They wrote, "From the moment that we placed the first '911' call until Hilda was safe in the emergency room, we sensed the deep personal involvement and commitment to the care of your fellow human that you each so freely gave."

Labeling the rescuers as "compassionate" and "caring" people was the most predominant identity theme in the letters.[15] The lost snowshoer's letter said, "[My husband and I] are both so appreciative of the competent and brave volunteers who are such a fabulous resource to our community. . . . We truly live in a caring community." This letter implied that the group members as people, not as rescuers, helped to create Peak County's "caring community."

In addition to labeling the rescuers as caring individuals, the snowshoers' letter showed that competence and bravery, which were used so frequently to characterize the heroic actions taken on missions, were also reinscribed onto the individual personalities of the rescuers performing these acts. Thus, the rescuers themselves were perceived to be competent and brave people, even outside of the rescue context.

Two other common identities attributed to the rescuers in the thank-you letters were selflessness and generosity, identity characteristics victims and families probably gleaned from rescuers' self-sacrificing behavior on the missions. The woman who threw out her back on the hiking trail said,

"Your generosity in donating your personal time and effort is extremely appreciated. It is nice to know there are people like you who care enough about others to participate in the Rescue Group." One of Polly's letters also alluded to generosity by thanking rescuers for being selfless: "Your unselfish giving of time and talent along with lots of heart are gifts to behold." These letter writers were not unique in attributing kind identities to rescuers. Research has shown that people are more likely to attribute kindness to others when the others' actions are not clearly motivated by self-interest, when the actions fulfill no social obligations, and when actors received no benefits (as is the case with volunteers helping strangers).[16]

Some letters blatantly ascribed heroic identities to the rescuers by defining their heroic actions as true reflections of their heroic selves. For example, the neighboring county's sheriff wrote Peak a letter after the five rescuers participated in the nationally renowned search for the missing skiers: "The real heroes in such an endeavor—those members of rescue organizations like yours who devote themselves to the preservation of life, often at the risk of their own—should and must be acknowledged and receive our heartfelt gratitude." The sheriff implied that not only do heroes perform risky actions to help others, but they are devoted to doing so. The sheriff's attribution of heroic identities to rescuers for their consistent actions in helping others mirrors other social psychological research showing that when individuals help many different people, others are likely to attribute the cause of their behavior to who they are (internal causes) rather than situational factors (external causes).[17] Thus, individuals' commitment to repeatedly performing heroic acts served as evidence of their heroic identities. Peak's members themselves also defined such commitment as a core feature of heroism, as has been discussed.[18]

Polly's family, too, in their letter to the group, expressed the nature of the rescuers' heroic identities: "The seven of us who kept vigil [during the search for Polly] came away marveling at the sacrifices all of you made to find a stranger and were deeply affected by your selflessness and compassion. . . . All of you are our heroes."

7

The Emotional Rewards
of Rescue Work

Rescuers overwhelmingly considered their main rewards to be emotional in nature. When asked what they got out of participating in Peak, they often began their responses with the words, "That good feeling you get when . . . ," and commonly labeled such good feelings as "euphoria," "joy," "excitement," and "self-satisfaction." The rewards they described fell into four main categories.

Increased Self-Efficacy

One reward rescuers described was an increased feeling of self-efficacy, or a feeling that they were active agents in the world who had the power to cause certain things to happen.[1] Peak's successful missions made rescuers feel like they were accomplishing something, which is a common reward for members of other types of groups as well, such as professional fire fighters, EMTs, and those who volunteer their time for community service.[2] One source of accomplishment was felt through hard physical activity in the field on missions. Gary told me that he preferred being in the field over being in the base, for example, running the radio or talking to family members during missions. I asked him why he found being in the field most rewarding:

> It's hands-on. I'd much rather be out getting dirty and sweaty and breathing hard. It's more fun. It's more exhilarating. You feel like you're accomplishing more [than if you're in the base]. Even though you're not necessarily accomplishing more, it feels like you are. It definitely feels like you

are. It feels good, just physically, to get out there and hump a bit [work hard physically].

Roy, the 15-year member and our trainer, echoed Gary's sentiments, saying that the feeling of accomplishment from missions was a reward in itself:

It's fun. I mean, it's fun because we go and do these [all night] carry-outs. It's a show of the human spirit, and how it can go all night long. Endurance. It's an accomplishment physically and mentally for the people effecting the rescue. The beneficiary of all that is the victim. They have a nice, quiet, smooth ride out. And [are] delivered to the ambulance or their loved ones.

It is interesting that Roy saw saving the victim as a reward secondary to the rescuers' own feelings resulting from a good performance. It seemed as though Roy was particularly rewarded by being challenged and succeeding, a view others held as well.

Vince, the member in his early twenties who dropped out of college to become a paramedic, was a member for three years. Although relatively inexperienced, he had been highly involved since he joined the group, attending every mission he could. On one occasion, he was sent in to tend to Smitty, a 69-year-old man who had become lost on Blue Hair Hill. Smitty, a small, frail-looking man, had gone hiking on a Monday and gotten lost on his return. By the time he realized that he had descended too far below the trail, he was too exhausted to climb back up through the boulders and dense forest to reach it again. He had signed the trail register when he began his hike and was under the mistaken impression that forest rangers checked it every night, so they would soon realize he was missing. He decided to lay out a large, highly visible orange tarp and wait for searchers to find him. He laid waiting for four days. By Friday, he had almost given up hope. Having had no food and drinking only stream water, he was extremely weak and could barely move, much less climb out of the area he was in. He resigned himself to dying up there.

Meanwhile, three tourists in their mid-twenties, Todd and his two friends, had gone off the trail and were tromping through the woods in search of a fishing hole when they spotted Smitty's orange tarp from afar. They were not sure what it was and wanted to check it out. They decided that Todd would make his way down there, and if someone was hurt, he would wave his arms in the air—a signal for the other two to go for help. When Todd reached Smitty, he was shocked and scared to see Smitty's condition; at first he thought he was dead. He gave him some food and signaled for his friends to get help.

When Peak got the ambiguous report—"someone off the trail needs help"—members did not know what to think. Peak put Vince and Gary in the field to find the reporting parties (the two friends), who were camped several miles up the trail. By the time Gary and Vince got there, Todd had returned to camp and was able to give them a more thorough report on Smitty's condition. The rescuers were immediately alarmed, considering the situation one of life-and-death. They decided that Vince, though relatively inexperienced, would accompany Todd back down to Smitty because he was a paramedic (more medically qualified than Gary, the EMT). Gary would hike out and marshal a team for Smitty's evacuation.

Vince and Todd hiked through the darkness for over an hour before they reached Smitty, whose condition had improved somewhat because he had eaten something and was, according to Vince, "happy as hell" to see them. After an initial medical evaluation, Vince ascertained that Smitty was in stable condition, so Elena, the mission coordinator, decided to wait until dawn—about eight hours—to dispatch the evacuation team. Vince and Todd camped out with Smitty that night, and Vince spent the night stoking a fire, monitoring Smitty's vital signs, and listening to him talk. In the morning, Vince radioed Elena and suggested that the evacuation team come up a different trail on the other side of a major river, because he thought the bushwhacking he and Todd had done to reach Smitty was too difficult and dangerous for an evacuation. Vince was able to get Smitty down to the edge of the river to wait for the evacuation team that was ascending a trail on the other side. When the team got there, they threw a line to Vince and together they set up a clothes-line-type system to pass Smitty and Vince across the river (Todd hiked back up to his friends). The team carried Smitty down seven miles of trail while he lay in the stretcher, talking.

Vince felt proud of the job he had done in effecting Smitty's rescue. He said he felt as though he had achieved a major accomplishment:

> That was the most involved that I had ever been. That was the most responsibility that I had undertaken, up to that point in time. I think a lot of what happened on that mission falls back onto my shoulders and deci-

sions that I made in the early hours of that mission. . . . I *was* the team. There was no one else to consult, essentially. . . . And then to stay out there all night with him and kind of see it through to the end was pretty cool. . . . On a personal level, to be able to do the work that I did that night, and to be able to accomplish what I did personally, for me, is great. I went to places where I'd never been before, accomplished things that I had not done before, had responsibilities that I'd never held before, and in the end it all worked out really well. So it's a huge personal success story for me. Or that's how I see it. I enjoyed the challenge.

Vince considered his experience a "personal success story," and felt like the decisions he made were influential in the team's ability to accomplish the rescue. By thinking about the situation and making decisions that others listened to, Vince increased his sense of control over the situation and thus was able to incorporate that feeling of efficacy into his self-concept. Other research supports this finding, showing that workers experience higher rates of self-efficacy when their jobs are more complex and challenging, as well as when their jobs allow them a great deal of independence and autonomy.[3]

Other members also felt that they performed well when challenged, and as a result, they felt good when they proved to themselves that they could do something they had not been so sure they could. Jim told me that when he traveled to the other county and took over the state-run, nationally renowned mission for the missing skiers, he felt genuinely rewarded when he found them alive. He said that the mission had presented him with some unique challenges, and he was forced to be creative to overcome them:

I remember trudging up there [to brief the pilot at the helicopter landing zone] and showing him on the map [where I wanted him to fly] and the pilot saying, "Where are we?" And I'm like, "*Great*! We've got a fuckin' pilot that doesn't even know where he is!" I wanted him to fly right down this little drainage, right through these trees, but he didn't know where I wanted him to go. So I remember going back to the [site where the searchers were gathered] and we lined everybody up in an arrow in the snow, and the helicopter got up, and it circled and came right over the arrow and went right down [the correct drainage]. Fifteen minutes later they found 'em. I mean, that's what [search and rescue's] all about. That's what it's all about. . . . And it was neat. It was neat to be a part of that at a level where I honestly felt like my decisions made a difference. That's neat.

Because it wasn't happening. They were in disarray ahead of time. I'm sure that there are other people that could've pulled that thing together, it just happened to be me. They called, I got to go, it worked. What a neat deal.

It is clear that Jim felt good about his performance and, in part, attributed the success of the mission to the decisions he made and the innovation he used in accomplishing the task.[4]

Several members went farther in describing their feelings of self-efficacy, relating them to "personal growth." Meg, for instance, told me how participating in rescue work, particularly her intense work with families during searches, had changed her:

I'm a little more confident of my own personal abilities. And I think as you become more confident as an individual in different things that maybe aren't so familiar to you, that's kind of rewarding. So I guess I've learned some things about myself. You know, I never participated in anything like hospice or grief counseling, or going out and finding somebody [who is lost]. I never participated in anything like that before I moved out here. So you accomplish something like that, and you walk away and you say, "Huh. I did okay." And that's rewarding. That's the growth part of it, and that's the learning experience part of it, and that's the part that makes you feel good. I mean, I want to feel like I helped someone, or I accomplished something for myself where maybe I thought I was pushing my envelope—whether it's in the field or inside [comforting family members], or whatever. That's the growth part for me.

Other members said they could see this type of growth in other rescuers. Oliver, the ex-police officer, said at times he could "see the light[bulbs] come on [above others' heads], and they realize they can do something maybe they didn't think they could do."[5]

This sense of self-efficacy extended beyond members' concrete experiences, however. Rescuers believed that they could conquer not only the specific challenge they had just overcome, but also, more abstractly, anything that they might encounter in the future. This confidence, however, tended to be more of a male phenomenon, as I have discussed previously. I asked Roy to explain the "self-satisfaction" that he experienced after a mission:

If there is a need for it, you can handle anything that comes up out there and get it done. No matter what comes your way—what curve ball they throw at you, what kind of trick nature plays on you or whatever—that you can just do it all. It's a real inner feeling that you *did* it. You started out walking in, and it's supposed to be a simple thing [mission], and it changed hour by hour, and it turns into a huge thing, and you still did it.

Special Bonds

A second source of good feelings rescuers experienced was the special bonds that they developed with other rescuers while on missions. Some research has shown that relationships with other volunteers is one reward that keeps people involved in volunteer groups.[6] Many rescuers were quite fond of the camaraderie built on missions, and they considered most missions to be fun because of it. Oliver felt that the connections that members made with one another on missions were the most rewarding feature of participation. He said that "fellowship, the connection when you're on a mission—that common bond that you feel—is neat." Several rescuers told me that even if a mission was very difficult, physically uncomfortable, and not enjoyable to experience—a "shit mission"—they were often able to look back the next day and realize it was a good time, mostly because of their interactions with other rescuers. Tyler, the eight-year member who evacuated the victim by piggyback, told me that the special relationship he had developed with other rescuers was the reason he enjoyed search and rescue:

> I think the biggest thing I get out of mountain rescue is the people I've met, the friends I've made. More than anything. Because there really isn't a whole heck of a lot else. You know, you get a little bit of knowledge here and there, you get to help some people, but the main thing is the people I've met; that's what keeps me coming back, is being with some of the people.

Of all the group settings, he thought missions were the most fun because of the camaraderie that developed:

You can have some absolutely great laughs. . . . We've had numerous missions that we still talk about—Mt. Lando was an absolutely hilarious mission. The mission in itself was a mess. It was being run by another county. But we had a great group of people that was there. There was just a lot of humor involved in it—we just laughed like idiots for 24 hours straight. And of course, we were somewhat sleepy and kind of punch-drunk. . . . It was fun. So I still look back on that particular mission, and still grin because it was a lot of fun.

The particular mission Tyler referred to involved discovering and recovering a frozen hiker's body. Yet he still considered it one of the most "fun" because of the bonds that he formed with other rescuers. Other researchers have shown that camaraderie is a major reward for volunteers.[7]

Like Tyler, other rescuers, too, thought that laughing and remaining lighthearted were important features of missions that led rescuers to bond with one another. Benny, the seven-year member who was a divorced father, also thought one particular mission—an all-night carry-out—was particularly useful in forming group unity. He chose this mission as an example because it happened at a time when group members were highly divided, intensely involved in some intragroup conflicts:

It was really good because it came out so well, where you got to know everybody in the group. See, that's where you get to know people [on the missions]. That's where it changed for me. I got to know people that I didn't really respect that much, like Russ, 'cause he's so headstrong, but there he was, [carrying the stretcher] right across from me the whole time. I mean we worked so well as a team. . . . It solidified the group so well [because of] the lightness that came out of it. You know, the telling of jokes, the singing of songs, the laughter—if you can't laugh, then it's all work. And when you laugh, it changes the whole thing into a team: a bunch of people having a hard time—and it was a scary time going down there—but over all we worked real well together. We came together, and it was like *family*, you know?

Benny was not alone in his use of the word "family" to describe the group members' relationships with one another. I suspect several rescuers used this term to describe the closeness they felt with other members, even if they did not see eye-to-eye on major issues. Members were proud that as a group, they could overcome their differences or dislike for one another during missions and work together effectively, as Benny described above in his experience with Russ. Oliver used the term "family," too, in describing how he felt rewarded when members pulled together to help others, which was a dynamic that he enjoyed seeing:

> Could you imagine calling a search and having nobody show up? [*Laughs nervously.*] That scares me, the fact that sometimes [we don't have many people show up]. But it always seems [that] enough people pull together. Like the search for the woman. Here Maddie pulls in, and Roger comes in—just people that you haven't seen for ages, but people pull together. That's neat, you know, I think that's really neat when everybody pulls together like that. And faces you haven't seen for a long time come around. I think you really feel like a family. And you're all pulling together trying to help another family out. And that's probably the satisfaction of it as much as anything.

For Oliver, this display of solidarity was in itself rewarding.

Finally, several members felt rewarded by their enduring connections with other rescuers, even after they had quit the group. Maddie, the 10-year member, told me that she had made life-long friends from her participation in Peak, something she realized very soon after she met them early on in her career:

> I knew these guys would always be there for me and I would always be there for them—the way you would for any really good friend. . . . I mean, a lot of those guys are still my closest friends, although a lot of them are not in the group anymore. If something [a big mission] happened, and we needed more people, I could still call them and say, "Hey, could you come help us out?" If there was any way they could, they would. I mean, they'll drop anything for you. Those are the kind of people that they are.

Maddie felt a sense of security from her close relationship with many members. The "type of people" that were in Peak provided her with the rewarding feelings that they would always be there to support her, whether it be in Peak or in her personal life. They were a special sort of trusted and dependable friends. Other research has shown that volunteers feel rewarded when they make friendships that last beyond the volunteer context itself, and that dangerous and risky activities, such as police work, volunteer fire fighting, and ambulance work promote similarly high levels of rewarding trust, dependability, and solidarity among team members.[8] In this way, Peak's members felt rewarded by the friends they made and their ability to overcome their differences in order to work well together during missions.

Moral Achievements

A third way rescuers felt rewarded was through the feeling that they accomplished something socially good or morally worthwhile, a reward found among members of various community-service groups.[9] One type of moral achievement was felt most strongly by Jim, the only remaining founder of the group. Recall that he had been instrumental in recruiting members to help the group grow and get established in Peak's early days. His goal was not necessarily to build the group under his own direction, but to create a humanitarian organization—one that served others—that could perpetuate itself. He described how his two search and rescue mentors advised him on his goals back in the early days:

> Basically, they set the example, and they set the tone for me. They guided me in the fact that a group that's dependent on an individual is no group at all. And [they said], "If you really wanna make a mark in search and rescue, create a group, Jim, that will go on beyond you. Because you have created a group, . . . but will it survive without Jim?" And that was the challenge.

Jim was proud because he had succeeded in establishing a self-perpetuating, community-service group; it was a moral achievement.[10] Jim was, however, still protective of his group:

> I guess I see myself more as the—I don't know—the *patron* [of Peak]. You know, we've established something, and I wanna make sure that the traditions are followed; that the same commitment to gettin' up in the middle of the night in the worst kind of weather—without questioning why—is done so that the victim has the best possible chance of survival. That's what it's all about. That's what was drilled into my head in the Marine Corps, that's what was drilled into my head by [my two search and rescue mentors]. They said, "It's not about *you*, Jimmy. It's not about you gettin' up and goin' out. It's about giving the victim the best possible chance of

survival. Without endangering yourself." And I believe in that. Whole-heartedly.

Oliner and Oliner (1988) showed that people who give to others at the expense of themselves enact a "moral heroism" because they are acting out of compassion, concern, and a feeling of social obligation.[11] Jim was aware that his victory was a moral one, in the strongest sense of the word, and he felt good about achieving it. He derived even further satisfaction from the fact that a member whom he had recruited years earlier had established a brand new rescue team in another town after moving away from Peak County. Jim thought it was "neat to see the whole thing grow and evolve like that."

Other members felt rewarded morally by being able to make a difference in others' lives. Patrick told me that he felt rewarded when he used his rock climbing skills for a higher purpose:

[I get] personal satisfaction that I'm going to use the skills that I've learned and practiced over a long period of time for something other than just—I hate to say "worthless recreation," but, I mean, these are recreational skills. When I first started doing this [rock climbing], I was just doing it for the fun, and now I'm actually doing it for a purpose, and that's kind of fulfilling. . . . I like to think I "did something good" as opposed to just "did something." I kind of like helping people, I kind of think it's neat. Making somebody happy when they're unhappy: "I'm lost!" "No you're not, walk that way." "Oh! Thank you! Thank you!" . . . I get a kick out of it, I like it.

The rewards Patrick received were similar to the rewards reported by other volunteers. First and foremost, they felt good about "doing something worthwhile," and second, they enjoyed using their specialized skills and experience to help others. Patrick also stated that he felt rewarded when he relieved others' suffering—"making somebody happy when they're unhappy"—which is a common reward for rescuers and emergency workers in other settings.[12] Other scholars have also shown that a focus on others is one of the most socially valued traits individuals can possess, and thus a highly moral one. As a result, it is often considered heroic.[13]

Rescuers also expressed satisfaction from seeing things put right—a restoration of the moral order—whether or not they themselves played a pivotal role in it. Jim, again, stated this vividly:

[Mountain rescue] is about finding a six-year-old and his grandmother up on Blanca Mountain after they spent the night out in a snowstorm. That's what it's about. Ain't no glory in that. The helicopter spotted 'em [*laughs*]. We spent all night up to our waists in snow lookin' for these people. They were fine. We never found 'em. The helicopter spotted 'em. But I've never seen a prettier sight than Hal getting off that helicopter with the six-year-old wrapped in his mountain rescue parka. Walkin' outta that helicopter with a big smile on his face. That's what it's all about. If those are the kinda things that get you going, then you're in the right place.

Kevin also said that he felt rewarded from playing a part in a larger effort, regardless of what role that was. He recounted the story of finding Polly, the 68-year-old hiker who was the first in the wave of senior citizens to get lost on Blue Hair Hill. Kevin and Martin had been put on the search helicopter, and as Martin described previously, it was by a "miracle" that he spotted Polly. The pilots and searchers decided that to reach her, they would have to perform a risky helicopter maneuver right then and there because, after five days, she was barely able to wave at them, much less sustain herself for another day until a ground team could reach her. Since the mountainside was so steep they could not land, the pilots hovered the aircraft inches above the rocky terrain while a third rescuer jumped out to get her. This maneuver was even more risky because of the tight spot the helicopter had to fit into. Kevin's job was to watch the tail rotor and warn the pilots when they were drifting toward the trees behind them, and Martin's job was to lay on his stomach with his head out the door, peering under the belly of the ship to warn the pilots when they were getting too close to the giant boulders below. Minutes later, Polly was in the ship, and they were on their way. The pilots (who had never participated in a rescue before) and the rescuers were euphoric.

Kevin told me about two conversations he had with the helicopter pilots that day, one before they found Polly and one after:

[While we were searching], one of [the pilots] inquired as to how much money we make to do this. I said, "We don't get any pay for this. In fact, it could be looked at as an expense." And they were a bit puzzled; they were like, "Huh." But after we picked her off [found and rescued Polly], and they were flying back, they were elated also. And I said, "Do you understand why I don't need to be paid to do this?" And they said, "Oh yeah! We wish we could be stationed in your neighborhood!"

There is no amount of money that you could pay me to feel that joy of having successfully completed a mission. . . . I felt as if we had—and I say "we"—we had accomplished something. There was some personal satisfaction, but the personal satisfaction came from being involved in an effort that was successful. It wasn't "pin a star on my chest," you know, because the two days before [I did unexciting jobs]. I staked out the camp one day and ran the landing zone another day. It didn't matter to me. But it was nice to be part of an effort that brought closure to an event. And that works for recovery of bodies [too]. I mean, you're bringing closure to an event for the families, for the people that have been involved in the search or whatever. But it feels good.

Kevin's satisfaction arose from making a difference in someone's life. The emotional reward that he felt was worth more to him than any amount of money. Other research has shown that rewards that are altruistically satisfying can be the sole reason for continued altruistic actions, and that offering volunteers money to do something they want to do can actually diminish the internal reward they feel.[14]

Many members, including Kevin, incorporated these feelings of moral achievement into their sense of self, considering their work with Peak to be influential in who they were. Kevin felt this way:

I'm a better person for being involved in Peak because it's a positive group. It does positive things. It's enriched me in a number of different ways, and if it's not here I will always think back to "Well, I was able to make a difference. I was able to be part of a team, an organization, a group of people that meant well and were well intentioned." I'm a better person for having done that. And hopefully there are people that I've been involved with that are better people for having been involved with me through the group. And there are certainly people who have had their lives saved through what we've done. So, yeah, it's a good thing, it's something that's been a part of me, will always be a part of me, but it does not define Kevin. It is not his life; it's a portion of it.

Other members felt that the group had influenced who they were in more concrete ways. For example, Nick told me how he had changed:

Nick: I think I'm more considerate on helping people. I'm more likely to. Like if somebody's broken down on the side of the road, even.

Because I realize that they appreciate it. . . . It's a weird feeling, like when somebody's stuck [in a snow bank] on the side of the road, and you pull 'em out, and they offer you money, and you say, "No, that's not the reason I did it. I did it just to help ya."

Jen: It's a weird feeling not to take the money?

Nick: To a point, yeah. When I was younger I'm sure I was like [*extends palm*], "Pay up!" before I even helped [*laughs*]!

Nick believed that performing good deeds and receiving gratitude had changed him. Some other research has supported this finding, showing that helpers who are thanked are more likely to help in the future, and that some volunteers who do charity work depend on gratitude to make their work emotionally rewarding.[15]

Inspirational Lessons

The fourth way rescuers were rewarded was through feeling inspired by successful missions. The predominant lesson rescuers took away from these inspirational experiences was never to give up. Many rescuers learned this for themselves when they found victims they thought they would never find, or when they encountered a victim who had survived seemingly impossible odds.

For example, Vince thought Smitty was particularly inspiring because, at 69 years old, he had survived five days without food in the rain:

I was expecting [that he would be in] much, much worse [condition when I got to him]. Just because of the general circumstances of that situation, you know, a man that's close to 70 years old spending five nights out by himself at that elevation, with no food or water, and with the weather we had had in that time period, or even that afternoon—there was some pretty harsh rain coming down up there—that's pretty amazing. So I was expecting much worse. I was impressed by his strength and his manner—his "will to live" I guess I should say.

Smitty's ability to survive during his ordeal impressed Vince and many other rescuers as well. Nancy, a six-year member in her early fifties (another one of my cohort-peers), told me that she had a long chat with Smitty on the hike out, and she asked him why he had been hiking alone.

He laughed. "Who could I get to come with me? All my old hiking buddies either just want to sit in their rockers, or they're dead!" Nancy told this story to several other rescuers, and they all marveled at this man's zest for life. In this way, rescuers were inspired. They were able to gain strength themselves from hearing that others had survived such hardships.

Rescuers were also able to bank these inspirational experiences and draw on them during subsequent missions when they began again to feel like their efforts were futile. For example, Jim fought the urge to give up while coordinating one particularly difficult search, the one for the 22-year-old hiker who was killed after falling 1400 feet off the top of Mount Alpine. Jim was frustrated when, by day six of the mission, searchers had not found even a single clue. This mission was particularly troubling for Jim because he had a good record. In his 20 years as a mission coordinator, he had found—dead or alive—everyone he had ever looked for. To inspire him during this search, he drew on his previous experience, holding steadfastly to what he knew would work—the systematic search process that had served him well in the past—despite strong opposition from the family members, who insisted that their son had met with foul play.

And [the sixth] night [of the search] we met with the family. And this meeting was not going the right way because the mother and the father were relying on the roommate and some psychic's advice. As opposed to my facts and figures—my computer-analyzed search statistics that told me that we were doing the things that we needed to do; that we were slowly but surely grinding out the elimination of these [search] areas. And there was huge speculation that this kid had been done-in somewhere else. And that this whole thing was a cover-up for the fact that he may have been murdered, and drug off someplace else, and who knows what. And the mother and the dad were just [hounding me, saying], "Well, his roommate says he would have gone here." And I just looked at the dad and I said, "Who the fuck's the roommate? Sir, we've *been* there. We were there. Is this the same roommate that waited *four days* to report your son missing?" I said, "I'm sorry, but either you've got to trust the process that I'm trying to do here, or you can find somebody else to run your goddamned search!" And that's the first time in 20 years that I've ever gotten to that point. . . .

Although it was emotionally demanding on me, in the end it worked. And it reinforced everything that I've been taught. I mean, I pulled every trick out of the bag, you know? The rabbit had left, there wasn't anything left in my hat, except, "Let's get a smaller helicopter, let's get over on the dangerous East Face, and if the pilot can put me in there, then we're gonna go up and down every inch of that rocky crag. Because either he fell off the top [of the mountain] and fell into one of those rocky crags, or he's *not* there." And boom: there he was.

Although this experience was not a pleasant one for Jim, in the end it served as inspiration for him; its successful outcome validated his decision to stick with what he had been taught. He subsequently drew on this experience for inspiration on other missions—both for himself as well as for others. Several times I heard him refer to the circumstances of this search in motivating rescuers not to give up.

An especially inspiring mission was the search for Polly. After his team picked her up in the helicopter, Kevin was elated. He explained how his emotions affected him for the next few days as he relived the experience in his mind:

> You just felt good inside. You just had a smile, and a bunch of emotions that played with it. Played with it like, "I can't believe we found her; I can't believe she was alive; I can't believe there was 100 people involved in this mission; I can't believe it was five days!" So all those things play through, and you smile for the next couple of days. And then people [community members] come up and say, "They found her!" and you say, "Yeah, isn't that cool? Isn't that great?" We didn't give up, we were gonna follow it through. Whatever the conclusion might be, we were gonna follow it through. This was certainly the conclusion everybody was hoping for. I still smile about that. It's one of those ones—it's kind of a Ripley's Believe-it-or-Not!

Kevin also described the lesson he took away from that search, as well as how it continued to inspire him:

> [Beating the odds like we did with Polly] is the reason that you never give up. Because when you start to think that there is no way, and it turns out to be "[yes] way!"—that sustains you in other missions. It really does play into helping you get through the long nights of drudging in the rain, and no sleep, and [thoughts of] "I wish I had something warm to eat." It really helps you through because you know that even as hopeless as it is appearing, it's not without hope. You don't give up hope until the conclusion is determined.

Kevin was able to draw on his experience to manage his own emotions during difficult times; he was able to keep performing despite the temptation to give up.

Finally, rescuers used these inspirational stories to understand themselves. Oliver provided a good example when he described his most memorable rescue:

> I think probably the most amazing rescue to me was where we went out to [the cave]. This father and his two kids [ages seven and nine] had been in the cave all day. They had gone in with a flashlight, and they got lost in there. So they went to the back of the cave, and they sat there, and he [the dad] turned the flashlight off [to save the batteries]. And they were there from like 9:30 or 10 [in the morning] 'til we found 'em at 3:00 in the morning. And here these little kids sat in a pitch-dark cave the whole day. Can you imagine that? What that'd do to your psyche? You know, people lose their minds in situations like that. They don't have control. . . . I've been a caver for a lot of years, and I can turn the flashlight off for a while knowing that I can turn it back on, and still you don't see in front of your face. You don't see *nothin'*. You feel very much alone if you're in pitch darkness, even if your father and your brother's right there. You feel very much alone not being able to see them. For little kids not to freak out— that's so cool. . . . They just amazed the heck outta me, these kids. So that was rewarding. . . . And there again, that's a learning experience for me, because I thought, "Man, could I sit in the back of a cave for, like, 16 hours in the pitch darkness?" Gosh that amazed me. It amazes me to this day.

Oliver was able to use this experience to learn something about himself. He was inspired at this family's strength to endure what they did, and he was especially awed by the young boys' ability to do something he wondered if he himself could do.

8

Heroic Efforts

Throughout this book, we have explored the experiences of mountain-environment search and rescue volunteers. We examined members' motives for volunteering, their socialization to organizational norms, their participation on missions, their relationships with those they rescued, the gratitude they procured from victims, families, and the community, and the rewards they received. Several themes have run throughout the course of this study: heroism, the self and identity, emotions, gender, edgework, and relationships. Some of these themes intersect, and we turn now to analyze these intersections theoretically.

Heroism and Identity

Rescuers were granted heroic identities on two levels: they were awarded heroic group membership by insiders after conforming to Peak's rigid socialization demands, and they were labeled heroes by outsiders after successfully rescuing victims.

Heroic Socialization

When new recruits joined Peak, they confronted a series of stringent norms designed to socialize them to the heroic nature of the group. New rescuers had to conform to these norms along three dimensions: consciousness, resources, and commitment. Along each of these dimensions, rescuers moved through two membership stages as they shifted in status from new to peripheral member (mastering the self-oriented norms) and from peripheral to core member (mastering the group-oriented norms). Those who achieved core status along all three dimensions were not compensated with tangible rewards, and thus they appeared to receive nothing in return. Their behavior completely conformed to group-oriented norms, making them seem selflessly devoted to the group. Yet they were indeed rewarded individually for their conformity: they were granted individual heroic status and heroic group membership.

The symbolic reward of heroism operated in two distinct ways. First, core members sacrificed their own needs in the name of helping others, and they were gratified by this; living up to heroic norms made them feel like heroes. Second, they were considered integral to the group's functioning and became the bearers of its prestigious identity; achieving group-affiliated status made them appear as heroes to others. In these ways, the esteem gained from developing such a selfless identity was ironically self-gratifying. As a result, rescuers actively sought this esteem by adhering closely to Peak's norms.

For outsiders, the lure of this esteem made membership desirable. They wanted to associate themselves with the group so that they too could be viewed in a heroic light.[1] The group's voluntary nature, however, could endanger its prestige. Indiscriminately granting heroic status to anyone who volunteered could dilute the prestige of membership, so Peak conferred esteem only on select members who were considered above average—those who worked diligently to do what was necessary to move from peripheral to core membership within the three dimensions. This dynamic gave rise to a demanding socialization process that preserved the eliteness of core membership.

Organizational socialization often occurs in stages; several scholars have suggested models delineating them.[2] Wanous (1992) integrated several previous approaches into a comprehensive, four-stage model. In the first stage, newcomers confront the reality of the organization by having their preconceptions confirmed or disconfirmed; in Stage 2 they are introduced to their role and learn what is expected of them. In Stage 3 members conform to the organization's norms and adopt its ideology, and in Stage 4 they develop commitment to the organization and detect "signposts," or signals, of acceptance. This model, as well as the others it incorporates, asserts a fixed, linear progression through the stages, with the assumption that members' socialization (for example, learning role expectations or developing commitment) always occurs in the same order.

My research challenges this assumption of linearity by suggesting, at least for some organizations, a layered model that conceptualizes membership on several dimensions simultaneously. Like others, my model emphasizes the crucial dimensions of membership: consciousness (or ideology), resources (or role performance), and commitment. Unlike the existing stage models, however, the findings based on my research suggest that members can conform within these three socialization dimensions at different rates, thus occupying several stages at one time. For example, a rescuer may have mastered the norm of managing group skill (and therefore may be a core member along the "resources" dimension), but still may not willingly accept mundane roles on missions (thus maintaining only peripheral status along the "consciousness" dimension). The layered model allows these three dimensions of members' socialization to function independently of each other, making it a more flexible, more precise tool in assessing organizational membership. It helps to illuminate the complexity of organizational socialization processes and pinpoints the difficulties that aspiring members experience while trying to conform to group norms.

One reason that my model may differ from others is that the existing models of organizational socialization derive almost exclusively from research on organizations that control members with material rewards— "utilitarian" organizations (Etzioni 1964)—such as workplace environments, or medical and business schools.[3] These models have also sporadically drawn on research from organizations that control members through force—"coercive" organizations (Etzioni 1964)—such as Goffman's (1961a) study of total institutions and Irwin's (1970) work on prisons; however, these organizational types are underrepresented in the models of organizational socialization. Organizations that control members with symbolic rewards—"normative" organizations (Etzioni 1964)—such as the utopian communities studied by Kanter (1968), have been incorporated into the theoretical models even less frequently, and thus are the most underrepresented of the three organizational types. Although the existing literature has illuminated many of the theoretical dimensions and processes of organizational socialization, the models that have emerged are limited by a narrow focus on organizations that provide members with material rewards.

It is possible that the type of organizational control used to gain members' compliance significantly influences how these groups manage the tension between individual and group interests. The intricate demands of voluntary heroism—a symbolic reward—may explain why I found this layered model to be operating in Peak, a normative organization. By requiring rescuers to move along three dimensions of conformity instead of one, the group held core membership as highly elusive and thus maintained its elite status. This more demanding socialization process may be related to the symbolic nature of Peak's membership rewards; it may be that such rewards are manipulated more easily than material rewards. The value of material rewards offered by utilitarian organizations is relatively fixed: money, for example, cannot be made more valuable than it is. Symbolic rewards, however, can be increased in value and then used to induce desired behavior. By examining how Peak enhanced the prestige of membership through exclusively granting symbolic rewards, we expand our understanding of organizational socialization. My research indicates that the type of control used in organizations influences socialization processes and may produce configurations that differ significantly from existing theoretical models.

A second contribution of the stage model presented in this study is that the membership norms were progressive, focusing first on the self, and then on the group. This suggests a sequence of socialization from self-interest to collective interest. Hewitt (1989) discussed the relationship between self-interested individualism (which he called "autonomy") and self-sacrificing collectivism (which he called "exclusivity"), positing that the "meaning system" that surrounds each of these values places them in opposition to each other. These "axes of variation" create an inherent tension in American society, guiding individuals to simultaneously pursue these highly valued but contradictory interests.[4] To construct a self in accordance with only one of these axes is overdemanding and impractical. Most Americans, Hewitt contended, construct their self through "pragmatic compromise," choosing to emphasize some aspects of identity through community membership and other aspects as individuals. Pragmatic compromise allows individuals to construct a "personal meaning system" in which they selectively identify with features from each realm: the self becomes autonomous, and yet is anchored in a community.

Pillsbury (1998), in his study of college basketball players' choice of pronoun use, extended Hewitt's conception of pragmatic compromise by offering four specific strategies for self-construction. The players, through referring to themselves inconsistently as "I," "we," and "you," actively negotiated the tension created by the opposing forces of individualism and team membership. In this way, they constructed a self through pragmatic compromise, giving priority to autonomy at some times and to teamwork at others. Pillsbury demonstrated how individuals balanced individualism and collectivism in a specific organizational context, namely college basketball teams. My research with Peak takes a slightly different tack: I examine how the organization's norms aided members in achieving that balance. As a result, I uncover a unique process of self-construction, previously unidentified by Hewitt or Pillsbury.

Peak's norms created an organizational structure that did not present individualism and collectivism as opposing forces, but rather created an opportunity to *resolve* the tension between self-interest and self-sacrifice by allowing them to build on each other. First, members were required to be self-oriented; second, to be group-oriented. Only after achieving group orientation within all three membership dimensions were they rewarded with a prestigious individual status—the esteem they gained by being so collectively oriented. There was no need for the "pragmatic compromise" described by Hewitt; rescuers could achieve the best of both realms simply by adhering strictly to Peak's organizational norms. The group and the community recognized them as selflessly devoted communitarians, and for that they were recognized as exceptional individuals.

This dynamic may be explained by the meaning system created by Peak's norms—one built around the symbolic idea of heroism. Heroism, as a construct, encapsulates both individual and collective interests. In his cross-cultural synthesis of heroic myths, Campbell (1968:30) characterized "separation, initiation, and return" as the universal path to becoming a hero. Mythic heroes leave their homes and embark on journeys, where they encounter obstacles that test their individual fortitude. Their journeys are explorations of the self: the heroes develop on their own and become something more than they were. They return home with "the power to bestow boons on [their] fellow man." This theme is reflected in Peak's norms: heroes must develop fully as individuals before they can be empowered to help others. Goode (1978:345) also suggested that heroism hinges on this relationship between individual and group—that it symbolically "represents an *extreme conformity with the ideal of putting group interests ahead of one's own*" (emphasis added). Goode, however, pushed this relationship further by revealing the underlying paradox of heroism, that subsuming the self to the group results in exalted individual status. The norms prevailing in Peak socialized members to do just this. In the final stages of socialization, members were required to place the group's interests ahead of their own, and then were rewarded with a prestigious individual status. Goode offered a functional explanation for this paradox, reasoning that such prestige is the only way to "persuade" individuals to put the group's interests first.

Though Goode's work comprehensively theorized the cultural foundations of American heroism, it seems to miss some subtleties that microlevel analyses are more likely to illuminate. For instance, my research demonstrates how social actors created and sustained a particular definition of heroism by subscribing to Peak's organizational norms, which then guided their future action and interpretation. By focusing on these actors' construction of heroic membership, we can reach a deeper level of understanding than given by Goode's analysis. This focus reveals not only how heroic status was used as an incentive for conformity, but also how the underlying meaning of heroism was instrumental in this process.

My research shows that Peak defined the reward of heroism in such a way that it symbolically promised to resolve the tension between individual and group interests. This discovery suggests that this symbolic reward—the reconciliation of the opposing values of individualism and collectivism—may hold great power in American culture. Specifically, it may operate in similar heroic environments, such as fire fighting, police work, ambulance work, and the military, where, although workers are paid to undertake a substantial amount of risk, they are also given the opportunity to be heroes: to go beyond the call of duty by voluntarily putting themselves in extreme danger to help others.

The Heroic Label

Many victims, families, and community members regularly labeled the rescuers heroes in their thank-you letters to the group, basing their claims on very limited interaction with them. Letter writers often recounted the events of the mission by highlighting the heroic nature of rescuers' actions, and then assigned them heroic identities based on these actions. Becker (1963) noted how important others' reactions are in constructing identity, and Mullaney (1999), building on Becker's work, theorized that the concepts of "doing" and "being" are often easily confounded when attributing identities to individuals. She asserted that different features of an "act" determine its "social weight" in identity attribution, such that the more weight an act carries, the more likely others are to perceive it as representative of the actor's identity.

One feature of an act that determines its social weight—how much it "counts" toward identity attribution—is the *frequency* with which it is performed. The more often someone performs an act, the more likely others are to attribute the characteristics of the act to that actor's identity. For example, one person may be labeled a "runner" because she runs five days a week; another may not be considered a runner because she only runs a few times a year.

A second important factor in determining the social weight of an act is what Mullaney called *markedness*, or how much an act deviates from the norm. The less normative an act, the more weight it carries in identity attribution: "We assume that, since 'everyone' is *not* doing these things, they must indicate something important about who the person (or group) *really* is" (Mullaney 1999:272; emphasis in original). When acts are highly marked, or out of the ordinary, it may only take a one-time performance to have it weigh heavily on the actor's identity. For example, if someone were to start a bar fight, he might be immediately labeled a "trouble-maker" and banned from the bar.

A third important factor in weighing an act, according to Mullaney, is the *context* in which it is performed. Different situations can cause different meanings to be assigned to an act, and thus each contextual meaning carries with it a different social weight. For example, the act of killing carries various social weights as our legal system punishes killers to different degrees: someone who spontaneously commits homicide in self-defense is less likely to be labeled a killer than someone who preplans and carries out a cold-blooded murder.

Mullaney's theory may explain the heavy social weight given to rescuers' heroic acts, and thus victims', families', and the community's propensity to assign them heroic identities. First, although victims, families, and community members may have only observed one rescue, they were aware that rescuers performed these acts on a regular basis (increasing the "frequency" dimension), which may have added to the social weight they accorded to rescuers' actions. Second, rescuers' heroic behavior was markedly different from everyday behavior, leading victims and families to characterize it as exemplary and assign it more weight in the identity attribution process. Indeed, scholars have asserted that heroic acts, by definition, are exceptionally different from everyday acts, which suggests, in light of Mullaney's theory, that such acts may carry extreme social weight in identity attribution.[5] Third, some of these heroic acts may have been accorded more social weight because they were performed in life-and-death contexts; rescuers were not just helping others, they were risking their own lives to do so.

Given that some acts "count" more toward identity attribution than others, and given that cultural definitions of heroism tend to carry much social weight in the markedness and context categories, my research suggests that those who perform heroic acts, even if they are few and far between, are likely to be quickly attributed heroic identities by others. That these inherent features of heroism lend themselves to a great deal of social weight may explain why heroic identities cannot be self-proclaimed, but rather must be granted by others.

Although Mullaney's theory is useful in understanding the link between heroic actions and heroic identity attribution, it is unable to explain why families did not write letters or label rescuers heroes when their loved ones were killed. According to the theory, rescuers' actions should have been accorded very nearly the same weight for several reasons: the frequency dimension was scarcely affected by any one rescue since this group was well established and had performed hundreds of missions in the past; the members engaged in the same types of "markedly different" actions whether victims survived or died; and the contexts, or the "how," of the acts were comparable in each case—rescuers risked their lives to save a victim regardless of that victim's fate. What my research suggests, which Mullaney's theory overlooks, is that the *consequences* of an act are a significant factor in identity attribution. Overwhelmingly, families wrote rescuers and labeled them heroes only when they saved their loved ones' lives. Becker (1963) noted a similar phenomenon when he suggested that it is the reaction of others that sets the deviant labeling process into motion— a reaction that can vary depending on the consequences of the deviant act. My research with Peak suggests that, at least in some cases, identity attribution is largely dependent on the consequences of the act.

This finding has implications for professional emergency workers and military personnel who may or may not be labeled heroes after risking their lives to help others. If, as my research suggests, those who sacrifice their own well-being to help others are only accorded the status of "hero" in the event of a "save," unsuccessful heroic attempts to help others may fail to allow risk takers to consider their actions heroic. Thus, the would-be hero may become demoralized as well as unmotivated to assume risk in the future.

Crisis and Emotional Culture

Critical and dangerous missions threatened to produce disastrous emotional responses in rescuers, victims, and their families. As a result, rescuers' beliefs about how emotions operate under these intense circumstances became important factors in how they managed their own emotions as well as those of the victims and families they helped.

Gendered Edgework

Rescuers' own emotions were an important part of performing edgework during missions. There were four stages of edgework that were marked not only by the flow of rescue events but also by the corresponding emotions they evoked. Rescuers risked both their physical and emotional well-being before, during, and after the missions, and maintaining a sense of order was a key concern in each stage. Because each of these four stages was characterized by different emotions that threatened their sense of order, members utilized several types of emotion management strategies as they prepared for, performed on, exceeded, and redefined the edge. Moreover, these feelings and management techniques varied by gender. The men in the group tended to feel confident and excited on critical missions and to display emotional stoicism at negative outcomes. Conversely, the women tended to feel trepidacious and fearful on the critical missions and to express their upset feelings in their aftermath. Thus, the dynamics of edgework, emotions, and gender converged to create the distinct model of emotional culture presented in this book.

The emotions Peak's members experienced during certain stages of a mission, as well as the consequences of those emotions, prompted rescuers to recognize their importance and to attach meaning to them. Members developed beliefs about which emotions were useful or appropriate in each stage, and constructed norms to help them achieve these desired emotional states. For example, they believed that emotions such as uncertainty, urgency, fear, upset, vulnerability, and guilt were undesirable because these powerful feelings were potentially disruptive; they could interfere with members' performance, causing them to sacrifice the efficiency of the mission as well as the safety of other rescuers and the victims. Working off this assumption—that during missions all emotions were dangerous obstacles that needed to be overcome—Peak's members constructed an emotional culture that prioritized suppressing all emotions while on missions and releasing them only after the crisis ended.

The belief that negative emotions are undesirable and should be suppressed is not unique to Peak. Stearns (1994) examined this idea in detail in his historical analysis of emotional culture in middle-class America.

During the last 100 years, there has been a strong trend toward remaining emotionally "cool" in social interactions, and doing so is believed to be evidence of superior self-control. The worth of "negative" emotions such as anger, guilt, jealousy, fear, and grief has declined sharply, and thus the cultural directive to suppress them has become increasingly strong. Maintaining emotional cool is especially important when interacting with others; thus, suppressing negative feelings generally occurs in the public realm. However, these negative emotions have not lost their potency; in fact, expressing them is now perceived to be more socially disruptive than it was in the Victorian era. Furthermore, present-day American emotional culture fosters the belief that when individuals suppress these intense emotions, the emotions become bottled up and subsequently need to be released. Culture mandates that individuals release these negative feelings in private. Stearns (1994) called this suppression-release pattern a "ventilating" model of emotional culture. Irvine (1999) termed this model "hydraulic," giving empirical support for the cultural belief that emotions must be released or "dealt with," otherwise they have the power to come bursting out in unpredictable ways.

These assumptions in American emotional culture clearly influenced Peak's members, as they used them to construct and understand their edgework experiences. Members who could successfully suppress their negative feelings and remain cool during the most demanding situations demonstrated extraordinary self-control and were thus considered the best rescuers. Members also believed there was a need to ventilate these feelings after missions. They spoke of "unwinding," as well as releasing the "tension" and "pent-up stress" they incurred from critical incidents. Thus, these larger cultural assumptions about how emotions work may explain why members' emotional experiences in unsuccessful missions yielded the management stage model presented here.

Furthermore, the concept of emotional cool is useful in understanding the connection between emotions and edgework, a link that has not yet been explored. Although edgeworkers are drawn to high-risk activity by the emotional highs they experience, and although edgeworkers share beliefs about what emotions are desirable and why, little consideration has been given to what appears to be the prominent emotional culture of edgework.

My research reveals the integral part that emotional suppression, or emotional cool, plays in performing edgework. By extension, then, edgework can be considered a strict application of the tenets of emotional cool.

Edgework challenges individuals' ability to maintain self-control by evoking intense, life-threatening emotions that *must* be suppressed. Failing this, the consequences are dire. Thus, it appears that edgework operates as the ultimate test of emotional cool—a test that gives edgeworkers the opportunity to live up to cultural ideals regarding emotional expression.

Yet Peak's tendency to epitomize emotional cool does not explain the two gendered models of emotion management that emerged from my research. Peak's women and men shared the belief in the "hydraulic" model of emotional culture, agreeing on the potentially disruptive nature of emotions as well as on the corresponding need to suppress them and remain cool during crises. They also agreed on the need to privately ventilate these pent-up feelings after crisis situations. However, they differed in the steps they took to bring themselves in line with these cultural beliefs. The abstract assumptions about emotions were shared, but the norms instituted to achieve them differed along gender lines.

These two ways of accomplishing edgework constitute two distinct "emotion lines," which Hochschild called a "series of emotional reactions [resulting from] . . . a series of instigating events" (1990:123). For example, women and men in Peak tended to interpret missions' "instigating events" differently, which set off a chain of feelings and management techniques unique to each gendered emotion line. The masculine emotion line was constructed around the interpretation of edgework as exciting. The men in the group were confident in their abilities even before they knew what a mission might require of them, and they held the belief that the more demanding the mission, the better. They looked forward to being challenged by very difficult situations, and their vocabulary reflected this as they referred affectionately to these situations as on the verge of "going to shit" and to themselves as being "put in the hot seat." They thrived on excitement during the missions, interpreting their heightened arousal as urgency, and continued to expect that they would succeed. When missions ended unfavorably, they did not release the built-up tension all at once, but let it leak out slowly, referring to it with telling metaphors such as "unwinding." Later, they neutralized their failure with emotional "justifying ideologies" (Cancian and Gordon 1988) which helped them maintain a positive self-image. Thus, it appears that the men approached and engaged in edgework with positive feelings (perhaps already suppressing negative feelings), and in the event of failure, released these pent-up emotions slowly; they followed an "excitement/slow leak" emotion line of failed edgework.

The feminine emotion line was based on the idea of edgework as anxiety producing. Peak's women tended to be unsure of their ability to engage in edgework and were anxious in anticipation of many physically and emotionally challenging situations. They openly questioned their potential for physical competence and emotional self-control. During critical missions, they remained anxious, often interpreting their heightened arousal as fear and constantly worrying that they might fail. When missions ended unfavorably, they released their emotions abruptly by bursting into tears. They later used emotional justifying ideologies, like the men did, to reconceptualize their actions, which neutralized potentially damaging definitions of the self. Thus it appears that the women in the group enacted an "anxiety/outburst" emotion line of failed edgework.

These separate gendered emotion lines, however, were not equally respected ways of enacting edgework. In fact, the distinction between the two stratified the group members, creating a hierarchy of emotional competence for edgework, with men at the top. When members evaluated the gendered ways of preparing for and enacting edgework, both men and women recognized the superiority of masculine "excitement" over feminine "anxiety." Although most women reported managing their anxiety in a relatively effective way (i.e., they were able to perform edgework competently), they viewed themselves as "emotional deviants" (Thoits 1990) when it came to the first two stages: preparing for and acting in crisis.

Thoits (1990) hypothesized that people who are marginalized in a subculture may recognize their own emotional deviance more frequently than nonmarginal members because their own emotions often conflict with those dominant in the subculture. By virtue of their fringe status, marginal subcultural members might, for example, feel pulled between two different emotional subcultures: the one in which they are marginal, and another with different norms and values, in which they better fit. The women in Peak accepted their status as emotional deviants. They rarely challenged the low expectations others had for them and often held low expectations for themselves, generally believing that their feelings and management techniques were inferior to men's. They readily admitted that they might not be able to handle the emotional demands of a mission, often deferring to others, usually men, who outwardly displayed no reservations about entering potentially challenging, upsetting, or gruesome situations. Clark suggested that when it comes to emotions and status, "[h]aving no place, or feeling 'out of place,' can be more painful even than having an inferior place" (1990:314). Thus, Peak's women validated their membership by volunteering to do less challenging tasks. In this way, they used inferior "place claims" (Clark 1990) to accept and reinforce their emotional place—subordinate though it was—in Peak's missions.

In the period after the missions, however, Peak's women did not feel that their norm of "outburst" was inferior to men's "slow leak" method of ventilating emotions. In fact, they viewed their method as superior to men's and disparaged the "slow leak" norm, because they believed that it caused negative emotions to become trapped and to fester. In this way women made superior place claims in the group, insisting that the men were too constrained by strict gender roles to display their negative feelings through an emotional outburst. Yet women's superior emotional place claims went unacknowledged. Peak's men did not accept an inferior status when it came to their slow leak method of releasing emotions. They paid no attention to the women's denigration of their management technique, and thus ignored the women's place claim to superiority in the emotional ventilation arena. Thus, the third phase of edgework, releasing emotions, was contested gender terrain; both women and men vied for the right to define normative ventilation methods.

It is possible that many women in the group perceived their position as inferior when it came to accomplishing edgework because voluntary risk taking is a traditionally masculine domain.[6] After the danger had passed, however, when it came to dealing directly with emotions, women may have considered themselves the "emotional specialists." In her landmark study of a male-dominated corporation, Kanter (1977) identified this common stereotype of women, noting that both genders assumed women to be better equipped "naturally" to deal with emotional issues. More recently, other scholars have found evidence of this pervasive stereotype in more contemporary male-dominated settings as well, which suggests that specializing in emotional issues is still a core feature of "doing femininity" (West and Zimmerman 1987).[7] Given this powerful belief, on the one hand it is easy to see why Peak's women felt justified in asserting the superiority of their "outburst" norm; by the same token, however, it is interesting that women's place claims in the emotional realm were given little credibility by Peak's men.

One explanation for this phenomenon might be that norms of masculinity, including the norm of masculine emotional stoicism, were so strongly entrenched and intricately connected to the edgework subculture that it gave men the "means of emotional culture production" (Cancian and Gordon 1988): they controlled the standards by which edgeworkers were judged.[8] Furthermore, if emotions were the main avenue through which men distinguished themselves from women before, during, and after edgework, they may have felt that their appropriate gender performance—their very masculinity—would be threatened if they were to display emotions associated with a feminized edgework performance. This interpretation resonates with Connell's (1987) conception of "hegemonic masculinity," which is sustained because it dominates over other gendered forms, such as alternative masculinities held by gay men or nurturing fathers, and any kind of femininity.

My research shows that there can be contested emotional terrain within one emotional culture. Cancian and Gordon (1988), in their historical analysis of shifting love and anger norms in twentieth-century women's magazines, demonstrated emotional culture contradictions. Their work illustrated how the messages being sent to women helped define the acceptable dimensions of their emotions. At times the messages were consistent, at other times they were not. Although Cancian and Gordon's content analysis was extensive and thorough, it was unable to assess how individuals received these conflicting cultural messages. My research uncovers this aspect of an emotional culture. It shows how Peak's women evaluated themselves in terms of these discrepant cultural messages and how these self-interpretations guided their future action. In some cases they acted to resist their subordinate position, drawing from the larger emotional culture to bolster their claims to a more respected place in the group. In other cases they drew on gendered emotion norms to reinforce their subordinate status. Similarly, the men in the group accepted women's place claims in some cases, yet denied them in others. By examining how women and men reacted to gendered cultural messages about emotions, my research reveals how gender may be constructed selectively by relying on culturally specific (and occasionally contradictory) emotion norms.

These gendered emotional dynamics may be useful in understanding female edgeworkers' place in many high-risk realms. Women who engage in risky leisure—in male-dominated activities such as rock climbing, mountaineering, whitewater kayaking, skydiving, and adventure racing, to name a few—may face experiences similar to those of Peak's women. These gendered emotional dynamics are also likely to hold true in risky occupational settings, which also tend to be highly male dominated, such as emergency work and the military. While many women in high-risk leisure and occupations often experience marginalization because of their relative lack of physical strength, my research reveals that it also may be useful to understand how cultural ideas about emotions—gendered patterns and stereotypes—influence women's marginalization in such risky arenas.[9]

The Emotional Culture of Interpersonal Emotion Management

In addition to managing their own emotions on missions, rescuers had to control the feelings of the victims they rescued as well as those of the families awaiting news of a lost loved one. They achieved this emotional control by defining the situation, the norms, and the participants' roles either tightly or loosely. During crises, rescuers were helping victims and families manage more than just their emotions, however; they were helping them manage their selves. When victims and families suppressed, transformed, or expressed their feelings, they managed not only their emotions per se, but more broadly, their "self-in-emotion" (Hochschild 1983). Both victims and families demonstrated that they could evoke a self in control by bringing their emotions into line with the norms rescuers dictated and the roles they required them to enact. Kotarba (1984:226) claimed that the self is constantly being "actualized only through social roles that must be shaped and even created to meet the needs that emerge as the self confronts itself." Victims and families experienced a newly constructed sense of self, then, by trying to meet those emerging needs—victims did it by suppressing and transforming their feelings; families did it by identifying, analyzing, expressing, and transforming them. By helping victims and families manage their own emotions, rescuers played an important part in helping them do "identity work" (Snow and Anderson 1987), or construct this new sense of self. This idea coincides with some of the basic premises of sociology (the self is developed in relation to others' reactions), and is a theoretical proposition that has been supported by the literature on interpersonal emotion management (others can help you develop your self-image by helping you manage your emotions).[10]

Furthermore, rescuers may have helped victims and families construct a particularly momentous and lasting sense of self because they were in crisis situations. Douglas (1984:77–78) suggested that physical and emotional crises may threaten individuals' "inner sense of self" and, to different degrees, threaten to disrupt and disorient the person, depending on the severity of the crisis. He offered an extreme example in which the individual is confronted with a fear of death:

The dread of death is one of man's most powerful and overriding emotions . . . because . . . this dread of the destruction of the self would override and sweep away all of our everyday concerns and programs, producing a panicky disorientation and disruption—a paralysis—of everyday life. . . . But any degree of dread of death . . . is enough to produce an extreme degree of self-awareness and self-examination, and these commonly lead to attempts to escape, to escapism, or to mourning for the self and to some effort to reconstruct the self, which decreases the dread.

To adapt under this threat to their selves, people become highly self-aware and may redefine their selves during crises. Suttles commented on a similar phenomenon, noting that highly "engrossing activity," such as mountaineering, can be appealing because it helps us experience a novel self; it provides us with an opportunity for "re-creation" (in Mitchell 1983:ix). Thus, it seems plausible that rescuers played a part in helping victims and families reconstruct their selves during these crisis situations by helping them manage their threatening and disruptive emotions.

One significant finding from my research is that victims' crisis experiences were distinct from those of families, which resulted in the two groups experiencing different emotions and using different management techniques (with rescuers' help) that influenced how they constructed their selves. Victims' selves were predicated on adhering closely to a narrow definition of the situation, enacting a specific role, and controlling their emotions—strategies that helped them physically survive the crisis. Families' selves were predicated on accepting several definitions of the situation, experiencing their brute feelings associated with them, and expressing their emotions—strategies that helped them emotionally survive the crisis.

That people may construct their selves within varying frameworks is not a new idea. Turner (1976) contended that when people rely on "institutional" anchors in conceiving of their selves, they adhere closely to the norms and roles inherent in the social structure. Other people may consider institutional anchors to be stifling to their idea of who they are, and choose to rely on their own desires, motivations, and urges—or an "impulsive" framework—to define their selves. Zurcher (1977) extended these ideas, positing that people may also develop the ability to regularly shift between realms when environmental conditions warrant, thereby controlling in which framework they anchor their selves. Zurcher termed this adaptability the "mutable self."

Gordon (1989) advanced these ideas, and using Turner's institutional/impulsive dichotomy, showed how people's interpretations of their emotions can provide the basis for self-construction in one realm or the other. People who hold an "institutional" emotional orientation restrain intense feelings so that they do not disrupt the social order, despite feelings and urges to the contrary. In this way, they use their emotions to uphold social convention and conform closely to institutional roles and norms. People who construct their selves within an "impulsive" emotional orientation remain unrestrained and express their immediate feelings. In this way, they use their emotions to defy social structure and yield to their urges.

My research shows that distinct situational conditions—rescues and searches—created a similar division of self-construction and emotional patterns for victims and families. By maintaining a great deal of emotional restraint, victims constructed their selves within an institutional framework. They developed highly efficacious, survivor identities by denying their problematic feelings and controlling their emotions in order to effect their own rescue. Families, on the other hand, who were in a different, more ambiguous situation, constructed their selves within an impulsive framework by expressing their emotions. When they survived their emotionally distressing experience (especially in cases where their loved one survived too), they realized they had shown incredible emotional strength. Depending on the severity of the situation, these accomplishments could impact victims' and families' identities in particularly significant and lasting ways, as it did for some who said their lives were changed as a result. It is interesting that the situations the victims and families were in warranted different types of self-construction, suggesting, as Zurcher does, that because social circumstances vary, the self must be mutable, able to adapt to changing environmental conditions.

My research, however, goes beyond these conceptualizations to show that, through manipulating individuals' emotions, others can control the realm of their self-definition. When rescuers tightly managed victims' emotions, they were the ones who demanded that victims emotionally control themselves and deny their problematic feelings. By doing so, rescuers imposed an institutional emotional orientation on victims, forcing them to adopt a specific role in the rescue as well as to interpret their emotions—and experience an unprecedented but crucial sense of self—within this framework. In loosely guiding families' emotions, rescuers imposed an impulsive emotional orientation on them, forcing them to construct an unprecedented but crucial sense of self around experiencing their brute feelings associated with several potential realities. By demonstrating how rescuers managed victims' and families' emotions to help them articulate a positive sense of self under these distinct but intense circumstances, my research illuminates how others can set the interpretive rules for self-construction, an aspect of emotional culture that has been previously unexplored.

Emotions and Relationships

In performing interpersonal emotion management for victims and families, rescuers formed intensely intimate bonds with them during the ordeal. Afterward, victims and families repaid rescuers with different forms of gratitude and, in some cases, tried to extend the bond they had formed during the crisis by pursuing a relationship with rescuers.

Exclusively Validating Interactions

The important role that rescuers played in helping victims and families experience an unprecedented and crucial sense of self may also explain why rescuers developed such quick and intensely intimate bonds with victims and families, another interesting finding of my research. Many scholars agree that intimacy is formed when people think another truly knows them.[11] Victims and families met this criteria: they experienced particularly novel selves through rescuers' help and deep involvement in their emotional experiences. Perhaps victims and families felt that rescuers truly knew them because rescuers were the ones who helped them construct and validate this novel, unprecedented self. Yet victims and families were also *dependent* on rescuers for developing this newly constructed definition of self, perhaps so dependent that this novel self could not be evoked outside of their relationship with rescuers. It might be said, then, that victims and families experienced an *exclusively validating interaction* with rescuers. These unprecedented, crucial selves were selves that were constructed and corroborated only through their intense interaction with specific others.

It seems that the concept of an exclusively validating interaction might be similar to intimacy development processes because in both cases the self is intimately known by another. Yet my conception of an exclusively validating interaction differs in that it targets those aspects of the self that can *only* be constructed through an intense interaction with another. Intimacy can be achieved by having another understand and validate the self, but establishing intimacy with another does not necessarily construct an unprecedented self.

Furthermore, the literature on intimacy development tends to conceptualize the process within an impulsive emotional orientation. Much of this work specifies the importance of emotional revelation, a feature of impulsive emotional orientation, in becoming closer to another.[12] Other literature asserts that people form intimate bonds when they deviate from the norms of propriety and find acceptance from others, despite their deviation; in other words, when they adhere to impulsive emotional orientations by engaging in unrestrained action that deviates from institutional norms.[13]

These conceptualizations are unable to explain how intimate bonds may develop from an encounter in which the participants define their self, and thus share it with others, within an institutional emotional orientation: by adhering quite closely to institutional norms. My research demonstrates that the self can be constructed from both an impulsive and an institutional self-orientation, thus it more broadly captures these distinctive ways of forming intimate bonds with others.

Socioemotional Exchanges

Another interesting feature of rescuers' relationships with victims and families was that the newly and quickly formed intimate relationships tended to persist when the victims survived, yet were terminated when the victims were found dead. Clark's (1997) conceptualization of the "socioemotional economy" may be useful in explaining this pattern.

Clark based her conceptual development of the socioemotional economy on Hochschild's (1989) idea of the "economy of gratitude," in which she showed how the wives and husbands she studied were happiest when they exchanged gratitude for acts intended to benefit the other. Clark (1997) broadened Hochschild's notion of gratitude exchange to encompass the social exchange of a variety of different emotional resources. She specifically examined sympathy as an important emotional resource that is exchanged between people. When we give sympathy to others it connects us in profound ways because we are indicating that we care about their problems. By accepting our sympathy, others indicate that they appreciate our concern. In this way, we give and take emotions, like sympathy and gratitude, as part of a social exchange, and we build relationships with others, in part, based on this ongoing exchange of emotions. Clark further elaborated on this economic model, showing how people can build up lines of "credit" by giving more emotional resources (like sympathy, love, attention, esteem) than they have received, and likewise, people can build up "debt" by accepting more than they have given. These exchange principles correspond with those in other social-psychological theories on relationships, such as distributive justice, reciprocity, and equity theory, yet Clark's work uniquely illuminates how emotions can operate as the medium of social exchange.[14]

Rescuers engaged in socioemotional exchanges with both victims and families, yet the reciprocity norms varied depending on the outcome of the missions. It appeared that when victims were found dead, socioemotional norms dictated that the families' emotional grief and bad fortune far outweighed the emotional support the rescuers had provided during the missions. Rescuers owed the family members sympathy for their misfortune, which is consistent with Clark's analysis of sympathy in the socioemotional economy. They offered up their sympathies in fairly formal ways that indicated they were merely acquaintances, and the relationship was terminated. (Recall when Meg noted how the negative outcome of a mission moved families' relationships with rescuers from ambivalence to certainty: "It's time for them to move on . . . to a reality of death, but when you're working with them, you're in that gray area.")

Families did not pursue the relationship either, perhaps because the rescuers symbolized the death of their loved one—an emotionally traumatic event they would rather not relive. Families disengaged from the intimate relationships they had developed with rescuers, returned to the normative structure of their everyday lives, and probably received ongoing emotional support from close friends and family at home.

Clark's idea of the socioemotional economy can also explain the outcome of the successful missions. When victims emerged from the missions safely, they and their families were overwhelmingly grateful to rescuers—not only for saving the victims' lives but also for providing them with the emotional goods they needed to get through the ordeal: caring, empathy, and sympathy. Victims and families had survived the crisis and, because of rescuers' help, were able to return to their normal lives. Thus, socioemotional norms dictated that victims and families then owed the rescuers for their help, which they most often repaid with gratitude. They expressed their appreciation in the form of kind words and monetary donations that they themselves acknowledged as merely symbolic gestures of their deep gratitude. They also, in some cases, deepened the emotional exchange by intensifying their attachment to rescuers and sustaining the intimate bonds they had developed on missions.

Yet my research reveals another important sector of the socioemotional economy that has not been previously explored: the emotional *service* of interpersonal emotion management. Clark defined the socioemotional economy as the exchange of emotional *resources*: gratitude for sympathy, affection for esteem, distrust for insincerity. Yet these are exchanges of emotional *goods*. My research with Peak suggests that interpersonal emotion management—helping others manage their own emotions—plays an important role in the social exchange of emotional resources. Aside from thanking rescuers for their sympathy and caring, victims and families also thanked them for helping them control their feelings. At times, rescuers performed this service in conjunction with offering emotional goods, such as when they comforted crying family members while also helping them maintain hope. Other times, interpersonal emotion management seemed to operate as an emotional service independent of emotional goods, such as when rescuers demanded specific emotional reactions from critically injured victims to prevent them from going into shock. It is further evident that interpersonal emotion management served this important role in the socioemotional economy because victims and families specifically thanked rescuers for it; it was a service worthy of repayment. By revealing how interpersonal emotion management can be the basis of exchange in interpersonal relationships, my research begins to map out the previously unexplored service sector of the socioemotional economy.

These findings may be useful in understanding emergency workers and volunteers' relationships with those they help during crisis situations. My research suggests that there are different ways that victims may be helped by strangers, and that these different forms of assistance have consequences for how victims come to understand their experiences, as well as for how they come to define their relationships with those who assisted them. Police officers and rape crisis workers, for example, may find different emotion management techniques more effective, depending on whether those they are trying to help are experiencing a physical or emotional crisis at the time. Furthermore, my research suggests that the helpers' involvement in the victims' or family members' emotions, and the resulting relationship formed during the crisis, may be important components in victims' and family members' postcrisis identities.

Heroism and Emotions

Throughout this study, we have explored several ways that emotions play an important role in the social construction of heroism. For example, in their thank-you letters to the group, victims and families labeled rescuers heroes while simultaneously noting that rescuers' emotions, such as compassion and sympathy, were instrumental in compelling them to help strangers. That these emotions are significant in motivating people to help others at their own expense is well documented by other research on altruism. For example, several scholars have demonstrated that empathy for another's plight leads people to help others, and Oliner and Oliner (1988) showed empathy, care, compassion, and concern for others to be major factors in explaining why non-Jews put their own lives at risk to rescue Jews in Nazi-occupied Europe.[15]

My research, however, differs from these accounts of altruism and heroism in that it shows that rescuers themselves rarely attributed their decision to become involved to these other-directed emotions. Instead, rescuers often described self-interested, nonemotional reasons as their main motivations to participate in Peak initially (such as acquiring skills and meeting people). In deciding to join, they often considered the benefits strangers would receive as an added bonus resulting from their participation. Conforming to group norms and gaining experience on critical missions, however, developed these other-directed feelings in rescuers. They began to understand, as Cyndi put it, "the point" of rescue work, and they learned to internalize their rewards, constructing them largely in emotional terms. In this way, rescuers were similar to Piliavin and Callero's (1991) sample of blood donors who progressively internalized their motivations throughout their donating careers, expecting and requiring less in the way of extrinsic rewards. Moreover, Piliavin and Callero demonstrated "that there is a link between the emotions felt during an experience and the development of a sense of self invested in that activity" (1991:195). My research supports this finding by showing that when Peak's rescuers internalized their rewards, they considered them not only part of their heroic selves, but also part of their emotional selves. Yet my research goes beyond this finding to show four specific ways that rescuers' rewarding emotions were considered to be positive reflections of their selves—selves that comprised, in part, their feelings of self-efficacy, their special bonds with others, their own moral achievements, and the inspirational lessons they learned.

The prestige and status the rescuers received through their participation in Peak also shows, in two ways, how emotions contribute to the social construction of heroism. First, others' admiration is an important emotional component in our cultural ideas of heroism because without social recognition, heroes cannot exist.[16] Thus, it was victims', families', and the community's *feelings* of admiration toward rescuers that made the latter's heroic status possible in the first place. Second, this type of esteem in the eyes of others made rescuers feel proud and admired, yet cultural emotion-norms dictated that they deny these feelings in order to sustain a humble, and thus properly heroic, emotional self-presentation.[17] Thus, members downplayed the status they had attained, conforming closely to the group's norm of self-denial—an important "feeling rule" (Hochschild 1983) to which most rescuers conformed, although sometimes with quite a bit of emotion management. These insights are significant because they show how these two emotions—admiration and humility—are both necessary and interdependent in constructing heroes.

Rescuers' superior emotional self-control during critical situations demonstrates a third way emotions are important in the social construction of heroism. Such tight control of their own emotions was the primary means through which rescuers were able to engage in edgework and thus perform heroic deeds. Victims' and families' thank-you letters to the group also highlighted these emotional features of rescuers' heroism during the missions, such as the courage and bravery they displayed in the face of danger. These features of heroism—courage and bravery—have been identified by other scholars, but despite the fact that these features are largely emotional, these previous conceptualizations stereotype heroes as emotionally stoic, implying that they avoid strong feelings altogether.[18] My research, however, reveals how potent emotions were evoked by critical incidents, how rescuers employed complex and skilled techniques to control them during missions, and how their surfacing feelings affected them after the heroic acts were attempted. These findings are significant because they uncover the emotion work that heroes engage in to achieve this end product: an emotionally stoic self-presentation. Some research on altruism in emergency situations tangentially deals with emotions, such as the absence of fear, for example when people run into burning buildings to save others without thinking of the danger to themselves.[19] Other altruism research carefully deals with the cognitive processes present in evaluating the costs and benefits of undertaking risk to help someone else.[20] Yet none of this literature focuses on the strong emotions that heroes must experience, at least in some of these cases, nor does it focus on the ways heroes deal with these feelings.[21]

Gendered patterns of emotion management reveal another way that emotions play a part in the social construction of heroism. Several scholars have noted that heroism is greatly or entirely a masculine domain because of the highly physical nature of many heroic activities, such as military and sport accomplishments.[22] However, my research suggests that the biggest impediment to women gaining heroic status in Peak was not physical, but rather emotional. Women were ostensibly given the same opportunities as men to perform physically demanding tasks; but when it came to controlling their emotions, women were stereotyped as weaker than men and thus less able to perform heroic duties. In addition, the tendency to assign women to stay with family members (because they were believed to be emotionally better suited to deal with them) resulted in women more often staying in the base than men, which provided women with less opportunity to perform physically heroic acts in the field. In Peak, beliefs about emotional capabilities contributed more to the masculine character of heroism than did beliefs about physical capabilities, which is an idea that has not been examined in the literature on heroism.

Peak's rescuers' ability to control victims' and families' emotions represents a final way that emotions play a part in the social construction of heroism. This type of interpersonal emotion management was an important way for rescuers to gain victims' and families' compliance, which allowed them to perform their heroic duties. Thus, it appears that definitions of heroism involve not only the ability to manage one's own emotions during crises but also the superior ability to pass along that emotional control to others in distress. This aspect of heroism has also been overlooked in the scholarly literature on heroism and altruism. It seems, however, that it would be a salient feature of both phenomena. For example, if much altruism is motivated by a desire to relieve others' suffering—to eradicate or reduce their painful emotions—then it stands to reason that interpersonal emotion management could play an important role in this process.[23] My research shows that it is indeed an imperative component of heroism, at least in some cases.

In these ways, my research with Peak Search and Rescue demonstrates the important role that emotions play in the social construction of heroism.

My findings suggest that it may be useful to consider emotions (including the suppression of them) for people who are routinely engaged in heroic activities, such as emergency workers, police officers, military personnel, and fire fighters. The emotional culture Peak's rescuers created to negotiate the physical, emotional, and social demands of heroism reveals that emotions are an integral part of the heroic experience, and that how heroes deal with these emotions can have significant consequences in their lives.

Notes

Notes to the Introduction

1. All names of people, places, and organizations are pseudonyms.

2. See Piliavin and Charng (1990) for a comprehensive review of the altruism literature.

3. See Kohn (1990), Oliner (2000), Oliner and Oliner (1988), and Piliavin et al. (1981) for examples. While these researchers study altruism, they have taken a special interest in delineating instances of altruism that pose great risk to helpers, such as running into a burning building to save a stranger.

4. Several scholars have theorized about the nature of heroism in society, most notably Campbell (1968), Edelstein (1996), Goode (1978), and Klapp (1962), but see also Adams (1987), Berkowitz (1987), Featherstone (1992), Morton and Conway (1977), and Swierczewski (1978).

5. For a discussion of the social function of heroes, see Edelstein (1996), Featherstone (1992), Goode (1978), and Klapp (1962).

6. See Klapp's (1962) descriptive survey of social types and Riemer's (1998) content analysis of "heroic suicide" for minor exceptions.

7. These ideas are couched in the theoretical tradition of symbolic interaction and are consistent with the ideas of the self first put forth by Cooley ([1902] 1964) and Mead (1934).

8. Schachter and Singer (1962) contended that emotions are not solely the result of physiology, but rather arise when people interpret these physiological reactions within a particular social context. Other scholars have examined particular emotions within historical and/or geographical context, such as love and anger (Cancian and Gordon 1988; Stearns 1994), jealousy and guilt (Stearns 1994), and sympathy (Clark 1997).

9. Gendered emotion norms and stereotypes have been examined by several scholars. For analysis of masculinity and emotions, see Connell (1987), Kimmel (1996), and Messner (1992). For discussion of primarily feminine emotion norms and stereotypes, see Cancian and Gordon (1988), Hochschild (1983), and Kanter (1977). For comparative gendered discussion, see Pierce (1995) and Stearns (1994).

10. Clifford (1995) published a journalistic account of his experiences with Mountain Rescue–Aspen.

11. For discussion of risk in the emergency medical field, see Mannon (1992), Metz (1981), Palmer (1983), and Palmer and Gonsoulin (1990). For the military, see Woodward (2000). For police work, see Hunt (1984), Martin (1980), and Van Maanen (1976b).

12. For discussion of risk in mountain climbing, see Mitchell (1983); in whitewater rafting, see Holyfield (1999) and Jonas (1999); for high ropes courses see Holyfield (1997) and Holyfield and Fine (1997).

13. Lyng borrows the term "edgework" from Hunter S. Thompson (1971).

14. Palmer (1983) termed many of the paramedics and EMTs he studied "trauma junkies," because they cast their need to experience these highs as similar to drug addicts' need for another hit.

15. For further discussion of adrenaline rush experiences during risky activity, see Lyng and Snow (1986), Mannon (1992), Metz (1981), Mitchell (1983), and Palmer (1983).

16. See Hunt (1984) and Martin (1980) for discussion of gender and police work. See Yoder and Aniakudo (1996, 1997) for discussion of African American women in professional fire fighting. See Campbell with D'Amico (1999), Miller (1997), Sadler (1999), and Williams (1989) for discussion of women in the military.

17. One of the interesting features of heroism, as I discuss in chapter 3, is that individuals cannot proclaim themselves heroes—it is not heroic to do so. The title must be granted socially by others. Although Peak's rescuers did not refer to themselves as heroes, I do so here because others labeled the rescuers as heroes. This happened frequently, for example in the local newspaper's headlines: "Rafter Saved after Heroic Efforts by Peak," or in thank-you letters sent to the group: "I thought I was going to die. You are all my heroes." Thus, while ethnographers generally do not refer to their subjects in terms the subjects themselves do not use, the term "hero" stands out as an exception to this rule.

18. This idea is prevalent in the theoretical literature on heroism. See Adams (1987), Berkowitz (1987), Edelstein (1996), Goode (1978), Morton and Conway (1977), Oliner (2000), and Riemer (1998).

19. See Edelstein (1996) for a summary of the Carnegie Hero Fund award qualifications. See Riemer (1998:106) for a summary of the Congressional Medal of Honor criteria.

20. See Perkins (1987), Perkins and Metz (1988), and Thompson (1993) for studies of the culture of volunteer fire fighters. See Riemer (1998) for the content analysis of the dedications that accompanied the award of the Congressional Medal of Honor. See Oliner and Oliner (1988) for a comprehensive examination of the factors compelling non-Jews to rescue Jews in Nazi-occupied Europe.

See Moran, Britton, and Correy (1992) for a pilot study of volunteer rescuers. The researchers conducted a small survey of State Emergency Services volunteers in Australia, who mostly responded to calls for search and rescue. They surveyed members' motivations for joining the service as well as the stress levels they experienced and the corresponding coping strategies they employed. While this study is the only one that exists on search and rescue volunteers, its authors caution that the data and analysis are preliminary. Although the questionnaires took between two and three hours to complete, the limited sample size (23 nonrepresentative respondents) did not allow the researchers to draw generalizable conclusions about search and rescue volunteers. Furthermore, due to the inherent limitations of survey designs, the researchers were not able to examine these issues—motivation, stress, and coping—in depth. Since this empirical setting is relatively untapped in the scholarly literature, a qualitative study on search and rescue volunteers—one that can gather a great deal of data, generate tentative theories, and suggest promising areas of theoretical interest—may be better suited to the exploratory nature of this topic. Empirically, my study fills this gap.

21. Because membership fluctuated over the course of six years, I am only able to estimate the number of members who possessed any trait at any given time.

NOTES TO CHAPTER 1

1. See Guba and Lincoln (1994) and Prus (1996) for detailed discussions of the ontological and epistemological issues in field research.

2. See Blumer (1969) and Glaser and Strauss (1967) for detailed discussions of the strengths and weaknesses of ethnographic research.

3. Blumer (1969), Lofland (1976), and Prus (1996) discuss similar issues relating to the generalizable aspects of ethnographic research.

4. Van Maanen (1991:40) contends that when researchers become "caught up in the same life situation and circumstances" as their subjects, they develop a rich and "empathetic" understanding of their subjects' lives.

5. See Jorgensen (1989) for a discussion of the benefits of the "everyday life" perspective.

6. Fine (1998:191) noted that this "tension exists between teaching and shunning a novice" in voluntary groups because it is risky to trust newcomers with sensitive, intragroup secrets. I later discovered additional reasons why rescuers were not friendly to newcomers, which I discuss in chapters 2 and 3.

7. Martin (1980) experienced some of the same feelings of apprehension when she joined a police force.

8. Jorgensen (1989) noted that team researchers' differing personality styles, like mine and Barbara's, can broaden rapport development.

9. Years later, after Elena and I became friends, she told me that she was so curt to me in the beginning because she had just spent a year trying to establish a place for herself in the group—an accomplishment that had taken so much work that she

felt her unstable place might be threatened if she became too allied with unproven newcomers. It is a common sociological observation that the newly initiated frequently become the most stringent gatekeepers, perhaps for this exact reason.

10. See Fine (1993), Goffman (1989), Shaffir (1991), and Wax (1971) for extensive discussion of fieldworkers' embarrassment and awkwardness in the early stages of research.

11. See Mannon (1992), Metz (1981), and Mitchell (1983) for similarly derisive terms connected with thrill-seekers' self-glorification.

12. Lofland and Lofland (1984) referred to this "persona" as the "socially acceptable incompetent." See Mitchell (1991) and Van Maanen (1991) for similar ideas.

13. See Wolf (1991) for a similar unfolding of events.

14. Gans (1968) and Lofland and Lofland (1984) also noticed that subjects often "forget" that the field researcher is studying them.

15. Similarly, Van Maanen (1991) and Hunt (1984) found that safety violations were one of the most severe mistakes police officers could make, resulting in a loss of status with their colleagues.

16. In this way, I went from an observer-as-participant (Gold 1958) to a complete member (Adler and Adler 1987).

17. See Fine (1993) for discussion of the myth of the "chaste ethnographer."

18. See Jorgensen (1989) for discussion of the benefits of the "native's" perspective in the field research setting.

19. Douglas (1976) detailed the benefits of team research techniques.

20. See Mannon (1992) for a description of a similar event in his research on ambulance workers.

21. Metz's (1981:126) ambulance workers were also more disturbed by the "emotional demonstrations of the survivors" than by the dead bodies themselves.

22. See Kleinman and Copp (1993) for discussion of emotions and researcher roles as they pertain to fieldwork.

23. Jorgensen (1989) and Lofland and Lofland (1984) noted that it is typical for field notes to become more focused as researchers' time in setting progresses and they become more selective with their observations.

24. Other fieldworkers have encountered similar problems, such as having to buy "professional," setting-appropriate clothes on a student's budget (see Griffin [1991] and Gurney [1991]).

25. See Adler and Adler (1991) for discussion of maintaining relations with different interest groups in the field.

26. See Adler and Adler (1987) for a comprehensive review of the pitfalls of different researcher roles.

27. Warren (1988) suggested that female fieldworkers are seen as "more open to emotional communication" than men. See Wax (1979) for similar ideas about gender and fieldwork.

28. Several female researchers have also encountered physicality and risk issues in highly masculine domains. See Altork's (1995) research on smoke jumpers, and Hunt's (1984) and Martin's (1980) research on the police.

29. Fine (1993) called this level of deception being under "shallow cover."

30. See Gallmeier (1991) for discussion about the emotions researchers feel when disengaging from a research setting.

31. After we moved, we continued to have contact with members of Peak. Gary has even considered joining the mountain search and rescue team in our new hometown. Thus, because we like these people (see Taylor 1991) and because we are likely to maintain "structured contact" (Stebbins 1991) with them through future search and rescue activity, it is likely that we will carry on personal and professional relationships with many of Peak's members for some time to come.

NOTES TO CHAPTER 2

1. See Cohen (1973), Porter, Lawler, and Hackman (1975), and Wanous (1992) for discussion of newcomers' expectations of and encounters with a new organization.

2. Roy's motives were not unique; competence in certain skill areas has been shown to be a motivator to join voluntary organizations (Thornton 1991) as well as to increase the likelihood that people will spontaneously help in situations where those skills are needed (e.g., Peterson 1983a,b).

3. Acquiring skills is a common joining-up motivation for other search and rescue volunteers (Moran, Britton, and Correy 1992) as well as for other voluntary group members such as mushroom collectors (Fine 1998).

4. The police recruits Van Maanen (1976b) studied, the search and rescue volunteers Moran and her colleagues (1992) surveyed, and Metz's (1981) ambulance workers were also lured to these activities by the thrilling and exciting nature of the work.

5. Palmer and Gonsoulin (1990) and Mannon (1992) also noted the role of the emergency-type television shows in their research on paramedics and EMTs in the early 1990s.

6. Fine (1998) noted that people are often pulled to voluntary groups because of the identity groups can provide their members.

7. Prestige was certainly a draw for the search and rescue volunteers Moran and her colleagues (1992) studied. See also Fine (1998) for a discussion of group prestige and recruitment.

8. Other research supports this idea. Many people are introduced to and drawn into voluntary organizations through friends and acquaintances (see Fine 1998; Hodgkinson and Weitzman 1992; Thompson 1993).

9. Van Maanen (1976b:50) noted a similar solidarity dynamic with the police recruits-in-training that he studied.

10. This pattern is similar to one in Piliavin and Callero's (1991) study on altruistic identities in which they found that many regular blood donors began donating after experiencing an occasion where they, their family, or friends needed blood.

11. Van Maanen (1976a) and Wanous (1992) showed that it is common for new organizational members to revise their motivations for participation once they gain experience with and are socialized to the group.

12. That some people develop altruistic motivations only after performing altruistic acts is a phenomenon found in some empirical research on altruism (e.g., Piliavin and Callero 1991) and an important element in some theoretical models of prosocial behavior (e.g., Eisenberg 1986).

13. According to Schein (1978), upon meeting new recruits, it is common for the established organizational members to evaluate how well the recruits fit the organization's needs.

14. Other research has uncovered similar organizational emphases on physical prowess and strength, particularly in highly masculinized domains. In recreational settings, Messner (1992) and Whitson (1990) found physical strength to be a core value in sport and Mitchell (1983) discussed its central importance to some mountaineers. Professionally, Williams (1989) showed it to be an integral part of status in the Marine Corps, and Yoder and Aniakudo (1996, 1997) have revealed its salient role in marginalizing professional female fire fighters from the mainstream fire-fighting culture (see also Altork 1995; Harrell 1986; Hunt 1984; Lyng 1990; Martin 1980; Metz 1981; Moran, Britton, and Correy 1992; Perkins 1987; Perkins and Metz 1988; and Thompson 1993).

15. Other research has shown, however, that the presence of children (ages 5–18) in the home increases individuals' likelihood to remain in the volunteer workforce because children may increase parents' degree of social integration, a factor that has been shown to correlate positively with propensity to volunteer (Wilson and Musick 1999). Clearly, this relationship did not hold in Peak (nor did it hold for Metz's [1981] ambulance workers or Thompson's [1993] volunteer fire fighters), most likely because the spontaneous and risky nature of emergency work varied from that of other volunteer organizations, such as PTA membership or Little League coaching.

16. This pattern is not unique to Peak. Other research has shown that when people have less time they are less likely to help others spontaneously (Darley and Batson 1973) or to volunteer their time regularly (Wilson and Musick 1999).

17. During the course of this study, there were two active members who were mothers, but their children were of college age and did not live at home. In contrast, all of the fathers' children were under 18.

18. This finding contradicts that of Wilson and Musick (1999), who not only

found a positive correlation between parenthood and volunteer work, but also found that this effect was stronger for mothers than for fathers because volunteering is closely associated with the role of being a mother. This finding coincides, however, with research on high-risk, masculine environments like the military. Segal and Segal (1993), for example, found that the role of "soldier" was less compatible with the roles of "mother" and "wife" than with the roles of "father" and "husband" (see also Sadler 1999).

19. The Australian search and rescue group Moran, Britton, and Correy (1992:209) studied was entirely male, despite the fact that the group was "an equal employment opportunity organization."

20. Jim's portrayal of Brooke's actions coincides with Kanter's (1977) finding that women in organizations are often viewed as incompetent and dependent.

21. Other research has shown that failing tests of physical strength can make some women feel marginalized in the male-dominated, highly masculinized culture of fire fighting, both in volunteer (see Perkins 1987) as well as in professional organizations (see Yoder and Aniakudo 1996, 1997).

22. Messner (1992) also found that his subjects—male ex-athletes of all levels—had trouble dealing with their declining physical ability because they connected the prowess they achieved through sport with a certain idealized image of masculinity.

NOTES TO CHAPTER 3

1. See Introduction for discussion of common definitions of heroism.

2. Etzioni (1964) has suggested this typology of organizations based on the kind of control they use to gain members' compliance: "coercive" organizations, such as prisons or mental institutions, control their members by physical means such as weapons or confinement; "utilitarian" organizations, such as work or business environments, control their members with material rewards like money; and "normative" organizations, such as churches or community service groups, control their members with symbolic rewards like prestige or acceptance. These are ideal types; in reality, organizations may use a combination of these approaches. For instance, a company might offer an employee the symbolic prestige of a job promotion in lieu of a material reward such as a salary increase.

These different types of organizational control may also represent different ways in which organizations may play a part in constructing an individual's sense of self and identity. For example, some coercive organizations, like the total institutions Goffman (1961a) studied, may engage in practices that strip individuals of their old identities and encourage new ones that, ideally, more closely meet institutional needs. A more cooperative way organizations can affect individuals' sense of self may appear in normative organizations, where membership is voluntary and rewards are symbolic. For example, Kanter (1968) studied how people give up their sense of self in exchange for group acceptance as they commit to "utopian" organizations like communes. Several other researchers have also examined these dynamics in normative organizations. In his study of basketball teams belonging to the National Collegiate Athletic Association's Division III, Pillsbury (1998) focused on the strategies that the players used in selectively constructing their selves within the organizational context. At times the players considered themselves to be distinct individuals, yet at other times, they considered themselves to be part of the team. Wuthnow (1994) also examined how individuals constructed and redefined their selves through their participation in small, spiritually oriented groups, noting the importance of their group affiliation in this process. For Irvine's (1999) subjects, members of a self-help group for codependents, group affiliation was also crucial in helping members invent their "true" selves because the group provided the ideology members could use to reconstruct their "dysfunctional," inauthentic selves.

3. This concentric-circle configuration of membership has been found in other groups as well; see Fox (1987).

4. Schein (1968) termed these essential elements for acceptance "pivotal norms and values"; Caplow (1964) identified them as constituting the "normative system."

5. Schein (1968) referred to socialization to core membership as the organizational "inclusion" dimension.

6. Downplaying egoism is a common feature of other high-risk-taking groups as well; see Mannon's (1992) and Metz's (1981) studies of ambulance workers, and Mitchell's (1983) work on mountain climbers.

7. Measures such as suspension and expulsion are commonly imposed by groups as "mortifying sanctions" in response to members' excessive autonomy (Kanter 1968).

8. See Edelstein (1996) for discussion of the aspects of Greek mythology that underlie our current definitions of heroism.

9. This dynamic, known as "BIRGing," or "basking in the reflected glory" of the group, was found by Cialdini and his colleagues (1976) in their study of football fans' identification with winning teams.

10. See Oliner and Oliner (1988) for discussion of heroes' anonymity.

11. Van Maanen and Schein (1979) termed this level of conformity the "custodial response," wherein newcomers conform completely to the organization's existing roles and do not question the status quo.

12. Kanter (1968) characterized this aspect of group commitment as "sacrifice."

13. Woodward (2000) also noted the need for both individualism and teamwork in her research on the British military's construction of the "warrior hero."

14. See Edelstein (1996) for discussion of the Greek roots in present-day conceptions of heroism.

15. Riemer (1998) also found leadership to be linked to heroism.

Notes to Chapter 4

1. See Lyng (1990) for a comprehensive theoretical argument on the sociology of "edgework" and voluntary risk taking behavior.

2. See Gordon (1989) and Cancian and Gordon (1988) for discussion of emotional culture and its implications. See also Stearns (1994) and Irvine (1999).

3. Hochschild (1979, 1983) contended that emotion management is a central medium through which we interact with others and thus develop perceptions of ourselves. She suggested that what we "feel" depends on how we define particular social situations. Interpreting what is going on around us allows us to assess what emotions we should feel by drawing on what she called "feeling rules," as well as to assess what emotions we should express by drawing on what she called "display rules." In examining these concepts, Hochschild highlighted how the subjects she studied—flight attendants and bill collectors—"managed" select emotions in order to bring them into line with occupational norms. Additionally, Hochschild suggested that emotion management has implications for self-conception; how closely people can accord their feelings and displays to the "rules" gives them important insights into who they are (or who they must be). For discussion of how the self may be constructed through emotions and emotion management, see Gordon (1989), Holyfield and Fine (1997), Irvine (1999), and Yang (2000).

4. While some scholars have examined emotions in stressful situations such as dealing with death in medical settings (Smith and Kleinman 1989), surviving rape (Konradi 1999), counseling rape victims (Jones 1997), and handling frantic callers to emergency hotline phone numbers (Jones 1997; Whalen and Zimmerman 1998), this work has focused mainly on emotional crises. Little sociological attention has been devoted to emotions during physically dangerous situations. Holyfield's (1997, 1999; with Fine 1997) work, however, is a notable exception. Tying emotion management to the sociology of adventure, she showed how emotions can be manipulated to alter the experience of high-risk leisure activity. Thus, the emotional cultures created around physically risky activities are likely to differ from emotional cultures created solely around emotionally stressful events.

5. For discussion of gender and emotion norms, see Cancian and Gordon (1988), Hochschild (1983), Irvine (1999), Kimmel (1996), Pierce (1995), and Stearns (1994).

6. Other research has also noted that high-risk takers sometimes prepare for risk by predicting and planning for a variety of potential outcomes. See Holyfield (1997) and Lyng (1990) for examples.

7. Lyng (1990) noted a similar tautological relationship between perceptions of skill and success in his study of skydivers. Successfully performing at high levels (surviving) served as "proof" that a skydiver had "the right stuff," while failing (dying or becoming critically injured) served as "proof" that one never had it. Woodward's (2000) study linked such confidence to masculine heroism in the

British military: the "warrior hero" is "brave, adventurous, and prepared to take risks."

8. In Fine's (1998) study of mushroom collectors, men also had more frequent and hazardous exposure to risk than women did.

9. The female ambulance workers in Metz's (1981) study also felt disadvantaged in the masculine environment of emergency medicine.

10. See Lyng (1990), Mannon (1992), Mitchell (1983), Riemer (1998), and Woodward (2000) for discussion of how high-risk takers value clear thinking and rationality.

11. Schachter and Singer (1962) demonstrated that the physiological arousal associated with adrenaline does not signify a particular emotion in the absence of other situational information. This finding corresponds with sociologists' view of emotions as socially constructed (see Introduction).

12. See Holyfield and Fine (1997) for a discussion of paralyzing fear and high-risk behavior.

13. See Mills and Kleinman (1988) for discussion of how battered women's overwhelming emotions may prevent them from making self-indications.

14. Segal and Segal (1993) also found that young, inexperienced soldiers on peacekeeping missions often expressed a desire to be sent to a new place so they could see some "action," while experienced combat soldiers did not express these same desires.

15. For discussion of this narrowing focus process in risky adventure, see Holyfield (1997), Lyng (1990), and Mitchell (1983). For examples in risky occupations, see Mannon (1992) and Metz (1981).

16. For discussion of the ways people emotionally detach during threatening situations, see DeCoster (1997), Jones (1997), Mannon (1992), and Smith and Kleinman (1989).

17. Mannon (1992) noted that the ambulance workers he studied also released stress in this way.

18. For Lyng's (1990) skydivers, the whole point of edgework was to experience this intense invulnerability after a jump.

19. Recurring memories of disturbing scenes are a common reaction for rescuers in other settings as well; see Moran, Britton, and Correy (1992) for discussion about search and rescue volunteers in Australia, and see Oliner and Oliner's (1988) work on rescuers of Jews in Nazi-occupied Europe.

20. Smith and Kleinman (1989) detailed medical students' reactions to their first dead bodies, and others have discussed this phenomenon for emergency workers (see Gibbs et al. 1996; Mannon 1992; Metz 1981; Moran, Britton, and Correy 1992).

21. Vulnerability has been shown to be a common feeling for rescuers after gruesome accidents (see Gibbs et al. 1996; Segal and Segal 1993).

22. This suppression-release pattern is a prevalent one for other types of emergency workers as well (see Mannon 1992; Metz 1981).

23. See Mills and Kleinman's (1988) study on battered women for a similar pattern of losing and regaining self-reflexivity. For discussion of crying and emotions, see Katz (1999).

24. There are several studies that have demonstrated men's tendency to cope through "conduct disorder," and women's tendency to cope emotionally. See Gove, Geerken, and Hughes (1979), King et al. (1996), Mirowsky and Ross (1995), Moran, Britton, and Correy (1992), Roehling, Koelbel, and Rutgers (1996), and Thoits (1995) for examples.

25. Mirowsky and Ross (1995) and Thoits (1995) show that men's alcohol use is often related to cultural norms that encourage them to hide their feelings. Segal and Segal's (1993) study of military personnel who survived after their comrades were killed in a plane crash offered some empirical evidence that supports this claim.

26. See Robinson and Johnson (1997), Roehling, Koelbel, and Rutgers (1996), Patterson and McCubbin (1984), and Sigmon, Stanton, and Snyder (1995) for discussion of the inconclusive findings about gender and effective coping mechanisms.

27. Gibbs and her colleagues (1996) also noted this pattern in their study of disaster volunteers.

28. The ambulance workers in Mannon's (1992) and Palmer and Gonsoulin's (1990) studies also neutralized their negative feelings in these ways, feeling relieved when they found out that patients died from causes beyond the medics' control.

29. Lyng's (1990) skydivers and Mitchell's (1983) mountain climbers used similar rationalizations to explain why their colleagues died or became injured. Social psychologists have termed this phenomenon—attributing others' failures to internal causes, even when clear situational causes are present—as the "fundamental attribution error."

30. The tendency for rescuers to attribute their own successes to internal causes (e.g., their personalities) while attributing their failures to external causes (e.g., extenuating circumstances) is known in social psychology as the "self-serving bias." This phenomenon is not only found among other edgeworkers (see Lyng 1990; Mannon 1992), but is also an everyday strategy people use to protect their self-esteem.

31. Metz (1981) reported that his ambulance workers also considered saving someone's life to be the most rewarding aspect of their jobs.

Notes to Chapter 5

1. For further discussion of interpersonal emotion management, see DeCoster (1997), Francis (1997a,b), and Thoits (1996).

2. Hochschild (1983), Rafaeli and Sutton (1991), and Sutton (1991) discuss how bill collectors manipulate their own and others' emotions. Rafaeli and Sutton (1991) also examine how criminal interrogators manage criminals' emotions.

3. For discussion of interpersonal emotion management in therapeutic settings, see Francis (1997a,b), Irvine (1999), and Thoits (1996); for doctor/patient interactions, see DeCoster (1997); for crisis hotline interactions, see Jones (1997); for parent/child interactions, see Chin (2000).

4. Clark (1990), Exley and Letherby (2001), Hochschild (1983), and Lively (2000) also discussed how emotion management can influence the status of the interactional participants, and thus their relationship.

5. For discussion of how stranger norms change in crisis situations, see Clark (1997) and Goffman (1963a).

6. Goffman (1974) termed such redefining "reframing" (see also Francis 1997a).

7. For sociological discussion of emotions and social situations, see Francis (1997a,b), Hochschild (1979, 1983), Holyfield (1997), McCarthy (1989), Schachter and Singer (1962), and Thoits (1984).

8. I borrow these terms from Goffman's (1963a) idea that social interaction is governed by varying degrees of formality and scriptedness. Highly formal and scripted interaction is "tight," while interaction that is less formal and scripted is "loose."

9. See Goffman ([1956] 1982) for detailed discussion of poise and embarrassment.

10. See Goffman (1963b) for detailed discussion of the spoiled identity and its consequences.

11. For a description of how ambulance workers often enter patients' backstage region, see Metz (1981).

12. See Cahill and Eggleston (1994), Goffman ([1956] 1982), and Gross and Stone (1964) for discussion of embarrassment.

13. Cahill and Eggleston (1994) discuss ways in which those who are embarrassed try to facilitate the flow of social interaction. Goffman ([1956] 1982) discusses ways in which audience members try to alleviate embarrassment for others to facilitate social interaction.

14. Goffman (1963a:105) notes that making oneself "accessible" to others is one way to develop a sense of "mutual obligation."

15. This strategy—setting the emotional tone for the interaction so that others interpret their experience accordingly—is known as "front-loading" (Holyfield 1997).

16. Goffman ([1955] 1982) calls these subtle messages "hints."

17. See Holyfield (1999) for a vivid and sociological account of a swim through the rapids.

18. See Metz (1981) and Palmer (1983) for discussion of how EMTs who work on ambulances also try to appear confident to their patients.

19. Jenkins (1996) discussed how one's emotional state can affect physical well-being, and Folkman (1984) showed that increasing one's sense of control lowers stress. Bolton (2001) showed how nurses often present different "faces" to their patients to manage both their own and the patients' emotions.

20. Clark (1997) argued that women are often expected to provide sympathy and understanding to others in everyday life; Hunt (1984) discussed this same phenomenon in her research on police work. Goldsmith and Dun (1997) showed that this belief is prevalent in popular thought.

21. See Goldsmith and Dun (1997) for a review of the literature on gender differences in social support.

22. See Fehr (1996) for a review of the literature on gender and intimacy development.

23. Other emergency workers have also been found to serve as "grief managers" under certain circumstances (Palmer 1983).

24. See Clark (1997) for discussion of the uncertainty surrounding displays of sympathy.

25. Jones's (1997) study of a rape crisis hotline demonstrated how the hotline volunteers felt more confident and willing to talk to callers in crisis after they had completed their formal training, largely because they were able to rely on "scripts" given to them by the crisis center which guided them through the call and gave them specific suggestions for things to say.

26. See Jenkins (1996), Thoits (1986), and Wells (1993) for discussion of how people fare better on measures of emotional health when they receive support from someone they think can understand their predicament.

27. There were a few emotions rescuers did not validate for families. An important one was anger toward the searchers. Meg told me that, in talking to the family members, she purposely introduced certain information to ward off any hostility the family could direct at the group members. She told me:

> I've never had a situation where . . . the people have been angry at the res-
> cuers. I mean, I make it also very [clear] to them that our people are in
> jeopardy every time they go out into the field. I try to talk a lot about what
> the rescuers are doing, [and] what their risks are in trying to make the situ-
> ation right, so that they see the whole picture.

28. See Brabant (1997) and Walter (1995) for sociological discussions of grief counseling. See also Jones (1997) for discussion of how the crisis hotline

volunteers she studied were instructed to be "supportive listeners" and always to validate the callers' feelings.

29. Lay-psychology's appropriation of Kübler-Ross's (1969) work to describe the (now-famous) five stages of the grief process serves as an example of this idea.

30. See Jones (1997) for a discussion of the relationship between crisis hotline call takers and callers.

31. Clark (1997) suggested that sympathy is a key factor in developing relationships with others because it allows us to care about each other's problems.

32. See Kübler-Ross (1969) and Mishara and Giroux (1993) for discussion of how maintaining optimistic yet realistic expectations reduces stress.

33. See Wells (1993) for discussion of how social workers try to prepare family members for a loved one's potential death by keeping them informed; see Kübler-Ross (1969) for discussion of the same dynamic among medical staff.

34. See Fine and Holyfield (1996), Fothergill (1999), and Oliner and Oliner (1988) for discussion of how sharing intense emotions during times of danger may contribute to increased solidarity.

35. Clark (1997) discussed the many ways in which sympathy facilitates relationships.

36. Jones (1997) found a similar dynamic between the volunteers and the callers to the rape hotline she studied.

37. Goffman ([1955] 1982) noted that when two people greet each other, the nature of the greeting operates to reestablish the relationship's intimacy that has faded since the last interaction.

38. See Bell (1981) and Fehr (1996) for discussion of the characteristics of friendships.

39. Clark (1997) wrote extensively on the relationship between sympathy and gratitude, showing how gratitude is the normative repayment for displays of sympathy.

Notes to Chapter 6

1. See Edelstein (1996), Goode (1978), Klapp (1962), and Swierczewski (1978) for theoretical discussion of why heroes must be granted the label by others.

2. Berkowitz (1987), Campbell (1968), and Swierczewski (1978) all suggested that part of the nature of heroism is the capacity to change the course of some event. Schulman (1996) suggested this also, terming this ability "transformational heroism" because the essence of such heroism lies in its capacity for change.

3. Interestingly, both of these letters were in reference to the same dead victim, Arnie, a well-known local skier who was killed in an avalanche.

4. Dead-body recoveries constituted well more than 5 percent of missions. Rough estimates ranged from 10 to 17 percent, depending on what was considered a mission.

5. See Goode (1978) for detailed discussion of how heroism is related to success.

6. See Berkowitz (1987), Campbell (1968), Schulman (1996), and Swierczewski (1978) for discussion of how a key characteristic of heroism is the ability to overcome great odds.

7. See Goode (1978) for discussion of amount of risk and personal investment in heroism.

8. See Gibbs et al. (1996) and Moran, Britton, and Correy (1992) for discussion of how rescuers become demoralized after recovering dead bodies.

9. For discussion of sacrifice as a component of heroism, see Berkowitz (1987), Goode (1978), Oliner and Oliner (1988), Schulman (1996), and Yang (2000).

10. For discussion of the links between heroism and risking one's life, see Campbell (1968), Edelstein (1996), Goode (1978), Oliner (2000), Oliner and Oliner (1988), and Piliavin et al. (1981).

11. See Campbell (1968) and Edelstein (1996) for discussion of the role of skills and competence in heroism.

12. See Campbell (1968), Edelstein (1996), and Swierczewski (1978) for discussion of physical strength as an element of heroism.

13. See Batson and Coke (1981), Batson et al. (1988), Eisenberg (1986), Oliner (2000), and Oliner and Oliner (1988) for discussion of caring and compassion in altruism.

14. People commonly attribute identity characteristics to others based on their actions. Mullaney (1999) discussed this phenomenon in depth (see also Becker 1963; Kelley 1972). This dynamic is also similar to one identified by Adler and Adler (1989) in their study of college basketball players. They found that the media and fans often attributed "gloried" identities—outstanding personal characteristics—to the players based on their actions within and outside of the athletic context.

15. This discovery is consistent with Oliner and Oliner's (1988) finding that the majority of the rescued individuals they studied (83 percent) tended to attribute caring identities to their own and others' rescuers.

16. See Baldwin and Baldwin (1970) for examples of when people are likely to attribute kindness as the cause of others' actions.

17. See Leahy (1979) for discussion of how people attribute the causes of behavior differently, depending on the circumstances.

18. Oliner and Oliner (1988) found that commitment to performing heroic acts is part of the "altruistic personality."

Notes to Chapter 7

1. See Gecas (1989) for a comprehensive review of the theory and research on self-efficacy.

2. Yoder and Aniakudo (1996) found that feelings of accomplishment were a rewarding aspect of African American women's jobs as fire fighters; Metz (1981) found this to be true for the ambulance workers he studied; and Stebbins (1996) found this to be a reason people engage in the "serious leisure" of volunteering.

3. See Kohn (1977), Kohn and Schooler (1983), Mortimer and Lorence (1979), and Mortimer, Lorence, and Kumka (1986) for discussion of job characteristics related to workers' sense of self-efficacy.

4. Palmer and Gonsoulin (1990) found that the EMTs they studied enjoyed the innovative aspect of their work as well, which sometimes forced them to improvise life-saving techniques while adapting to unique emergency circumstances.

5. These reactions are similar to those of the clients who passed through the therapeutic adventure programs Holyfield studied (1997; with Fine 1997).

6. For discussion of how relationships with others can be viewed as a main reward for participation in voluntary groups, see Fine (1998), Moran, Britton, and Correy (1992), Pearce (1993), Stebbins (1996), and Wilson and Musick (1999).

7. Fine (1998) and Stebbins (1996) have illustrated the importance of camaraderie in voluntary groups. Indeed, Perkins (1987; with Metz 1988) claimed that for the volunteer fire fighters he studied, such camaraderie and solidarity were the only rewards.

8. Thornton (1991) showed that volunteers may feel rewarded when they make friendships that transcend the voluntary group. Other scholars have shown how trust and dependability can increase, and thus be rewarding, in a risky subculture, such as police work (Van Maanen 1976b), fire fighting (Perkins 1987; Perkins and Metz 1988, and Thompson 1993), and ambulance work (Mannon 1992).

9. See Stebbins (1996) and Yoder and Aniakudo (1996) for discussion of how community volunteers and professional fire fighters can feel morally rewarded.

10. In this way, Jim was similar to the kidney donors in Fellner and Marshall's (1981) study, who reported feeling good about themselves because of their altruistic donations.

11. See also Yang (2000) for discussion of the "moral grandeur" that people may seek through heroic actions.

12. For discussion of the good feelings rescuers and emergency workers experience, see Moran, Britton, and Correy (1992), Metz (1981), and Oliner and Oliner (1988).

13. Berkowitz (1987), Edelstein (1996), Goode (1978), Klapp (1962), and Mannon (1992) all have shown how heroism is linked to the idea of morality by focusing on others.

14. Piliavin et al. (1981) have shown that people may continue to act altruistically because the rewards for doing so are satisfying. Thornton (1991) has found that offering volunteers money to do something they want to do can dilute the intrinsic reward they gain from acting altruistically.

15. Piliavin et al. (1981) have found that helpers who are thanked are more likely to help in the future, and Stein (1989) found that the soup kitchen volunteers he studied felt rewarded only when they were thanked.

NOTES TO CHAPTER 8

1. Cialdini et al. (1976) have referred to the phenomenon of associating oneself with a prestigious group as BIRGing, or "basking in the reflected glory" of the group. See also Goode (1978) and Wanous (1992) for similar ideas.

2. For discussion of the process of organizational socialization, see Baum (1990), Buchanan (1974), Feldman (1976), Porter, Lawler, and Hackman (1975), Schein (1978), and Wanous (1992).

3. For discussion of the research included in the organizational socialization models, see Van Maanen (1976a), Van Maanen and Schein (1979), and Wanous (1992).

4. Hewitt borrowed the term "axes of variation" from Erikson (1976).

5. Berkowitz (1987), Edelstein (1996), Featherstone (1992), and Goode (1978) have all noted that heroic acts are exceptionally different from everyday acts.

6. For discussion of voluntary risk taking as a masculine domain, see Harrell (1986), Hunt (1984), Lyng (1990), and Sadler (1999).

7. See Hochschild (1983) and Pierce (1995) for discussion of women and emotional stereotypes.

8. See Connell (1987), Kimmel (1996), and Messner (1992) for discussion of masculinity and emotions.

9. For discussion of physical strength issues in male-dominated domains see Altork (1995), Campbell with D'Amico (1999), Connell (1987), Harrell (1986), Hunt (1984), Lyng (1990), Martin (1980), Messner (1992), Metz (1981), Miller (1997), Mitchell (1983), Moran, Britton, and Correy (1992), Perkins (1987), Perkins and Metz (1988), Thompson (1993), Whitson (1990), Williams (1989), and Yoder and Aniakudo (1996, 1997).

10. Cooley ([1902] 1964), Mead (1934), and Goffman (1959) discuss how the self develops as a result of social interaction with others. Francis (1997a,b), Holyfield and Fine (1997), Irvine (1999), Thoits (1996), and Wolkomir (2001) discuss how interpersonal emotion management may lead to a change in self-image.

11. Altman and Taylor (1973) and Simmel (1950), for example, assert that intimacy is achieved when people think another truly knows them.

12. Altman and Taylor (1973), Bell (1981), Clark and Reis (1988), Honeycutt (1986), Knapp (1983), Reis and Shaver (1988), and Rubin (1985) focus on emotional revelation as a key component in intimacy development.

13. Denzin (1970), Kurth (1970), and Suttles (1970) assert that people form intimate bonds when they deviate from the norms of propriety, yet find acceptance from others.

14. Homans's (1984) notion of distributive justice, Gouldner's (1960) conceptualization of normative reciprocity, and Walster, Walster, and Berscheid's (1978) work on equity theory all contain the idea that exchange is an essential feature of social relationships.

15. For discussion of how empathy operates in altruism, see Aderman and Berkowitz (1970), Aronfreed (1970), Batson and Coke (1981), Batson et al. (1988), Cialdini et al. (1987), Eisenberg (1986), and Piliavin et al. (1981).

16. See Edelstein (1996) and Goode (1978) for discussion of why heroism must be socially recognized.

17. Edelstein (1996), Featherstone (1992), and Goode (1978) also found that humility and self-effacement are core features of heroism, yet they have not examined these features as emotions.

18. See Campbell (1968), Edelstein (1996), Featherstone (1992), Goode (1978), and Woodward (2000) for discussion of the courageous and brave, but emotionally stoic hero.

19. See Piliavin et al. (1981) for discussion of the absence of fear during heroic actions.

20. Eisenberg (1986) and Piliavin et al. (1981) offer discussion of how some altruistic acts may require a cost-benefit analysis.

21. Yang (2000) linked heroism to emotions in his study of the 1989 Chinese student movement. While he showed how the protesters engaged in a process of "emotional achievement," where they achieved "self-actualization" through their fearless and heroic efforts, his analysis did not focus on the role of emotions in heroism.

22. Because of the physicality required for many heroic acts, Campbell (1968) and Goode (1978) suggest that heroism is a largely masculine domain; for the same reason, Edelstein (1996) asserts it is an entirely masculine domain.

23. Batson and Coke (1981), Batson et al. (1988), Eisenberg (1986), and Oliner and Oliner (1988) all suggest that much altruism is motivated by empathy for others who are suffering and a desire to relieve that suffering.

References

Adams, David S. 1987. "Ronald Reagan's 'Revival': Voluntarism as a Theme in Reagan's Civil Religion." *Sociological Analysis* 48:17–29.

Aderman, David, and Leonard Berkowitz. 1970. "Observational Set, Empathy, and Helping." *Journal of Personality and Social Psychology* 14:141–48.

Adler, Patricia A., and Peter Adler. 1987. *Membership Roles in Field Research.* Newbury Park, CA: Sage.

———. 1989. "The Gloried Self: The Aggrandizement and the Construction of Self." *Social Psychology Quarterly* 52:299–310.

———. 1991. "Stability and Flexibility: Maintaining Relations within Organized and Unorganized Groups." Pp. 173–83 in *Experiencing Fieldwork: An Inside View of Qualitative Research*, edited by William B. Shaffir and Robert A. Stebbins. Newbury Park, CA: Sage.

Altman, Irwin, and Dalmas A. Taylor. 1973. *The Development of Interpersonal Relationships.* New York: Holt, Rinehart, and Winston.

Altork, Kate. 1995. "Walking the Fire Line: The Erotic Dimension of the Fieldwork Experience." Pp. 107–39 in *Taboo: Sex, Identity and Erotic Subjectivity in Anthropological Fieldwork*, edited by Don Kulick and Margaret Wilson. New York: Routledge.

Aronfreed, Justin. 1970. "The Socialization of Altruistic and Sympathetic Behavior: Some Theoretical and Experimental Analyses." Pp. 103–26 in *Altruism and Helping Behavior*, edited by Jacqueline R. Macaulay and Leonard Berkowitz. New York: Academic Press.

Baldwin, Clara P., and Alfred L. Baldwin. 1970. "Children's Judgments of Kindness." *Child Development* 41:29–47.

Batson, C. Daniel, and Jay S. Coke. 1981. "Empathy: A Source of Altruistic Motivation for Helping?" Pp. 169–88 in *Altruism and Helping Behavior: Social, Personality, and Developmental Perspectives*, edited by J. Philippe Rushton and Richard M. Sorrentino. Hillsdale, NJ: Lawrence Erlbaum.

Batson, C. Daniel, Janine L. Dyck, J. Randall Brandt, Judy G. Batson, Anne L. Powell, M. Rosalie McMaster, and Cari A. Griffitt. 1988. "Five Studies Testing Two

New Egoistic Alternatives to the Empathy-Altruism Hypothesis." *Journal of Personality and Social Psychology* 55:52–77.

Baum, Howell S. 1990. *Organizational Membership: Personal Development in the Workplace.* Albany: SUNY Press.

Becker, Howard S. 1963. *Outsiders: Studies in the Sociology of Deviance.* New York: Free Press.

Bell, Robert R. 1981. *Worlds of Friendship.* Beverly Hills, CA: Sage.

Bellah, Robert N., Richard Madsen, William M. Sullivan, Ann Swidler, and Steven M. Tipton. 1985. *Habits of the Heart: Individualism and Commitment in American Life.* Berkeley: University of California Press.

Berkowitz, Bill. 1987. *Local Heroes: The Rebirth of Heroism in America.* Lexington, MA: Heath.

Blumer, Herbert. 1969. *Symbolic Interactionism: Perspective and Method.* Englewood Cliffs, NJ: Prentice Hall.

Bolton, Sharon C. 2001. "Changing Faces: Nurses as Emotional Jugglers." *Sociology of Health and Illness* 23:85–100.

Brabant, Sarah. 1997. "Guilt and Shame: Problematic Emotions in Grief Counseling." Pp. 103–24 in *Social Perspectives on Emotion,* vol. 4, edited by Rebecca J. Erickson and Beverley Cuthbertson-Johnson. Greenwich, CT: JAI Press.

Buchanan, Bruce II. 1974. "Building Organizational Commitment: The Socialization of Managers in Work Organizations." *Administrative Science Quarterly* 19:533–46.

Cahill, Spencer E., and Robin Eggleston. 1994. "Managing Emotions in Public: The Case of Wheelchair Users." *Social Psychology Quarterly* 57:300–12.

Campbell, D'Ann, with Francine D'Amico. 1999. "Lessons on Gender Integration from the Military Academies." Pp. 67–79 in *Gender Camouflage: Women and the U.S. Military,* edited by Francine D'Amico and Laurie Weinstein. New York: New York University Press.

Campbell, Joseph. 1968. *The Hero with a Thousand Faces.* 2d ed. Princeton, NJ: Princeton University Press.

Cancian, Francesca M., and Steven L. Gordon. 1988. "Changing Emotion Norms in Marriage: Love and Anger in U.S. Women's Magazines Since 1900." *Gender & Society* 2:308–42.

Caplow, Theodore. 1964. *Principles of Organization.* New York: Harcourt, Brace, and World.

Chin, Tiffani. 2000. "'Sixth Grade Madness': Parental Emotion Work in the Private High School Application Process." *Journal of Contemporary Ethnography* 29:124–63.

Cialdini, Robert B., Richard J. Borden, Avril Thorne, Marcus Randall Walker, Stephen Freeman, and Lloyd Reynolds Sloan. 1976. "Basking in Reflected Glory: Three (Football) Field Studies." *Journal of Personality and Social Psychology* 34:366–75.

Cialdini, Robert B., Mark Schaller, Donald Houlihan, Kevin Arps, Jim Fultz, and Arthur L. Beaman. 1987. "Empathy-Based Helping: Is It Selflessly or Selfishly Motivated?" *Journal of Personality and Social Psychology* 52:749–58.

Clark, Candace. 1990. "Emotions and Micropolitics in Everyday Life: Some Patterns and Paradoxes of 'Place.'" Pp. 305–33 in *Research Agendas in the Sociology of Emotions*, edited by Theodore D. Kemper. Albany, NY: SUNY Press.

———. 1997. *Misery and Company: Sympathy in Everyday Life*. Chicago: University of Chicago Press.

Clark, Margaret S., and Harry T. Reis. 1988. "Interpersonal Processes in Close Relationships." *Annual Review of Psychology* 39:609–72.

Clifford, Hal. 1995. *The Falling Season: Inside the Life and Death Drama of Aspen's Mountain Rescue Team*. New York: Harper Collins.

Cohen, Peter. 1973. *The Gospel According to the Harvard Business School*. Garden City, NY: Doubleday.

Connell, R. W. 1987. *Gender and Power: Society, the Person, and Sexual Politics*. Stanford, CA: Stanford University Press.

Cooley, Charles Horton. [1902] 1964. *Human Nature and the Social Order*. New York: Schocken Books.

Darley, John M., and C. Daniel Batson. 1973. "From Jerusalem to Jericho: A Study of Situational and Dispositional Variables in Helping Behavior." *Journal of Personality and Social Psychology* 27:100–108.

DeCoster, Vaughn A. 1997. "Physician Treatment of Patient Emotions: An Application of the Sociology of Emotion." Pp. 151–77 in *Social Perspectives on Emotion*, vol. 4, edited by Rebecca J. Erickson and Beverley Cuthbertson-Johnson. Greenwich, CT: JAI Press.

Denzin, Norman K. 1970. "Rules of Conduct and the Study of Deviant Behavior: Some Notes on the Social Relationship." Pp. 62–94 in *Social Relationships*, edited by George J. McCall. Chicago: Aldine.

Douglas, Jack D. 1976. *Investigative Social Research*. Newbury Park, CA: Sage.

———. 1984. "The Emergence, Security, and Growth of the Sense of Self." Pp. 69–99 in *The Existential Self in Society*, edited by Joseph A. Kotarba and Andrea Fontana. Chicago: University of Chicago Press.

Edelstein, Alan. 1996. *Everybody Is Sitting on the Curb: How and Why America's Heroes Disappeared*. Westport, CT: Praeger.

Eisenberg, Nancy. 1986. *Altruistic Emotion, Cognition, and Behavior*. Hillsdale, NJ: Lawrence Erlbaum.

Erikson, Kai T. 1976. *Everything in Its Path*. New York: Simon and Schuster.

Etzioni, Amitai. 1964. *Modern Organizations*. Englewood Cliffs, NJ: Prentice Hall.

Exley, Catherine, and Gayle Letherby. 2001. "Managing a Disrupted Lifecourse: Issues of Identity and Emotion Work." *Health* 5:112–32.

Featherstone, Mike. 1992. "The Heroic Life and Everyday Life." *Theory, Culture, and Society* 9:159–82.

Fehr, Beverley. 1996. *Friendship Processes*. Thousand Oaks, CA: Sage.

Feldman, Daniel Charles. 1976. "A Contingency Theory of Socialization." *Administrative Science Quarterly* 21:433–54.

Fellner, Carl H., and John R. Marshall. 1981. "Kidney Donors Revisited." Pp. 351–65 in *Altruism and Helping Behavior: Social, Personality, and Developmental Perspectives*, edited by J. Philippe Rushton and Richard M. Sorrentino. Hillsdale, NJ: Erlbaum Associates.

Fine, Gary Alan. 1993. "Ten Lies of Ethnography: Moral Dilemmas of Field Research." *Journal of Contemporary Ethnography* 22:267–94.

———. 1998. *Morel Tales: The Culture of Mushrooming*. Cambridge, MA: Harvard University Press.

Fine, Gary Alan, and Lori Holyfield. 1996. "Secrecy, Trust, and Dangerous Leisure: Generating Group Cohesion in a Voluntary Organization." *Social Psychology Quarterly* 59:22–38.

Folkman, Susan. 1984. "Personal Control and Stress and Coping Processes: A Theoretical Analysis." *Journal of Personality and Social Psychology* 46:839–52.

Fothergill, Alice. 1999. "Women's Roles in a Disaster." *Applied Behavioral Science Review* 7:1–19.

Fox, Kathryn J. 1987. "Real Punks and Pretenders: The Social Organization of a Counterculture." *Journal of Contemporary Ethnography* 16:344–70.

Francis, Linda E. 1994. "Laughter, the Best Mediation: Humor as Emotion Management in Interaction." *Symbolic Interaction* 17:147–63.

———. 1997a. "Emotion, Coping, and Therapeutic Ideologies." Pp. 71–101 in *Social Perspectives on Emotion*, vol. 4, edited by Rebecca J. Erickson and Beverley Cuthbertson-Johnson. Greenwich, CT: JAI Press.

———. 1997b. "Ideology and Interpersonal Emotion Management: Redefining Identity in Two Support Groups." *Social Psychology Quarterly* 60:153–71.

Gallmeier, Charles P. 1991. "Leaving, Revisiting, and Staying in Touch: Neglected Issues in Field Research." Pp. 224–31 in *Experiencing Fieldwork: An Inside View of Qualitative Research*, edited by William B. Shaffir and Robert A. Stebbins. Newbury Park, CA: Sage.

Gans, Herbert. 1968. "The Participant Observer as a Human Being: Observations on the Personal Aspects of Fieldwork." Pp. 300–17 in *Institutions and the Person*, edited by Howard S. Becker, Blanche Geer, David Riesman, and Robert Weiss. Chicago: Aldine.

Gecas, Viktor. 1989. "The Social Psychology of Self-Efficacy." *Annual Review of Sociology* 15:291–316.

Geertz, Clifford. 1973. *The Interpretation of Cultures*. New York: Basic Books.

Gibbs, Margaret, Juliana R. Lachenmeyer, Arlene Broska, and Richard Deucher. 1996. "Effects of the AVIANCA Aircrash on Disaster Workers." *International Journal of Mass Emergencies and Disasters* 14:23–32.

Glaser, Barney, and Anselm Strauss. 1965. *Awareness of Dying*. Chicago: Aldine.

———. 1967. *The Discovery of Grounded Theory.* Chicago: Aldine.

———. 1968. *Time for Dying.* Chicago: Aldine.

Goffman, Erving. [1955] 1982. "On Face-Work." Pp. 5–45 in *Interaction Ritual: Essays on Face-to-Face Behavior.* New York: Pantheon.

———. [1956] 1982. "Embarrassment and Social Organization." Pp. 97–112 in *Interaction Ritual: Essays on Face-to-Face Behavior.* New York: Pantheon.

———. 1959. *The Presentation of Self in Everyday Life.* New York: Anchor.

———. 1961a. *Asylums.* Garden City, NY: Doubleday.

———. 1961b. *Encounters: Two Studies in the Sociology of Interaction.* Indianapolis: Bobbs-Merrill.

———. 1963a. *Behavior in Public Places: Notes on the Social Organization of Gatherings.* New York: Free Press.

———. 1963b. *Stigma.* Englewood Cliffs, NJ: Prentice Hall.

———. 1974. *Frame Analysis: An Essay on the Organization of Experience.* Cambridge, MA: Harvard University Press.

———. 1989. "On Field Work." *Journal of Contemporary Ethnography* 18:123–32.

Gold, Raymond L. 1958. "Roles in Sociological Observations." *Social Forces* 36:217–23.

Goldsmith, Daena J., and Susan A. Dun. 1997. "Sex Differences and Similarities in the Communication of Social Support." *Journal of Social and Personal Relationships* 14:317–37.

Goode, William J. 1978. *The Celebration of Heroes: Prestige as a Social Control System.* Berkeley: University of California Press.

Gordon, Steven L. 1989. "Institutional and Impulsive Orientations in Selectively Appropriating Emotions to Self." Pp. 115–35 in *The Sociology of Emotions: Original Essays and Research Papers*, edited by David D. Franks and E. Doyle McCarthy. Greenwich, CT: JAI Press.

Gouldner, Alvin W. 1960. "The Norm of Reciprocity: A Preliminary Statement." *Annual Sociological Review* 25:161–77.

Gove, Walter R., Michael Geerken, and Michael Hughes. 1979. "Drug Use and Mental Health among a Representative National Sample of Young Adults." *Social Forces* 58:572–90.

Griffin, Christine. 1991. "The Researcher Talks Back: Dealing with Power Relations in Studies of Young People's Entry into the Job Market." Pp. 109–19 in *Experiencing Fieldwork: An Inside View of Qualitative Research*, edited by William B. Shaffir and Robert A. Stebbins. Newbury Park, CA: Sage.

Gross, Edward, and Gregory P. Stone. 1964. "Embarrassment and the Analysis of Role Requirements." *American Journal of Sociology* 70:1–15.

Guba, Egon G., and Yvonna S. Lincoln. 1994. "Competing Paradigms in Qualitative Research." Pp. 105–17 in *Handbook of Qualitative Research*, edited by Norman K. Denzin and Yvonna S. Lincoln. Thousand Oaks, CA: Sage.

Gurney, Joan Neff. 1991. "Female Researchers in Male-Dominated Settings: Implications for Short-Term versus Long-Term Research." Pp. 53–61 in *Experiencing Fieldwork: An Inside View of Qualitative Research*, edited by William B. Shaffir and Robert A. Stebbins. Newbury Park, CA: Sage.

Harrell, W. Andrew. 1986. "Masculinity and Farming-Related Accidents." *Sex Roles* 15:467–78.

Hewitt, John P. 1989. *Dilemmas of the American Self*. Philadelphia: Temple University Press.

Hochschild, Arlie R. 1979. "Emotion Work, Feeling Rules, and Social Structure." *American Journal of Sociology* 85:551–75.

———. 1983. *The Managed Heart: Commercialization of Human Feeling*. Berkeley: University of California Press.

———. 1989. *The Second Shift*. New York: Avon Books.

———. 1990. "Ideology and Emotion Management: A Perspective and Path for Future Research." Pp. 117–42 in *Research Agendas in the Sociology of Emotions*, edited by Theodore D. Kemper. Albany, NY: SUNY Press.

Hodgkinson, Virginia, and Murray Weitzman. 1992. *The Charitable Behavior of Americans*. Washington, DC: Independent Sector.

Holyfield, Lori. 1997. "Generating Excitement: Experienced Emotion in Commercial Leisure." Pp. 257–81 in *Social Perspectives on Emotion*, vol. 4, edited by Rebecca J. Erickson and Beverley Cuthbertson-Johnson. Greenwich, CT: JAI Press.

———. 1999. "Manufacturing Adventure: The Buying and Selling of Emotions." *Journal of Contemporary Ethnography* 28:3–32.

Holyfield, Lori, and Gary Alan Fine. 1997. "Adventure as Character Work: The Collective Taming of Fear." *Symbolic Interaction* 20:343–63.

Homans, George C. 1984. *Social Behavior: Its Elementary Forms*. Rev. ed. New York: Harcourt Brace Jovanovich.

Honeycutt, James M. 1986. "A Model of Marital Functioning Based on an Attraction Paradigm and Social-Penetration Dimensions." *Journal of Marriage and the Family* 48:651–67.

Hunt, Jennifer. 1984. "The Development of Rapport through the Negotiation of Gender in Field Work among Police." *Human Organization* 43:283–96.

Irvine, Leslie. 1999. *Codependent Forevermore: The Invention of Self in a Twelve-Step Group*. Chicago: University of Chicago Press.

Irwin, John. 1970. *The Felon*. Englewood Cliffs, NJ: Prentice Hall.

Jenkins, Sharon Rae. 1996. "Social Support and Debriefing Efficacy among Emergency Medical Workers after a Mass Shooting Incident." *Journal of Social Behavior and Personality* 11:477–92.

Jonas, Lilian M. 1999. "Making and Facing Danger: Constructing Strong Character on the River." *Symbolic Interaction* 22:247–68.

Jones, Lynn Cerys. 1997. "Both Friend and Stranger: How Crisis Volunteers Build and Manage Unpersonal Relationships with Clients." Pp. 125–48 in *Social Perspectives on Emotion*, vol. 4, edited by Rebecca J. Erickson and Beverley Cuthbertson-Johnson. Greenwich, CT: JAI Press.

Jorgensen, Danny L. 1989. *Participant Observation: A Methodology for Human Studies*. Newbury Park, CA: Sage.

Kanter, Rosabeth Moss. 1968. "Commitment and Social Organization: A Study of Commitment Mechanisms in Utopian Communities." *American Sociological Review* 33:409–17.

———. 1977. *Men and Women of the Corporation*. New York: Basic Books.

Katz, Jack. 1999. *How Emotions Work*. Chicago: University of Chicago Press.

Kelley, Harold H. 1972. *Causal Schemata and the Attribution Process*. New York: General Learning Press.

Kemper, Theodore D., and Muriel T. Reid. 1997. "Love and Liking in the Attraction and Maintenance Phases of Long-Term Relationships." Pp. 37–69 in *Social Perspectives on Emotion*, vol. 4, edited by Rebecca J. Erickson and Beverley Cuthbertson-Johnson. Greenwich, CT: JAI Press.

Kimmel, Michael. 1996. *Manhood in America: A Cultural History*. New York: Free Press.

King, Gary, Steven R. Delaronde, Raymond Dinoi, and Ann Forsberg. 1996. "Substance Use, Coping, and Safer Sex Practices among Adolescents with Hemophilia and Human Immunodeficiency Virus." *Journal of Adolescent Health* 18:435–41.

Kitsuse, John. 1962. "Societal Reactions to Deviant Behavior: Problems of Theory and Method." *Social Problems* 9:247–56.

Klapp, Orrin E. 1962. *Heroes, Villains, and Fools*. Englewood Cliffs, NJ: Prentice Hall.

Kleinman, Sherryl, and Martha A. Copp. 1993. *Emotions and Fieldwork*. Newbury Park, CA: Sage.

Knapp, Mark L. 1983. "Dyadic Relationship Development." Pp. 179–207 in *Nonverbal Interaction*, edited by John M. Wiemann and Randall P. Harrison. Beverly Hills, CA: Sage.

Kohn, Alfie. 1990. *The Brighter Side of Human Nature: Altruism and Empathy in Everyday Life*. New York: Basic Books.

Kohn, Melvin L. 1977. *Class and Conformity: A Study in Values*, 2d ed. Chicago: University of Chicago Press.

Kohn, Melvin L., and Carmi Schooler. 1983. *Work and Personality: An Inquiry into the Impact of Social Stratification*. Norwood, NJ: Ablex.

Konradi, Amanda. 1999. "'I Don't Have to Be Afraid of You': Rape Survivors' Emotion Management in Court." *Symbolic Interaction* 22:45–77.

Kotarba, Joseph A. 1984. "A Synthesis: The Existential Self in Society." Pp. 222–34 in *The Existential Self in Society*, edited by Joseph A. Kotarba and Andrea Fontana. Chicago: University of Chicago Press.

Kübler-Ross, Elisabeth. 1969. *On Death and Dying*. New York: Macmillan.

Kurth, Suzanne B. 1970. "Friendships and Friendly Relations." Pp. 136–70 in *Social Relationships*, edited by George J. McCall. Chicago: Aldine.

Lazarus, Richard S., and Susan Folkman. 1984. *Stress, Appraisal, and Coping*. New York: Springer.

Leahy, Robert L. 1979. "Development of Conceptions of Prosocial Behavior: Information Affecting Rewards Given for Altruism and Kindness." *Developmental Psychology* 15:34–37.

Lively, Kathryn J. 2000. "Reciprocal Emotion Management: Working Together to Maintain Stratification in Private Law Firms." *Work and Occupations* 27:32–63.

Lofland, John. 1976. *Doing Social Life*. New York: Wiley.

Lofland, John, and Lyn H. Lofland. 1984. *Analyzing Social Settings: A Guide to Qualitative Observation and Analysis*. Belmont, CA: Wadsworth.

Lyng, Stephen. 1990. "Edgework: A Social Psychological Analysis of Voluntary Risk Taking." *American Journal of Sociology* 95:851–86.

Lyng, Stephen, and David A. Snow. 1986. "Vocabularies of Motive and High Risk Behavior: The Case of Skydiving." Pp. 157–79 in *Advances in Group Processes*, vol. 3, edited by Edward J. Lawler. Greenwich, CT: JAI.

Mannon, James M. 1992. *Emergency Encounters: EMTs and Their Work*. Boston, MA: Jones and Bartlett.

Martin, Susan Ehrlich. 1980. *Breaking and Entering: Police Women on Patrol*. Berkeley: University of California Press.

McCarthy, E. Doyle. 1989. "Emotions Are Social Things: An Essay in the Sociology of Emotions." Pp. 51–72 in *The Sociology of Emotions: Original Essays and Research Papers*, edited by David D. Franks and E. Doyle McCarthy. Greenwich, CT: JAI Press.

Mead, George Herbert. 1934. *Mind, Self, and Society*. Chicago: University of Chicago Press.

Messner, Michael A. 1992. *Power at Play: Sports and the Problem of Masculinity*. Boston, MA: Beacon Press.

Metz, Donald L. 1981. *Running Hot: Structure and Stress in Ambulance Work*. Cambridge, MA: Abt Books.

Miller, Laura L. 1997. "Not Just Weapons of the Weak: Gender Harassment as a Form of Protest for Army Men." *Social Psychology Quarterly* 60:32–51.

Mills, Trudy, and Sherryl Kleinman. 1988. "Emotions, Reflexivity, and Action: An Interactionist Analysis." *Social Forces* 66:1009–27.

Mirowsky, John, and Catherine E. Ross. 1995. "Sex Differences in Distress: Real or Artifact?" *American Sociological Review* 60:449–68.

Mishara, Brian L., and Guy Giroux. 1993. "The Relationship between Coping Strategies and Perceived Stress in Telephone Intervention Volunteers at a Suicide Prevention Center." *Suicide and Life-Threatening Behavior* 23:221–29.

Mitchell, Richard G., Jr. 1983. *Mountain Experience: The Psychology and Sociology of Adventure*. Chicago: University of Chicago Press.

———. 1991. "Secrecy and Disclosure in Fieldwork." Pp. 97–108 in *Experiencing Fieldwork: An Inside View of Qualitative Research*, edited by William B. Shaffir and Robert A. Stebbins. Newbury Park, CA: Sage.

Moran, Carmen, Neil R. Britton, and Ben Correy. 1992. "Characterising Voluntary Emergency Responders: Report of a Pilot Study." *International Journal of Mass Emergencies and Disasters* 10:207–16.

Mortimer, Jeylan T., and John Lorence. 1979. "Occupational Experience and the Self-Concept: A Longitudinal Study." *Social Psychology Quarterly* 42:307–23.

Mortimer, Jeylan T., John Lorence, and Donald S. Kumka. 1986. *Work, Family, and Personality: Transition to Adulthood*. Norwood, NJ: Ablex.

Morton, Marian J., and William P. Conway. 1977. "Cowboy without a Cause: His Image in Today's Popular Music." *Antioch Review* 35:193–204.

Mullaney, Jamie L. 1999. "Making It 'Count': Mental Weighing and Identity Attribution." *Symbolic Interaction* 22:269–83.

Oliner, Samuel P. 2000. "Extraordinary Acts of Ordinary People: Faces of Altruism and Heroism." Paper presented at the annual meeting of the Pacific Sociological Association, San Diego.

Oliner, Samuel P., and Pearl M. Oliner. 1988. *The Altruistic Personality: Rescuers of Jews in Nazi Europe*. New York: Free Press.

Olson, Mancur. 1965. *The Logic of Collective Action*. Cambridge, MA: Harvard University Press.

Palmer, C. Eddie. 1983. "'Trauma Junkies' and Street Work: Occupational Behavior of Paramedics and Emergency Medical Technicians." *Urban Life* 12:162–83.

Palmer, C. Eddie, and Sheryl M. Gonsoulin. 1990. "Paramedics, Protocols, and Procedures: 'Playing Doc' as Deviant Role Performance." *Deviant Behavior* 11:207–19.

Parsons, Talcott. 1951. *The Social System*. New York: Free Press.

Patterson, Joan M., and Hamilton I. McCubbin. 1984. "Gender Roles and Coping." *Journal of Marriage and the Family* 46:95–104.

Pearce, Jone. 1993. *Volunteers: The Organizational Behavior of Unpaid Workers*. New York: Routledge.

Perkins, Kenneth B. 1987. "Volunteer Fire Departments: Community Integration, Autonomy, and Survival." *Human Organization* 46:342–48.

Perkins, Kenneth B., and Carole W. Metz. 1988. "Note on Commitment and Community among Volunteer Firefighters." *Sociological Inquiry* 58:117–21.

Peterson, Lizette. 1983a. "Influence of Age, Task Competence, and Responsibility Focus on Children's Altruism." *Developmental Psychology* 19:141–48.

———. 1983b. "Role of Donor Competence, Donor Age, and Peer Presence on Helping in an Emergency." *Developmental Psychology* 19:873–80.

Pierce, Jennifer L. 1995. *Gender Trials: Emotional Lives in Contemporary Law Firms*. Berkeley: University of California Press.

Piliavin, Jane Allyn, and Peter L. Callero. 1991. *Giving Blood: The Development of an Altruistic Identity*. Baltimore: Johns Hopkins University Press.

Piliavin, Jane Allyn, and Hong-Wen Charng. 1990. "Altruism: A Review of Recent Theory and Research." *Annual Review of Sociology* 16:27–65.

Piliavin, Jane Allyn, John F. Dovidio, Samuel L. Gaertner, and Russell D. Clark III. 1981. *Emergency Intervention*. New York: Academic Press.

Pillsbury, Gerald. 1998. "First-Person Singular and Plural: Strategies for Managing Ego- and Sociocentrism in Four Basketball Teams." *Journal of Contemporary Ethnography* 26:450–78.

Porter, Lyman W., Edward E. Lawler III, and J. Richard Hackman. 1975. *Behavior in Organizations*. New York: McGraw-Hill.

Prus, Robert. 1996. *Symbolic Interaction and Ethnographic Research: Intersubjectivity and the Study of Human Lived Experience*. Albany: SUNY Press.

Rafaeli, Anat, and Robert I. Sutton. 1991. "Emotional Contrast Strategies as Means of Social Influence: Lessons from Criminal Interrogators and Bill Collectors." *Academy of Management Journal* 34:749–75.

Reis, Harry T., and Phillip Shaver. 1988. "Intimacy as an Interpersonal Process." Pp. 367–89 in *Handbook of Personal Relationships: Theory, Relationships, and Interventions*, edited by Steve W. Duck. Chichester, UK: Wiley.

Riemer, Jeffrey W. 1998. "Durkheim's 'Heroic Suicide' in Military Combat." *Armed Forces and Society* 25:103–20.

Robinson, Michael D., and Joel T. Johnson. 1997. "Is It Emotion or Is It Stress? Gender Stereotypes and the Perception of Subjective Experience." *Sex Roles* 36:235–58.

Roehling, Patricia V., Nikole Koelbel, and Christina Rutgers. 1996. "Codependence and Conduct Disorder: Feminine versus Masculine Coping Responses to Abusive Parenting Practices." *Sex Roles* 35:603–18.

Rubin, Lillian B. 1985. *Just Friends: The Role of Friendship in Our Lives*. New York: Harper and Row.

Sadler, Georgia Clark. 1999. "From Women's Services to Servicewomen." Pp. 39–54 in *Gender Camouflage: Women and the U.S. Military*, edited by Francine D'Amico and Laurie Weinstein. New York: New York University Press.

Schachter, Stanley, and Jerome E. Singer. 1962. "The Interactions of Cognitive and Physiological Determinants of Emotional State." *Psychological Review* 69:379–99.

Schein, Edgar H. 1968. "Organizational Socialization and the Profession of Management." *Industrial Management Review* 9:1–15.

———. 1978. *Career Dynamics: Matching Individual and Organizational Needs*. Reading, MA: Addison-Wesley.

Schulman, Paul R. 1996. "Heroes, Organizations, and High Reliability." *Journal of Contingencies and Crisis Management* 4:72–82.

Segal, David R., and Mady Wechsler Segal. 1993. *Peacekeepers and Their Wives.* Westport, CT: Greenwood.

Shaffir, William B. 1991. "Managing a Convincing Self-Presentation: Some Personal Reflections on Entering the Field." Pp. 72–82 in *Experiencing Fieldwork: An Inside View of Qualitative Research,* edited by William B. Shaffir and Robert A. Stebbins. Newbury Park, CA: Sage.

Sigmon, Sandra T., Annette L. Stanton, and C. R. Snyder. 1995. "Gender Differences in Coping: A Further Test of Socialization and Role Constraint Theories." *Sex Roles* 33:565–87.

Simmel, Georg. 1950. *The Sociology of Georg Simmel,* translated by Kurt H. Wolff. Glencoe, IL: Free Press.

Smith, Allen C. III, and Sherryl Kleinman. 1989. "Managing Emotions in Medical School: Students' Contacts with the Living and Dead." *Social Psychology Quarterly* 52:56–69.

Snow, David A. 1980. "The Disengagement Process: A Neglected Problem in Participant Observation Research." *Qualitative Sociology* 3:100–122.

Snow, David A., and Leon Anderson. 1987. "Identity Work among the Homeless: The Verbal Construction and Avowal of Personal Identities." *American Journal of Sociology* 92:1336–71.

Stearns, Peter N. 1994. *American Cool: Constructing a Twentieth-Century Emotional Style.* New York: New York University Press.

Stebbins, Robert A. 1991. "Do We Ever Leave the Field? Notes on Secondary Fieldwork Involvements." Pp. 248–55 in *Experiencing Fieldwork: An Inside View of Qualitative Research,* edited by William B. Shaffir and Robert A. Stebbins. Newbury Park, CA: Sage.

———. 1996. "Volunteering: A Serious Leisure Perspective." *Nonprofit and Voluntary Sector Quarterly* 25:211–24.

Stein, Michael. 1989. "Gratitude and Attitude: A Note on Emotional Welfare." *Social Psychology Quarterly* 52:242–48.

Strauss, Anselm. [1973] 1998. "America: In Sickness and in Health." *Society* 35:108–14.

Suttles, Gerald D. 1970. "Friendship as a Social Institution." Pp. 95–135 in *Social Relationships,* edited by George J. McCall. Chicago: Aldine.

Sutton, Robert I. 1991. "Maintaining Norms about Expressed Emotions: The Case of Bill Collectors." *Administrative Science Quarterly* 36:245–68.

Swierczewski, Ryszard. 1978. "The Athlete—the Country's Representative As a Hero." *International Review of Sport Sociology* 13:89–98.

Sykes, Gresham, and David Matza. 1957. "Techniques of Neutralization: A Theory of Delinquency." *American Sociological Review* 22:664–70.

Taylor, Steven J. 1991. "Leaving the Field: Research, Relationships, and Responsibilities." Pp. 238–47 in *Experiencing Fieldwork: An Inside View of Qualitative Research*, edited by William B. Shaffir and Robert A. Stebbins. Newbury Park, CA: Sage.

Thoits, Peggy A. 1984. "Coping, Social Support, and Psychological Outcomes: The Central Role of Emotion." Pp. 219–38 in *Review of Personality and Social Psychology*, vol. 5, edited by Phillip Shaver. Beverly Hills, CA: Sage.

———. 1986. "Social Support as Coping Assistance." *Journal of Consulting and Clinical Psychology* 54:416–23.

———. 1990. "Emotional Deviance: Research Agendas." Pp. 180–203 in *Research Agendas in the Sociology of Emotions*, edited by Theodore D. Kemper. Albany, NY: SUNY Press.

———. 1995. "Identity-Relevant Events and Psychological Symptoms: A Cautionary Tale." *Journal of Health and Social Behavior* 36:72–82.

———. 1996. "Managing the Emotions of Others." *Symbolic Interaction* 19:85–110.

Thompson, Alexander M. III. 1993. "Volunteers and Their Communities: A Comparative Analysis of Volunteer Fire Fighters." *Nonprofit and Voluntary Sector Quarterly* 22:155–66.

Thompson, Hunter S. 1971. *Fear and Loathing in Las Vegas: A Savage Journey to the Heart of the American Dream*. New York: Warner.

Thornton, Patricia. 1991. "Subject to Contract? Volunteers As Providers of Community Care for Elderly People and Their Supporters." *Journal of Aging Studies* 5:181–94.

Turner, Ralph H. 1976. "The Real Self: From Institution to Impulse." *American Journal of Sociology* 81:989–1016.

Van Maanen, John. 1976a. "Breaking In: Socialization to Work." Pp. 67–130 in *Handbook of Work, Organization, and Society*, edited by Robert Dubin. Chicago: Rand McNally.

———. 1976b. "Rookie Cops and Rookie Managers." *Wharton Magazine* 1:49–55.

———. 1991. "Playing Back the Tape: Early Days in the Field." Pp. 31–42 in *Experiencing Fieldwork: An Inside View of Qualitative Research*, edited by William B. Shaffir and Robert A. Stebbins. Newbury Park, CA: Sage.

Van Maanen, John, and Edgar H. Schein. 1979. "Toward a Theory of Organizational Socialization." Pp. 209–64 in *Research in Organizational Behavior*, vol. 1, edited by Barry M. Staw. Greenwich, CT: JAI.

Walster, Elaine, G. William Walster, and Ellen Berscheid. 1978. *Equity Theory and Research*. Boston: Allyn and Bacon.

Walter, Tony. 1995. "Natural Death and the Noble Savage." *Omega* 30:237–48.

Wanous, John P. 1992. *Organizational Entry: Recruitment, Selection, Orientation, and Socialization of Newcomers*. 2d ed. Reading, MA: Addison-Wesley.

Warren, Carol A. B. 1988. *Gender Issues in Field Research*. Newbury Park, CA: Sage.

Wax, Rosalie H. 1971. *Doing Fieldwork: Warnings and Advice*. Chicago: University of Chicago Press.

———. 1979. "Gender and Age in Fieldwork and Fieldwork Education: No Good Thing Is Done by Any Man Alone." *Social Problems* 26:509–22.

Wells, Paula J. 1993. "Preparing for Sudden Death: Social Work in the Emergency Room." *Social Work* 38:339–42.

West, Candace, and Don H. Zimmerman. 1987. "Doing Gender." *Gender & Society* 1:125–51.

Whalen, Jack, and Don H. Zimmerman. 1998. "Observations on the Display and Management of Emotion in Naturally Occurring Activities: The Case of "Hysteria" in Calls to 9-1-1." *Social Psychology Quarterly* 61:141–59.

Whitson, David. 1990. "Sport in the Social Construction of Masculinity." Pp. 19–30 in *Sport, Men, and the Gender Order: Critical Feminist Perspectives*, edited by Michael A. Messner and Donald F. Sabo. Champaign, IL: Human Kinetics.

Williams, Christine L. 1989. *Gender Differences at Work: Women and Men in Non-Traditional Occupations*. Berkeley: University of California Press.

Wilson, John, and Marc A. Musick. 1999. "Attachment to Volunteering." *Sociological Forum* 14:243–72.

Wolf, Daniel R. 1991. "High-Risk Methodology: Reflections on Leaving an Outlaw Society." Pp. 211–23 in *Experiencing Fieldwork: An Inside View of Qualitative Research*, edited by William B. Shaffir and Robert A. Stebbins. Newbury Park, CA: Sage.

Wolkomir, Michelle. 2001. "Emotion Work, Commitment, and the Authentication of the Self: The Case of Gay and Ex-Gay Christian Support Groups." *Journal of Contemporary Ethnography* 30:305–34.

Woodward, Rachel. 2000. "Warrior Heroes and Little Green Men: Soldiers, Military Training, and the Construction of Rural Masculinities." *Rural Sociology* 65:640–57.

Wuthnow, Robert. 1994. *Sharing the Journey: Support Groups and America's New Quest for Community*. New York: Free Press.

Yang, Guobin. 2000. "Achieving Emotions in Collective Action: Emotional Processes and Movement Mobilization in the 1989 Chinese Student Movement." *Sociological Quarterly* 41:593–614.

Yoder, Janice D., and Patricia Aniakudo. 1996. "When Pranks Become Harassment: The Case of African American Women Firefighters." *Sex Roles* 35:253–70.

———. 1997. "'Outsider Within' the Firehouse: Subordination and Difference in the Social Integration of African American Women Firefighters." *Gender & Society* 11:324–41.

Zurcher, Louis A. 1977. *The Mutable Self: A Self-Concept for Social Change*. Beverly Hills, CA: Sage.

Index

Admiration, 194

Adrenaline rushes: in rescuers, 5, 8, 83, 93–97, 102, 107, 198n. 15; in victims, 8, 97

Altruism, 53, 153, 167, 193–95, 202n. 12, 213n. 14, 214n. 15, 214n. 23; compared to heroism, 9–10, 197n. 3. *See also* Helping others; Heroism

Ambulance workers, 14, 200n. 21, 206n. 9, 206n. 17, 207n. 28, 207n. 31, 208n. 11, 212n. 8, 212n. 2. *See also* Emergency workers; EMTs (emergency medical technicians); Paramedics

Anxiety, 119–22, 127, 180

Avalanches, 9, 15, 16, 28, 34–35, 68, 73–75, 86, 88, 91, 95, 102–3, 105–6, 136, 138, 149–51

Bellah, Robert N., 64

Body recoveries, 9, 36–37, 89, 97, 98–100, 103–5, 106, 107–8, 110–11, 135–38, 149–50, 162, 167

Camaraderie, 161–62, 212n. 7

Campbell, Joseph, 176, 197n. 4, 210n. 2, 211n. 6, 211n. 10, 211n. 11, 211n. 12, 214n. 18, 214n. 22

Carry-outs, 122, 157, 162

Clark, Candace, 93, 115, 183, 184, 190–92, 208n. 4, 208n. 5, 209n. 20, 209n. 24, 210n. 31, 210n. 35, 210n. 39

Coping, 105–7, 129

Covert role, 28, 31, 42

Crying, 105–6, 126, 132, 133, 138, 139, 183–84

Deep acting, 107, 108

Display rules, 86, 205n. 3

Drinking alcohol, 106–7

Edgework, 13, 85–113, 205n. 1; and body recoveries, 99; and confidence, 89–93; emotional culture of, 181–82; and emotions, 85–113, 180–86, 194–95; and fear, 93–97; gendered emotional culture of, 182–86, 195; and gendered emotion lines, 182–86; and sense of urgency, 95–97; and worry, 87–89

Embarrassment, 116–19, 208n. 13

Emergency workers, 103, 165, 179, 185, 192, 196, 198n. 11, 209n. 23. *See also* Ambulance workers; EMTs (emergency medical technicians); Paramedics

Emotional cool, 181

Emotional culture, 11–12, 85, 179–89, 196, 205n. 2

229

About the Author

A native of New York State, Jennifer Lois received her B.A. in Latin American Studies from Dartmouth College and her Ph.D. in sociology from the University of Colorado–Boulder. She is currently an assistant professor at Western Washington University, where she teaches a variety of courses including field research methods, where she gets to share her research experiences with her students as they undertake their own ethnographic projects. Professor Lois's research interests include the sociology of emotions, gender, family, and social psychology. She is currently studying home-schooling parents ethnographically, specifically focusing on the emotional experiences of home schooling and the social construction of motherhood and family within the home-schooling subculture. She lives in Bellingham, Washington, and takes many hikes in the woods with her husband, "Gary," new baby, Calvin, and their "search pug," Francie.